The Patriots

An Inside Look at Life in a Defense Plant

by

Jean Alonso

To Dr. Beth Richie
and Dr. Cathy Cohen
Fellow writers and
steadfast leaders in
the social justice movement.
With affection and solidarity,
Jean Alonso
11/20/11

The Patriots

The Patriots

Author's Preface

When I began to write this book, in 1991, our country was, as now, in a war that seemed to offer an opportunity for U.S. predominance in the Middle East. I was against that war from inside one of its engines, the defense plant where I worked for fifteen years. *The Patriots* is the story of an investigation in that plant. Though it was not uncommon for government investigations to take place there, this one was a fifteen-month investigation by its workers.

I have chosen to write about our explorations in the genre of narrative non-fiction—that is, as a story, with ourselves as characters and our discussions set in scenes. By doing this I hope to make it enjoyable reading for a broad audience. However, our comments and observations are not fictional. They are real, carefully transcribed from taped discussions and from notes taken, with peoples' permission, during shop-floor conversations.

My friends at work were gracious, funny, and interested in sharing their experience with all people who work. They faced troubling issues and thought deeply about them. This book is theirs, and it is to them that I fondly dedicate it.

Jean Alonso
Boston, 2011

I

War Preparations

'*This* Scud's for you!' reads the cartoon taped to the gray cellar wall near my workbench. Saddam Hussein is riddled with bullets and dripping blood, his pants down and his genitals getting blown off by a missile. Nearby, another: Saddam is a camel with a missile in his mouth, sweating, his genitals on a chopping block, with an Arab man standing beside him, mallet poised. The caption reads "Iraqi Missile Launcher."

It is 1990. We are hard at work in a defense plant, making missile parts for the Gulf War and listening to war reports on our radios. I remember people listening like this around kitchen tables when I was a kid in 1941. Our department is awash with yellow ribbons, little cardboard American flags, "scud-buster" sweatshirts. People have been charting Scud hits like notches on a gun. Older women, fancying World War II movies, vow they'd like to go right over there and creep into Saddam's tent and seduce him then stick a knife in his back.

"Hey, we have to bomb Saddam," Sal opens his palms imploring me to embrace the common sense anyone in his neighborhood would have. Sal is a sensitive person, a musician. "Look, it always happens this way. You have a big guy walking along, minding his business and a little guy gets in his face. The big one says, 'hey, get out of the way'—it's always some little guy who's feeling big. You have to show him or he'll keep on picking on you. I don't see it as a power trip. It's just the way it is—the only way to get the respect of a bully is beat him. You would understand that, Jean, if you'd grown up as a guy."

I fidget in my seat. I've been thinking my own thoughts about this war. Last August I listened to Congressional hearings while I soldered. Congress was debating what to do about Saddam's invasion of Kuwait— stick with the embargo against Iraq or declare war? These are the notes I made. Congressman John Lewis of Georgia said, "War is obsolete as an instrument of foreign policy." Sam Nunn, chair of the Foreign Relations Committee, said, "Everyone expected the embargo would take at least a year to eighteen months to work. It is very puzzling how anyone could give up on it after five months." The new Senator from Minnesota, Paul Wellstone, said in his first speech on the floor, "It is a bedrock principle of world order that no country has the right to swallow up another country. Modern day warfare means mass slaughter. This policy will not create a new world order, but world disorder."

"If we win," said Senator George Mitchell of Maine, "it will be, in the minds of the Muslim world, the U.S. vs. Muslims. It will devastate our diplomatic relations in the world."

Now we are at war. A Middle Eastern world is beamed into our living rooms each night. The President's son, George W. Bush, who is Managing General Partner of the Texas Rangers baseball team and Director of Harken Energy Corporation of Dallas, Texas, has obtained an exclusive concession for drilling for oil off Bahrain. Recently he told Peter Brewton, of *The Houston Post,* that he didn't think there was a connection between Harken and U.S. armed forces at the ready to protect drilling rights in that area.[1] Hasboro Toys is using army specs to prepare a G.I. Joe doll with special desert equipment.

The back story is that American businesses are facing change. The May 1990 cover of *Business Week* featured a picture of "The Stateless Corporation." U.S. economic competitiveness is at risk, and so corporations are indeed packing their bags for a grand tour abroad. It's a time when Bruce Springsteen's songs of working-class pride have grown muted and sad, and President George Herbert Walker Bush, sensing the national ground giving way, is defending our turf. We will *own* this New World Order, he says, and we'll fight anyone who thinks different.

I wipe down my workbench with chloroethane solvent, removing sticky flux and solder from yesterday's out-put.

This is my second home, my second family, my life's work. I build transformers for missiles, and, in my dreams, at least, peace and grass-roots, rank-and-file power. I am devastated by this war at home. I'm fifty-three, with thirteen years on the job. Like most people here, I need the paycheck because I've had two children to support—I just got finished working a

---

1   Quoted in "It's Oil in the Family," *The Village Voice,* February 5, 1991.

second job to help them through college. In the shop I get lots of advice about the kids, my dates, my old car, the condo I finally managed to buy. Most of all people like to appraise my politics, which make them both wary and amused. Sometimes I feel on display—amazing, the pet radical, the only one in captivity, here at least. The one they have personally domesticated, fed, sheltered and taken civic responsibility to contain. Odd, but theirs, and useful at times. A few years ago they got fed up with how the union ignored all their grievances, so they unanimously voted me in as shop steward.

"You're a thorn in their sides, Jean," they would chuckle, knowing that for conservative folks like them to send a radical woman into the ranks of the union officials was a nice shot across the bow. And we did rock that boat.

"Hey, Miss Jean, you look down. Did you see PBS last night? *La Bohème!* Come on, let's sing!" Rudy knows it's my favorite. He sits at the bench just behind me, is sixty, blonde, stout, sensible and never misses a day of work. He grew up long ago in Sicily, where he was a barber. He knows every opera by heart and sings with a beautiful voice.

Julio taps my arm. "*Senorita Juanita, que te pasa?* Come on, cheer up," he says, flashing one of those spectacular grins that seem to be native to Puerto Rico. We speak Spanglish together. He's my buddy, *mi hermano, mi vida.* "Remember, *carita*"—he arches an eyebrow—"You're my pet, you know. That means you'll do just what I say, like my cat. So get me some coffee!"

"Miss Jean, take my advice. Do yourself a favor. Buy a nice blouse after work. It will do you good," says Eleanor. She's Irish, portly and ten years my senior. We call her Mother Superior because she expects that what she says goes, and it usually does. She looks spiffy in a large, pink and red plaid blouse that goes with her ruddy complexion and well coiffed blonde hair. She goes to the beauty parlor every week.

I'm rather embarrassed to admit that I've become known as Miss Jean, the preschool teacher of Boston television's "Romper Room," who was the heroine of all of our little kids years ago. Miss Jean used to look through her "magic mirror," name everyone waiting shyly at home, and mysteriously know the events of their lives. She would whisper softly, "I see Jackie, and Maria, and Bobby, and Sue. Magic mirror, tell me do, did all my friends have fun at play?" They started calling me Miss Jean, they said, because, by their robust standards, I have a soft voice, and because they assume that someone educated is probably a teacher. But I never was a teacher, except in the practical way they are, so I started calling them back 'Miss Eleanor,' 'Mr. Rudy,' 'Señor Julio.' Acting young and having fun is what's done here to pass the time and I've learned to do it too—tease, joke, play games of personal hide-and-seek, and make light of knowing things.

It has taken me quite a while to master the casual, light relations of this place—it feels as difficult and unnatural to me as ice-skating always did, with my weak ankles. At first I wobbled a lot but now I can glide playfully along with the best of them. I rarely risk coming to an abrupt stop, cutting an arc to face them and be myself. I grapple with the question of whether it might be all right, after all this time, to turn to folks with my own rather alien needs and worries. Except for day-to-day practical problems, it's really not done here.

There were guards on the roof this morning, and new coils of barbed wire spiked their way along the tops of the fence that surrounds the plant. The guards in the shack where we present our security badges started searching our bags. There was a new sign:

THE COMPANY WILL BE INSTITUTING
EXTRA SECURITY MEASURES DUE TO THE
SENSITIVE NATURE OF OUR INDUSTRY'S
ROLE IN THE GULF CONFLICT

"They think there could be terrorist attacks," Nina tells us confidentially. She's an attractive fifty-ish woman from Chile, who has an inside track with management. They say she used to date the boss. "I hear we better watch what we say outside. I'm afraid to say where I work these days. I'm afraid I'll go out some night and find my new Cougar smashed."

Beneath the daily banter, people seem grim lately, frightened of retaliatory attacks or frightened of getting laid off. Our budgets and our options are in the grip of a long recession. We're beginning to realize there are no new jobs out there. Young people with high mortgages and day care costs are facing the fact that, unless they get laid off, they aren't ever really "gonna get outta here one of these days."

There's been a flare-up of patriotism that has a strange, angry, sexually sadistic quality to it. I don't like the tension I see in people. They're like coiled cobras watching for targets. Racism and sexual harassment have increased. This morning we came in to find James, an elderly black south-ern gentleman, his face ashen, pointing to a noose someone had hung on his bench lamp. Several days ago someone had taped a centerfold of a black penis to Crystal's bench, knowing that, as an older, married woman, she would consider it especially offensive.

"What's going on in here?" I turn around and ask Sam, a Vietnam-era vet.

"Nobody is thinking here," he mutters, "This war is like a bandwagon that everyone's hopping on."

"It's like a football game!" Meg says, peering pointedly at him over her large Gloria Steinem-type glasses. She's a twenty-year-old feminist. "All that's missing is the beer and popcorn. It feels sick, how much people are getting off on the war. They called me a traitor after the union meeting when we made that motion to support sanctions."

"That was another great union meeting," I explain to Sam. "The Massachusetts Congressional delegation supported sanctions, we make a motion to support our delegation and we get booed." I shrug and smile at them both. "At least I'm not a weirdo in Dorchester. I was at a peace vigil there Sunday and all the drivers that went by gave us the peace sign."

"Jeannie, let me give you some advice," Sam grinned. "Don't try it in the parking lot here, all right?"

"Yeah I know." I really want to read them something I've been carrying around with me. "Can I read you guys this clipping, then I promise I'll shut up and let you get back to work."

"Go ahead," Meg says.

"I've been trying to figure out what's behind the war. Is it really Sadaam, is it oil or what? Listen to this guy—he's the financial editor of *The Chicago Tribune*—on why we should be in the war: 'there's no alternative for the U.S. but to exploit our virtual monopoly of force to gain funds and eco-nomic concessions from our rivals, Germany and Japan'. Then he goes on to say, 'We must charge them a fair price for our considerable services as the world's rent-a-cops. There will be criticism for this more open role as mercenaries but if we abandon that role, we will lose our control over the world economic system.'[2] How about that? In other words, we're no longer the top dog, so we have to sell ourselves as the world's Enforcer?"

Sam is shaking his head in disbelief.

2   Quoted by Noam Chomsky in an opinion editorial "The Danger of Mercenary Role In the Gulf," *The Boston Globe*, February, 1991. Documented in an article in *Z Magazine*, May 1991, as the opinion of William Neikirk, *Chicago Tribune*, Sept. 9, 1990.

All of a sudden Nina careens toward my bench and yells in my face: "You peace people oughta be shot!"

The room goes silent. I glance behind and see the boss, Shaunessy, is eyeing me, and picking up the telephone.

I decide to take cover for a while in the lady's room. Nora! Thank god she's here. She's smiling and shaking her head at me, stretched out on a couple of chairs. She's worked here for some time as a machinist but she's also a sculptor, a graduate of Rhode Island School of Design. We're not close friends—she's part of a younger crowd—but we've started an informal women's committee together here, and I always take heart from just hearing her artist's perspective, so clean and clear in this cellar.

"Hi there, how are you?" she says, applying some claret lipstick that highlights her black sculpted hair. She approaches life here, like her face, with quiet restraint and, when you least expect it, just the right vivid touch or thought.

"Oh great," I say. "I just opened my mouth about some peace stuff. That set Nina off—she's of the opinion that I should be shot—and now Shaunessy's on the phone, probably giving the higher-ups on mahogany row a thrill about how I'm in weekend peace vigils."

"I heard her. People are getting crazy in here."

"I'm so tired of it all. Everybody's so volatile. There's such meanness hanging in the air. I feel like I can't face another boring hour of tinning wires, never mind years. Am I starting to lose it, or is it just Friday?"

We sink down on the dirty green plastic chairs and stare at the round gray stone sink that looks like a feeding trough for animals, with a circular copper spigot and matching foot bar we press for common hand washing. Eleanor comes out of the stall area and gives the bar a decisive stomp. A circle of spray hisses out on all sides for a moment then shudders noisily to a halt as she blots her hands dry, raises an eyebrow at me and hurries away.

Nora turns to me gravely. "Jean, you know what I think? I don't see a way to change things here any more. Why are we here? I have to find a way to leave."

"You're not serious?" She nods and picks up a newspaper. We sit for a while in silence.

What can I say? War, like all crises, tears holes in reality, stalks us with questions. Why *are* we here?

Fifteen years ago, I had answers. Half the country was in the streets about civil rights or the war and it seemed as though we were on the verge of a second American revolution. How could we get working people to join? Where did they stand, anyway? It was obvious that we activists had better go into the regular workforce and find out. How filled with conviction I was then. How I took to heart Mao's precept 'If you want to know a certain thing, you must personally participate in the practical struggle to change reality. If you want to know the taste of a pear, you must change the pear by eating it yourself. All genuine knowledge originates in direct experience.'[3]

Now here I am absentmindedly picking at these old solder drops that have permanently welded themselves to my jeans, and wondering why I'm here. How murky the answer has been over the years. How easy it's been to lose myself in the practical struggle and turn away from questions and contradictions. Such as that American working people have stood up for union democracy and racial equality, and then again called for the punishment of "welfare queens" and a halt to affirmative action. The country is taking a turn to the right.

Nina hurries in past us, tight lipped. I glance at Nora but she's reading her newspaper. I don't know what to do. Where do they stand now? The question returns, like a midnight rap on the door. There's a recession and a crusade for national power, like pre-war Germany. How does fascism start? With little cardboard flags and dashed expectations? "Power to the people!" Did we ever question, when we said that, when we loved those words, what kind of power angry people might want? Maybe Nora is right to leave before things get ugly.

As she looks up at me I whisper "I know what you're saying. I'm beginning to feel like we're in a bad dream, one of those dreams where you're trapped in the spotlight in the wrong place at the wrong time. Or where you have a serious illness and you know you're not going to make it. But there's got to be something more we can do. I can't just walk out of here as if all these years we put in don't matter."

She nods and grimaces.

"Hey, there are signs up forbidding sexual harassment on every plant wall in the state," I remind her gamely, "We did that!"

---

3   Mao Tsetung, "On Practice," in *Five Essays on Philosophy* (Peking: Foreign Language Press, 1977), 7-8.

Our women's committee had pressured the union to negotiate a statement in the contract forbidding sexual harassment. The company put up signs to announce the new rule, and shop floor debates broke out all over the state, like talk shows. Then there were the hazardous chemicals. One day we found out that the chemicals dumped in drains in our shop floor were polluting a nearby river. Williamson, who's sixty five and a conservative, had beckoned to me. "Jeannie, come for a little walk," he said, and showed me where the drains led to the hidden pipe running out of the plant.

"Now," he said, "I want you to go for another walk at lunch. Cross the footbridge on D Street and look back at the riverbank. You know what you're going to see." Sure enough, I saw the mouth of that pipe in the riverbank, with a liquid stream pouring out. When I called in the E.P.A., they sent a young chemical engineer to do tests. She verified that there were carcinogenic chemicals in the drain, and told me later, in a confidential phone call, that she had been unable to get her supervisors at the E.P.A. to invest money to take on our huge company in a law suit. We were discouraged until one morning we found the millwrights filling in the drains with cement. They stopped the dumping.

"I know," Nora is folding her paper, getting ready to leave. "But Jean, you have to admit, things are different now. People won't do anything. Let's face it: the anger and depression and apathy in this place are like a poisonous gas. It gets in at the pores and permeates everything. It has us all paralyzed."

"Yeah, you're right. A poisonous gas. Maybe it's inflating us into giant mutations—war heroes."

"We're just hired guns," she shrugs and smiles. "Hey, these days, I prefer to hide in my headphones. Listen to this..." (she adjusts her headphones over my ears) "It's Springsteen...he's singing our song."

> *"I get up in the evening and I ain't got nothin' to say*
> *I come home in the morning feelin' the same way*
> *I ain't nothin' but tired, man, I'm just tired and bored*
> *with myself.*
> *...I check my look in the mirror*
> *I wanna change my clothes, my hair, my face!*

Man I ain't gettin' nowhere,

Just livin' in a dump like this

...You can't start a fire, you can't start a fire without a spark!

This gun's for hire, even if we're just dancin' in the dark"[4]

There's a blast from the buzzer, the end of afternoon break. Back to the bench.

I replace the blade in my beaver knife, and scrape away at the green plastic that coats the lead wires, baring the wire ends so I can tin them with solder. Friday afternoons always make us quiet, turning into ourselves, preparing for landing in this descent, at last, toward the weekend.

My thoughts turn to my kids, who've said they'll be in town for supper Sunday—"Make cheesecake, Mom!" They're still tolerant of my commitment to factory life and my hope that American workers will reform the country.

"Mom's eccentric," Marc tells his friends, and Melissa has amused hers by dubbing me "Mom the Com." I remember the Sunday night supper thirteen years ago when I broke the news to them that I was quitting my store-front counseling job to work here. My kids, my moorings and mainstays in our little three-person family—they accepted that with their teen version of equanimity. Marcus, age seventeen, had his head upside down tossing his waist-length hair in front of the oven to make it frizzy and wild looking.

"So you're going into a halfway house for the downwardly mobile?" he said. "That's okay. If that's what you really want, that's cool."

"Rosie the Riveter!" said Melissa.

It's never been any use trying to explain my beliefs, though, to these urbane kids of mine. My convictions, learned from small-town sermons and Memorial Day speeches on how all people are created equal, born again to me in the socialism of the '70s, tend to get lost in translation.

I paint a solder joint with the brown flux that smokes and makes the solder hot enough to flow into a tiny smooth seal, getting on with the afternoon's quota of wires to be soldered. But my angst returns in the deepening silence around me. When I have found myself building, in long intervals, no peace nor action, but only missiles, I have counseled myself to be, at least, loyal whatever happens—the person who stays. No short-term tourist, no looking back, no entertaining even a thought of leaving. But are my friends lost to me now? Are they going down a frightening road? I'm shaken to have admitted these doubts. I sit back in my chair and look with new eyes at the place. All these faces around me, bent over their work, all the years of slow-settling trust, the fragile resistance we've built, a day here, a week there, in this vortex of power—they all seem to fly out aimlessly now, like a cobweb I've cut. What's come over us? I should be clearer about it. I shouldn't make any hasty decisions. I have to know. I should try just asking.

Checking the mirror taped in my toolbox, which is trained on Shaunessy's desk, I see he's not here. So I get up, move quickly from one bench to another, and whisper "Can I ask you something? What's wrong with us?" I know I'm breaking shop-floor conventions, now, with such personal questions. "What are you feeling? How does this work make you feel?" Do they harbor regrets that our missile is killing Iraqi civilians, like I do? Or will they admonish me, partisans now of an imperial future?

Sam hesitates, giving me a long look. During Vietnam he was in Intelligence, hanging from a plane with a camera, doing air surveillance. He's very respected, handsome and quietly self-assured.

"The main way I feel about work? The way I always feel here? Inadequate. Stupid." They go on, with similar opinions, one after another. Their answers sound like unanimous votes, like keys tossed in a bucket:

"I feel like a zero."

"Incompetent."

"Inferior."

"Empty."

"Helpless."

"Alone. I guess I'm weird."

"I'm very depressed and anxious."

"I'm so unhappy here I get aches and pains from it."

"Apathetic. I can't do anything at home anymore but watch TV."

"I was a musician, you know, so I still need to write everyday— if you don't, you have no soul. But I go home and I'm too tired."

"There's no learning, no chance for advancement, no hope for the future."

"I feel like there's something crushed inside—I feel really defeated. It's like giving up your whole self in order to make a living—you can't figure a way out."

"Hey, cut that out, Alonso! What are you doing? Get back to work!" I didn't see Shaunessy come in. I obediently slip back to my bench, hunched over to be unobtrusive so that I can quickly write it all down and lock the notes in my steel toolbox before he confiscates them.

Now I am driving home past the small, white ranch-style houses next to the plant. They have snow-covered grape arbors, probably landscaped by the owner's Italian cousin. The neighborhood has painted green and red stripes beside the white ones on the major roads. I'm heading home into Boston's inner city, and soon I begin to pass indistinguishable, worn triple-deckers. Here, as my friend and neighbor Chelsea observed, the yellow ribbons that decorate our benches and every suburban door along the route cease abruptly. Dreams of victory in the Gulf are apparently no comfort here. This is the place of dreams deferred, not life on easy street, like life at the plant, with its good pay, where years of nouveau security have shaped our uneasy, guarded orthodoxy and casual surface relations.

But today all that surface cracked like thin ice. I pull to a stop in front of my house and reach for my travel mug, too absorbed to get out. What people said today has never been said in all our years together. They are always so stoic, so disciplined in accepting necessity's routine. They don't believe in complaining. It must have been hearing my desperation today that made them reach out to me in kind, as if offering condolences, and just speak from the heart. 'The truth about work? It's empty and crushing. The real way we feel? Like a zero, depressed and defeated.' I wait, looking around, in no hurry. Pretty soon the tall ash trees I love will again have yellow-green buds. Jonesy, my Siamese cat, hearing my familiar engine, has assumed his greeting place on my garden wall and is meowing at me, puzzled. They heard a different question about work than the one on my mind; they heard one that hit home. It was as if our shop floor camouflage got swept aside, and there it was in the underbrush— an unidentified casualty, not Iraqi but one of our own. I know the usual decorum here when people let down their guard and say too much: you're supposed to turn your back and act like nothing happened. I'm not going to do that. I feel that they honored me with the truth: we ourselves are in trouble. I need to think of a way to tell them I heard.

It's Monday. Workbench lights are flickering on around the room, soldering irons are heating, and the day starts with our usual polite greetings to each other. People are sipping coffee and shaking off sleep. Should I say something now, open my mouth so early? No, I'll wait. An hour passes.

Rudy is stretching. That's our signal to take a little unofficial break while the bosses are at their Monday meeting.

"So, Jeannie," he begins, "what did you do this weekend?"

"More standing on street corners, peacenik?" Julio asks—the trouble maker! The whole room goes quiet.

I take a deep breath and turn around to face them. "No. I thought about you. All weekend I couldn't stop thinking about what you told me Friday." I take out my notes and, without giving names, I read to them what each one said. You could hear a pin drop.

"Hey, what's your problem? You all are lucky to have jobs!" It's Jerry, the company snitch from the machine shop, so everyone clams up till he leaves.

"No, it's the truth," Sam says quietly. "I was glad, for a change, to be asked by *somebody* about *something*!"

They're with me, deeply interested.

Frankie has emerged from the oil room, apparently hearing our conversation. He's thirty-eight, with a past of fast living, hard drugs, but now that he's married and a dad, his hair is short and he's off the drugs. He still likes to twist his mustache and sigh as certain girls pass, "Oh Baby." He slouches in his oil-stained shirt and shrugs.

"Listen, it was me who said there's no hope for the future. We're all frigging depressed in here. There is something wrong, and it's something about work. But hey, what can you do?"

They're looking at me.

"I...don't know. But I think you uncovered something very important going on here. To me it's like an air raid warning, or like a sign we've got some sick building syndrome."

"Sick building syndrome of the mind—we're loco!" Julio grins.

Sal frowns at him: "Soul syndrome, man!"

"You said it!" Frankie gives us a crooked smile. "So what do we do about that, Miss Jean baby, hand the union a grievance?"

I take a step back and perch on a bench. "Yeah. Some other union, some other year. They hate us, ever since we voted against them in the union election. Can't you just hear them? 'Oh, the blue-shirt department is depressed? We'll be glad to put them out of their misery!'"

Frankie, who used to be a steward too, nods. "Right. Like out the door. So let's do something on our own."

"Well, okay, but if we were to make some demands to Shaunessy like we did about the bench ventilation, what would we say?" I'm thinking as I talk now. "We demand...what?' We don't really know what's causing the problem or what could fix it, do we? We might have to try to track it down somehow, like maybe study it."

Shaunessy strides in so we turn to our work. But all day, people approach me surreptitiously. They have ideas and they want to talk more, they say, but away from the plant—"the walls have ears."

I'm stumped. I'm afraid the days of routine will enclose us in apathy again. And study? This is no place to suggest study, with people who had a lot of disappointing study experiences in school. Plus they're pretty intimidated about coming together in groups on the floor to talk, even though that's "concerted activity" for the benefit of the members, protected as such under national labor laws. But the union would be checking out our concerted activity just as closely as the company does.

A week has passed, when one afternoon Nora beckons me out to the hall. "Listen. Tom and I have been doing some talking and we think we could have a study group. We've rounded up six people, and you and the two of us would make nine. They said they could handle meeting once a month. The topic would be simple—'how does our work affect our lives?'"

She's smiling at me. "So do you think this is another wild goose chase, Jean, or should we try it?"

"What's your take on it?"

"Well," she says, "For me, this week reality set in. Wanting to leave is one thing, affording to is another. I figure I have to stay till I pay down my mortgage a little...maybe I've got six months or a year. So why not? Life could get interesting. What do you think?"

"Well, I'll tell you," I grin at her, "wild geese make me think of my man Henry David Thoreau. In the last month of his life, when everything was wrong—he had TB and his younger brother had died, and nature was looking grotesque to him—he strapped on his skates one morning and wrote in his Journal in a shaky hand, 'I believe I'll take another turn around the pond.' So me too. I believe I will too."

She smiles, signals thumbs up and turns to leave.

"Nora?" I whisper as an afterthought, "We weren't alone after all, were we?"

Our discussion group continued meeting for fifteen months. Before I share with you what we investigated, let me try to give an overview of "American Missile and Communications Corporation." I have given the plant, and also people's names, a protective fictional coat of paint. But the essence of this story—the testimony in the form of comments and observations by the people at work—is all true and accurately transmitted: no white wash.

II

American Missile

View From the Top

Every year in May, Chelsea, Meg and I have exercised our rights, as holders of single shares of stock in American Missile and Communications Corporation, to attend the Annual Meeting of Stockholders.

I first met Chelsea as a result of powder-puff mechanics. The Human Resources Department, which ran a ride-sharing program, told me she lived near me and needed a ride.

"Hi!" she had greeted me as she hopped in my car. She was a striking black woman about ten years younger than me, in fitted jeans and a black silk shirt. "I had my engine apart—I like to fix my own car. I'm a feminist," she chuckled. "But I haven't gotten the darn thing together right yet. So I appreciate the ride." As we rode and chatted she said to me, "You remind me of Anne. Did you know her?" I didn't. "She left a few years ago when all those activists left. People called her a communist but I liked her. I've always questioned the system myself. In 1968, a group of us from U. Mass. went down on a bus to Washington to the Poor Peoples' March. I'll never forget it. Angela Davis spoke."

I noted her straight black pageboy. When I knew her better I would be asking her "where's Angela's Afro?" Now, I dropped her at her door, close to my street. Wow! I thought. I can't believe someone like her works here. I'd like to have her for a friend!

Meg has become our sidekick. She is very young, Irish, from a Right-to-Life family far away in a mill town. Meg, however, belongs to N.O.W. and supports abortion rights. She has chafed at American's bit, like most young people here, and gotten herself in trouble a lot, but always comes up fighting. She has informed us she plans to make herself a single mother, since she is fed up with men but loves kids. Chelsea and I, with grown kids, have tried to advise her to take an easier way, like marriage and divorce, which she finds irrelevant.

Once again this year, 1991, the three of us leave work at noon and put on high heels and suits to come here to corporate headquarters. We've parked my old car some distance from the entrance. The Gulf War is over. It is spring, the season of good will and optimism. Distinguished look-ing crowds are strolling up over the rolling lawns, through fuchsia azaleas and into the atrium where tables are set with linen and silver trays of *hors d'oeuvres* on little doilies. We exchange glances, rather impressed, but say-ing nothing. We have always made it our practice to be uncharacteristically quiet at these meetings, hoping to blend in with the other owners and the trustees, many of whom share joint positions on boards of local banks, insurance companies, and of course, of their long-time associate, Harvard University.

The ambiance of this afternoon puts me in the sophisticated frame of mind of that long-left alma mater of mine, as we withdraw and observe. This affair is, in fact, conducted with a very Harvard-like stateliness and mastery of every detail including taste and humor. There are magnificent wall-size color photographs hung for the occasion. We feel dwarfed by their images of American's awesome scale and global reach. Batteries of missile launchers in the Saudi desert, seismographic expeditions in the Steppes of Russia, enormous petrochemical plant construction shining against the blue skies of the Pacific rim, nuclear plants sprawling on the banks of the Mississippi, little reading groups of children with enthusiastic, innocent faces, sitting on the floor in a circle, clutching the texts of American's pub-lishing house acquisition.

American has grown from a little basement enterprise to a world-class industry, high in the Fortune 500. Its interests now lie at the heart of power and the national infrastructure— defense, surveillance, multi-national in-dustrial construction, massive energy and environmental projects. And the company dabbles, like the wealthy in thoroughbred racing, in influencing education and culture. Its negotiations now are with Pentagon chiefs, sena-tors and Saudi princes.

Yet American maintains a charitable human face, bloated to larger than life for these gatherings. Its magnified photos and public service ads tout its executives volunteering in soup kitchens or advising minority businesses, its record highs for employee giving in United Way Campaigns, and its initiation of local coalitions for waterway cleanup of industrial pollutants.

We file into the huge conference room with its vaulted ceiling and gold upholstered folding chairs, and take our seats halfway down, unobtrusive.

"Cucumber sandwiches!" Chelsea whispers. "White people's food!"

"They're good for you!" Meg hisses. "Vegetarian." I cross my legs and tug at my skirt, eyeing the expensive pearls on the silver-haired stockholder sitting in front of me. Fox Winship, the CEO, is stepping to the bank of microphones to address us. He is trim and immaculately suited, a gray-haired man clearly in full control of his own life and everything else, exuding vigor. As he gives his long report, he shares with us stockholders the festive self-congratulatory mood that comes of being accustomed to privilege and the habitual attainment of excellence.

"It's like a Harvard Commencement speech!" I whisper to my companions.

The officers of the corporation, Winship assures us, have maintained American's reputation for quality and reliability nearly untarnished, and have once again produced success from prudent planning. It seems that this year they have seized the market for beating swords into plowshares, contracting to do the clean-up of nuclear waste and the destruction of chemical weapons, while pruning and husbanding a smaller harvest of their own finest weapons, still in worldwide demand. Apparently having learned from past failures in the commercial sector, they now have the wisdom not to stray too far from the government funding arrangements, which have proven so convivial over the years. In closing, Winship makes a veiled reference to the possibility of future layoffs in the thousands, preferably to be avoided, of course, but a safeguard in place should it become necessary to hold the line in recessionary times. This is his real plum for the stockholders—a guarantee of stable or rising stock prices.

We sneak a furious glance at each other. This kind of information is why we come every year. The union will keep it quiet, upholding their end of the bargain—no labor unrest.

"Unless there are questions," Winship says, "Let me invite you to have refreshments and enjoy the special displays prepared for you today."

But a clergyman and two nuns rise.

"The Board of Pensions of the Evangelical Lutheran Church," says the Reverend, "would like to know, as stockholders, what American is going to do about the fact, recently exposed in the news, that it has long been a

major polluter of local waterways? Along with CERES, which is a broad
coalition of institutional investors and environmentalists, we call upon you
to dispose of waste through safe and responsible methods and to imple-
ment the nine other guides for production as stated in the Valdez Principles,
found in the company's proxy pamphlet." [1]

One of the nuns states that she represents The Sisters of Saint Joseph of
Peace. "We wish to take exception to American's plans to increase weapons
sales to the Third World, especially sales of components of mass destruction.
Along with the Domestic and Foreign Mission Society of the Episcopal
Church, the National Council of Churches of Christ in the U.S.A., and
scores of other institutional stock holders, we call upon you to adopt the
ethically responsible Military Contracts Criteria as stated in the proxy."

"The Grey Nuns of the Sacred Heart," says a second nun, "with the
American Baptist Church, The Corporation of Roman Catholic Clergymen,
and The City of New York Pension Funds, object to American's long business with apartheid. We call upon you to take all possible steps without
violating legal contractual obligations, to terminate remaining economic
relationships with South Africa at the earliest possible date."

Winship answers with cold courtesy that these resolutions have already
been voted down in the proxy ballots. Inspired by these unknown allies of
conscience, we ourselves decide on the spur of the moment to rise and ask
questions about equal employment. We elbow Chelsea: "You ask" knowing
that Winship might feel more compelled to call on an African American.

"I see you have one woman on the Board of Directors," she says, pro-
jecting her voice well. "As union members at American we are concerned
about the company's compliance with equal opportunity clauses in federal
contracts. Could you tell us how many women and minorities overall hold
management positions at American, and how many hold top level union
jobs?" One of the nuns turns toward us and smiles.

"I don't have those statistics. Do you have them Bill? No. You could
speak to Personnel about those."

"Oh, right!" we whisper. Several years ago Chelsea and I had done
that. We went to Personnel to read the affirmative action statistics, which,

<hr/>

1   While people's introductory remarks are fictionalized, the formal resolutions were in
fact put forth in Annual Stockholder meetings by these and other institutional stockholders at
corporations across the country in 1991. They may be found in their entirety, together with the
sponsors and the corporations at which they were actually presented, in *Church Proxy Resolutions*,
January, 1991. They are published in pamphlet form by the Interfaith Center on Corporate
Responsibility, 475 Riverside Drive, Room 566, New York, N.Y., 10115.

according to notices on the plant walls, were freely available to all as required by our federal contracts. The statistics looked incriminating—the company appeared to be way out of compliance. When we returned the next day, with notebooks in hand, we were told that the statistics had been impounded as "company secrets." We couldn't afford the legal work for the court order needed to release them.

The stockholders apparently find the idealism of all these questions and resolutions inconsequential, and the corporate chiefs are confident of their upper hand. Sure, I think to myself. They have the unflagging support of their banker and industrialist directors, and probably also of the funders of the university research and journals of government policy that might otherwise be expected to criticize their projects. The festivities close with congratulations to the Board, the management and the stockholders for another outstanding year. This self-congratulatory spirit is sometimes also handed out sparingly to employees in times of need, like Thanksgiving canned goods. In a company newsletter during the Gulf War, Fox Winship had written to employees: "Everything you do makes a difference. President Bush knew that ours is more than a missile, that it is a symbol of what we stand for as a country, and we know it symbolizes what American stands for as a company. Thank you for all you have done to remain true to its spirit. Let's keep that spirit burning bright."

Back on the shop floor the following morning, I report the reference to layoffs at the annual meeting. Then, on impulse, I ask people how they would describe the shop floor to someone who'd never worked in a factory, and they say:

"You're a nobody here, just a number. If I dropped dead in the aisle they'd step over me and say 'Fred who? Just do your job. It's shipping week.'"

"Unbelievable! You're thrown in with all kinds of people, some you want to know and some you'd never want to know. Apathy. Your brain goes to sleep. I'm a mindless robot!"

"Plastic and asbestos hanging, no ventilation, dirt, smoke, chemical fumes, noise all around. Favoritism, psychological reinforcement of acceptable behavior. Most everybody hates how they're treated but they're afraid to say it—they stay for the money."

View From the Bottom

I myself first saw American Missile and Communications Corporation on a peace map illustrating populations in the Northeast in danger in case of enemy attack. It was the center of all concentric circles—the hotspot. The real thing, with its sprawling plants and rotating radar towers, seemed to me a model of the military-industrial complex, set in concrete. I remember the place as I saw it on my first day of work in 1978. I was admitted behind the security gate and led from the Personnel Office by my pleasant new foreman, Charlie, on a meandering route through the sprawling plant—industry on a scale I'd never known. I remember feeling like I had taken the wrong turn in an airport, gotten lost behind some door in a huge hanger where the public didn't belong, where the announced international arrivals and destinations, the intersecting pathways of personal life and commerce, seemed reduced to wing parts and nuts and bolts lying about on the floor—the reality behind our anticipations of flight. As I passed endless rooms like storage areas, characterless, with wire bins of parts and tools and rows of people silently at work, there seemed no relation between these fragments and their owners' traffic in arms and international shifts in power and wealth. I was shown to a seat in the Light Assembly Department, where I was to be a taper and winder, introduced by Charlie as "the new hire—a working mother, a girl with nimble fingers." I liked having this more basic side of myself acknowledged— mother and life-long seamstress—instead of life-long student. I enjoyed the handiwork of wrapping wire then tape around little donut-shaped magnets, like crocheting, with its repetitive, neat production at my own hand. I found the manual work relaxing, if unchallenging. I liked that it left me time to think, and get to know the people around me, and figure out how to behave in this working-class factory culture that was so different for me. I used to tell myself that this change of pace would be good for everybody now and then.

Factory activists of another generation had a saying: "If you come from the middle class, it takes about ten years to be really integrated into the working class." I had already been working for years outside the middle class, in prison and storefront poverty counseling. Still, working here, I too gradually changed. It was at ten years that I found myself getting annoyed at my middle-class parties. I was resenting privileged types. Friends surprised me by commenting that I was talking most of the time with a different style than I used to. And one day I awoke to the fact that I had acquired the often disguised, hidden, internal hallmark of many working-class people: a sense of inferiority.

The work at American ranges from making tiny printed circuit boards, wired under a microscope, to construction of huge parts for submarines and missiles. We don't work on an assembly line because we make limited numbers of components for varied contracts, so assembly line production is impractical. We work alone with little reason organic to the work for interchange with each other. We drive to work in the dark, some of us for an hour or more, and hurry to the time clock at exactly 7:00 A.M. We work in a dirty and windowless cellar at Formica and steel workbenches, with florescent lights and long gray metal storage shelves, each neat and conforming to the others. No personal property is to be in evidence— military regulations. We tape pictures of our families inside the covers of our toolboxes, galleries that can be quickly closed if visiting Pentagon brass are expected. We use hammers, wrenches, wire cutters, pliers of different kinds, soldering irons, spools of lead and silver solder and containers of glue, flux and cleaning solvents. The air is soon heavy with a fog that smells acrid, or sweet, and burns the eyes. Bench ventilation we ask for would cost too much, the company says.

A few people who enjoy the special confidence of the bosses get to test or assemble somewhat interesting sets of components called power supplies. They are made of interconnected transformers, PC boards, diodes and resistors and supply electric power to missiles. They require learning a blue print or "spec." But most of us repeatedly do simple things for years, making the components of these power supplies. They are later assembled, tested, fastened in steel cases filled with transformer oil, welded shut then painted—desert sand, jungle camouflage, Nile green, space silver—with destinations we only guess at. They are reputed to range in price from one thousand to sixty thousand dollars. I hold a small, simple unit in my palm and wonder how it could be worth more than my car.

Problems with production are rare, solved long ago, but welcome when they happen because they're thought-provoking. However they have to be reported to managers who confer about them near our benches, backs turned to us, making it clear that we are out of the loop of advisors.

In fact it is we who know the answers, we who have possession of the little tricks of construction that mean the difference between success and failure of these components. It's we who know how many pieces of paper to put between the magnet faces to regulate the current flow, how much torque is required to bring them together just enough but not too much. These methods are on dog-eared pieces of paper, notes and diagrams we have made or inherited from workers now dead or retired. Our efforts to get these instructions and drawings transferred to the official government blue prints usually prove futile, and we are just as glad. It confirms the absurdity of the place, and shores up for us our own meager supply of power. We share them with each other.

Fundamentally everyone here is seriously under-employed, using only a fraction of his or her mechanical abilities. But, with the industry getting "leaner and meaner," advanced positions have been eliminated, so there's no way up but out. Now and then, on random hot afternoons, when the shop is hazy with smoke and chemicals and we are faceless, thoughts drifting, someone shares a wish to go to night school, learn a new trade, open an Amway business, start a day-care center, marry rich, have an industrial accident. "But you're still here, aren't you?" we point out to each other. "You love it here!" echoes a voice over the din of the oil room. "It's the best job you ever had! Is it 3:30 yet?"

In moments of desperation I take refuge in writing little dramatic lines to myself. "Another day, another dollar, Friday afternoon at the bomb factory," I scribble on a scrap of paper. "The black hole. We work silently, mechanically, long ago divorced from work we do, like shadows on a wall. The disappeared." Others clip grocery coupons, buy themselves some Avon products, think about the walk they'll take with their mates when they get home, or the extra lottery ticket today seems the right day to buy. We all seek what windfalls we can in these personal moments, something extra salvaged for ourselves out of the slim pickings of the workday.

III

What's The Problem?

Meeting

Joe Brown declined our discussion group. He was a former Golden Gloves boxer, a huge gentle black man. He hated boxing, just did it to put his six kids through college. He was a friend and advisor of mine—his unfailing judgment and intelligence had everyone's respect and earned him a lucrative group leader job in the skilled trades at American. "Listen, just take a stand, everybody's for it, then turn around and look over your shoulder. You'll be all alone!" he counseled me. "I did my stint in neighborhood organizing in the nineteen sixties. You knocked yourself out and people never showed up. I've had it. Never again. You'll be wasting your time, Jean. Don't say I didn't warn you!"

I drove into the church parking lot wondering if I had been too careless, choosing a meeting place so near the plant. Was it too risky, too intimidating? In this company town nothing went unseen, and on the shop floor the Star of the Day was the person able to break the monotony with the hottest gossip. Would this end, after all, in polite excuses tomorrow? I looked over my shoulder and watched eight cars pull in beside me.

It was a hot June afternoon, a few weeks before the plant shutdown for our standardized vacations, which prospect always put us in a buoyant mood. Now, car doors slammed and people strolled up ever so casually, but the grins gave us away—we were feeling downright excited and conspiratorial at this new, non-standardized project.

I turned the copy of the church key with which we had been entrusted and the heavy door of the parish house swung open. Behind the austere white panels all along one wall of the vestibule lay a large, lovely room the church had offered us for $25 a meeting. We had received a small grant from the Haymarket Foundation for this rent and for child care expenses. The room was serene and elegant, with fresh pale blue paint and long, old-fashioned windows framing birches stirring gently outside. A sanctuary.

"I think this will do," said Hildie matter-of-factly, surveying the damask drapes and long mahogany table with its plush armchairs. "It looks like a Board Room."

"It is now!" Nora smiled.

We made nervous small talk, unsure of what to do. We hardly knew each other, unless you counted seven years of casual comments about the weather and the work. Should we now rupture that restraint, so carefully cultivated?

"Okay," I said. "Want me to take notes? I'm really fast, and tape recorders make me paranoid."

"Your hands might be fast but your memory isn't!" Sean said. "Must be the fumes, Jean! For God's sake, get a tape recorder. We want you to get this right!"

"Look," Tom smiled, raising an eyebrow. "Just coming here is enough to put us on some Suspect Persons list! We're all in this together, so what harm can a tape recorder do?"

They laughed.

"That's right."

"Count me in!"

"That's fine. I'll practice my radio voice." So I did tape the subsequent sessions.

"Why don't we just start by going around the room and talking about what's on our minds, why we want to be here?" I suggested. We introduced ourselves in the following way. The italicized names and descriptions, slight disguises, were devised or approved by the group members themselves.

Dominic, age 29, Italian-American, a clean-cut, funny and sensitive guy, a holder of traditional values and beliefs yet open-minded and knowledgeable, especially about physical fitness and industrial health. (I have to add, he was awfully cute—stocky and unusually short. When the department jocks made fun of him for that, he sought consoling hugs from all the women, placing his head on our bosoms and mischievously eyeing the jocks, who looked disgruntled): "I've got ten-and-a-half years at American. The first two years I said 'I'll never stay here' but I got comfortable. I used to like to tell people I worked here—it meant prestige, big bucks, benefits, security. I was proud of it. Now I hope they lay me off. Forty more years here? I hope I fall down an elevator shaft—I hope I touch my soldering iron with wet hands! I used to go camping and do a lot of things after work. Now I just sit in front of the TV, no drive anymore. I feel like a retarded dog. I go home and say, 'I hate this job.' But I feel guilty complaining —at home they say 'be thankful you've got a job, you've got it made!' Ninety per cent of my family have worked at American. They say 'don't push it!' and remind me of how in their day the boss came to your house to see why you were out. I still have to hide now, from them, if I take a day off."

Ruth, African-American from the South. Tall and graceful with corn row braids and a smooth, milk chocolate complexion. A mother of two teenagers, she initially described herself as too shy to talk in the group, sure she had nothing to say. A dedicated leader in her community church. She was shy, but she soon had plenty to say. On the tapes she sounds like an anchor-woman with her graceful, modulated voice. Her association in the shop with us, her new friends, raised the hackles of her old crowd from the South, in the Coil Winding Department—"she's down there hangin' with the whities again!"

"I come from South Carolina, went to school in New York and then into the Job Corps. I loved Boston because I thought it was so quiet. Now I've got twenty years in electronics. I started out wanting to be an engineer, but I had kids to support, so I went to a technical institute. I like mechanical work. I can repair appliances, including my own washing machine. I used to do all kinds of mechanical work but now I have to force myself to do anything at home. I just go home and drop. My kids say 'Mommy, what's wrong with you? Why are you always so tired?' At that machine, winding hundreds of tiny coils under time pressure, I have been introduced to *stress* for the first time on a job. I was praying everyday. At church you're taught to be obedient to people around you, and I believe in the Lord, but the Lord didn't tell you to be no *fool!*"

Tom, dubbed "Tom Paine." Age 58, Irish-Jewish-American, father of five grown children, Korean vet and a hawk during the Vietnam War. Very well read, knowledgeable in history, politics, and finance. A skeptic, fairly radical now. He was a new person in our shop. I immediately liked his pugnacious, tough debating style and constant use of quotes from current non-fiction he was reading: "I've worked in factories, broadcasting, twenty years in marketing and sales. Let me tell you what people with a lot of money think about the average working person: they don't hold us in high esteem! They work at using psychological warfare on us through radio and TV, think we're easily swayed. Seldom do they deal honestly with you. I had to get out. So I came late to American. Here you work on the same piece of equipment, the same product all the time. If they find out you do a good job on one thing, God help you, you'll do it till hell freezes over. They won't promote anybody from the bench anymore—they're only taking people with college degrees. So I'm just waiting for retirement. For me, the week is nothing but a bridge to Saturday and Sunday. But our problems and the conformity here go beyond American—they pervade society."

Nora, Russian-Finnish-American, age 32. Progressive in her thinking, her artist's intelligence makes her a sensitive observer of human relations. Nora's fine-boned face and elegant appearance have the clean, well-wrought lines of the small, precise sculptures she has shown me in her studio. They are beautiful, shimmering mobile pieces in miniature steel cages. She manages to be aloof and friendly at once, cool and intense, which both attract and hold at bay her all-male co-workers: "I graduated from design school but I wanted to do big industrial-looking sculpture so I learned to be a machinist outside in a C.E.T.A. program. The defense industry was an opportunity for me, because of its affirmative action requirements, to get a job doing what I love to do—working with metal. But the conditions here have me so frustrated and depressed I find it difficult to work on my art. It's hard to change modes, from the passive to the creative. I usually think it's my own personal problem, a lack of ambition. But creativity is something that comes in a flow of energy that can't be turned on and off. The act of being creative makes you excited about life. The act of shutting down your creativity makes you depressed. It's such an anti-creative environment at work, in every way. I just go home and watch TV. My husband also doesn't understand—everyone thinks we have such great jobs. But they don't see that other things may be more important than what we're paid."

Suzanne, African-American and Delaware Indian, mother of a grown son, sometimes conservative politically but a fighter for neighborhood safety. A student of consumer and financial data, often sought out for help by people with problems. She is very pretty, with *café-au-lait* skin and an infectious smile. She has a second husband now, who surprises her with jewelry and dozens of roses in the shop on anniversaries—the envy of all us women. She sticks up for all the women, as a member of "Action," our women's group, especially for the ones with abusive relations at home: "I've also taken a number of electronics courses, and a college course in art. Once I worked in a department store—I wanted to be a buyer—but at that time they only let black women be elevator operators, so that's what I did. I came here so I could support my son too. The inspection work I do makes me feel intimidated. If you try to be aggressive or innovative you get stepped on. It kills your incentive. I go home at night—who wants to do anything? I'm mentally drained from the pressure, and my blood pressure is up. I don't sleep on Sunday night thinking of Monday. I used to like to do ceramics, go out dancing, but I have no energy for any of that anymore. TV is an escape—a way of climbing into another world. There's nowhere else to go now—I'm stuck in this job. It's sad."

Jasmine, of mixed European and African-American background, raised in both the South and North, an attractive 27 year old mother of one, a liberal and a good student who is in college at night, majoring in art. She is very striking, with high cheekbones and large eyes. She's quite reserved, not known by many of us because she has recently come from the night shift. We feel lucky her friend Hildegard has persuaded her to join us: "Some day I'd like to leave here, to do something for the betterment of society. But now I have to support my two-year old, and I need the benefits. At home I manage work, my household, and my son and still manage to work on my studies and my art. But here I'm treated, like we all are, as one of the children. I'm worried about what the job is doing to me psychologically. I feel isolated, suffocated and manipulated and not worth while. I'm really losing my self-confidence."

Myself, Jean, age 53, of Swedish and Yankee origins, mother of two grown children, a former public mental health worker, and a long-time activist and socialist: "What made me worried about work was that I found myself unable to read or think much in a conceptual way, or have imagination anymore. Sometimes I get asked to speak places but I always refuse because I have so little confidence in my ability to know anything worth saying. Now, since I have three college degrees, I knew I didn't used to be stupid, and yet now I feel I am, functionally. This loss of functioning scared me, and made me realize it must happen to everybody, no matter what education they started with. But this group gives me hope, trying to get at the truth of what it is like to be a human being in a factory. There are no right answers—there are many sides, many contradictions in the truth."

Hildegard, German and Scottish-American, a svelte grandmother of two who has learned many jobs in her time. Often conservative politically, an observer of social and industrial trends who characterizes herself as "a survivor." Hildie, with her neat silver pixie cut, likes to pose as one of the silent majority, but I know better. She's a sturdy realist and an astute and independent thinker: "I wanted to be in police work—a lot of my family were distinguished military men—but that wasn't open to women. So I have thirty years in electronics. I'm at a place where I don't want to get up in the morning and come to work. I hate it. I'm actively seeking a way out. I used to like knitting, crocheting—and motorcycle riding, just so you don't think I'm a deadhead! My motorcycle club reminds me of American—constant bickering! I came to American with a reasonably high IQ—I went to college at thirty-seven. Now I don't think I could function on the outside. I wonder does my brain still function, or am I on automatic pilot? I have an idea and do they want to hear it? No. 'You're just an assembler.' You know you're not stupid, and yet in a certain way you are."

Sean, age 38, a veteran, Boston Irish, a self-taught intellectual whose preoccupations are conscientious equal-time parenting of three young children, Democratic city politics and green technology. Sean has a teasing, infectious wit, freckles, a cowlick and the slouchy clothes of an Irish good ole boy, which he is not, mostly. He does, though, have the habit of suddenly appearing before my bench out of nowhere and doing a little jig. He has a lawyer's ability to make a good argument, which he likes to practice on me: "A study on boredom in the U.S. auto industry said those who got through it without going crazy were the ones with a goal of getting out in ten or twenty years. I have one hundred and eighty months to go. The day I got out of high school I was on a bus to the Army base. When I got out of the service I had a great job in a college library—working with twelve girls! But we had a new arrival and my father said this was too much of a good thing and not enough money, so he sent me up to American. Society gave us a false hope we could do better. It was supposed to take care of us—wages and earnings were going up. Not now. We can't leave because there are no jobs. Does it make it right just because we're lucky to have a job, that we work in a lousy and by the way very unsafe atmosphere? When I joined the union democracy campaign I got a rude awakening, getting taken out of my job like I did for three quarters of a year by the company to help the union incumbents punish people who opposed them— well, reality stepped in! To analyze our environment we have to look at all aspects—management, union, our fellow workers, the manipulation and negative self-image. The company, which everyone hides behind, is a non-person. What are you going to hate? Maybe that's the question for us."

"You know," Tom said, when it was time to leave, "It's so good to talk like real people for a change instead of the typical conversation on the shop floor—'How's it going?' 'It sucks!' Look at all the different backgrounds and interests we have, that we never *knew*."

Driving home, I recalled a comment Adrienne Rich once made about the first women's consciousness groups in the '60's: "We began by naming and acting on issues we had been told were too trivial to mention."[1] That was a lot like us. We all felt apologetic about having these little misgivings, so illegitimate to others, when we have such terrific jobs.

My counselor's ear, out of commission for thirteen years, tuned in on high frequency. In counseling, first sessions are always just the tip of the iceberg, but are very significant because people introduce fragments of the real problems to come. What we've got here, I thought to myself, taken together with what people said on the shop floor (not to mention what you find in yourself, Miss Jean!) are a whole bunch of symptoms that clinicians would take very seriously. They would hear problems with apathy, passivity, fatigue, low self-esteem, depression, anger, intimidation, physical symptoms, isolation, stressful working relations, self-blame, loss of skills, creativity and cognitive functioning, and guilt and confusion at a dissatisfaction and sense of loss or injury that was undefined. Maybe we are like the Detroit autoworkers in Arthur Kornhauser's classic study, *Mental Health of the Industrial Worker*. He found that forty percent had "low mental health."[2] And most of us are dealing with this by handling troubling circumstances, which in our case constitute a good part of our waking hours, by diminishing their importance with a defense called "marginalization"—work is only a bridge to the weekends.

Later, I fixed myself a glass of iced tea, and took to my wicker porch rocker, brushing aside some encroaching lavender wisteria. Revisiting the afternoon, I had the feeling of walking through a house and sensing that

1   "Blood, Bread and Poetry," *Radcliffe Quarterly*, March, 1992.
2   Quoted in *Work in America: Report of a Special Task Force to the Secretary of Health, Education, and Welfare* (Cambridge: M.I.T. Press, 1973), 83.

somewhere behind closed doors there is someone being kept in seclusion. The clinical symptoms don't matter, I thought. It's true that they show that we're not mistaken and something is wrong. But what matters are the ghosts there today—the memories of ourselves in the past, and the apprehension each of us feels that we are not the same people we used to be. The missing persons account.

I needed to sit with this a while, to step back and do some thinking in the month before our next session. I had also promised the group I'd do a little research, urging them to come along with me and read too. But now, and throughout the sessions, they kept declining. "Studying? Better you than me! You do it and tell us about it. We just like the discussions."

Determining the Problem

"This library should belong to all the townspeople some day, not just be open to card-carriers like me!" I pronounced irritably to myself as I climbed the vast marble steps of Harvard's Widener Library, pausing to catch my breath. Inside, I smiled at the huge reading room with its celestial blue vaulted ceiling and fifty tables, unchanged, where I once met Harvard boys for study dates. But I headed straight for the card catalogue room, anxious to see again the miles of drawers of index cards documenting hundreds of thousands of books, a whole world easily accessible to anyone who knew the alphabet. I remembered how thrilling these had been to me when I first saw them, more, even, than the sea of Harvard's ten thousand men. But…had the best library in the country done something so appalling and stupid? The drawers were gone—vanished as if by whirlwind or plague. Feeling a little like Blanche Du Bois, I relied on the kindness of a young man at the desk to show me how to punch out titles and subjects on a pitiful little screen. If I was a dinosaur here, at least I wore the proper camouflage—jeans just like everybody else's, except mine had solder drops and theirs rips in all the wrong places.

The computer directed me across Harvard Yard to the William James Library of Psychology and Sociology. Once there, I settled myself on an old wine-colored leather couch that was to become my beachhead in this small, manageable library, with its open stacks pleasantly designed as balconies wrapping around the top of each reading room, reached by little spiral staircases.

I needed to attempt some abstract thinking. What was the problem we were trying to grasp? How did we need to approach it?

I was troubled by this question: were we just dissatisfied with our jobs and so obviously, if we could possibly find other work, should all simply quit? That didn't quite fit. Our demoralization at work was really not the same thing as job dissatisfaction. That subtle difference was one of the most difficult and important points to figure out. Job dissatisfaction, a subject of great interest to industrial psychologists and a common reason for middle-class people to change jobs, is no big deal to working people. It is not a legitimate complaint. It is a given, something to be endured with toughness and humor.

"Is my wife happy with her job?" Rudy replied when I asked if work made him and his family happy. "Of course not. Me either. Work is not happiness. That goes without saying. Happiness is for later. Retirement is happiness. A trip to Italy is happiness."

"You shouldn't be worrying about job satisfaction," an organizer of southern African American textile workers cautioned me. "That's a middle-class problem. Working people's problem is how to survive—how to put bread on the table."

This tradition of work as a kind of curse to be endured extends from Biblical times to the present, borne out, I found, in a number of studies. Ambivalent responses about work on a multitude of surveys led one authority, Robert Kahn, to conclude that sixty percent of American workers' feelings could be summarized by the phrase "Work is necessary but not enjoyed."[3] Most people pronounced themselves moderately satisfied with work. But when he asked more searching questions which were designed to get at intrinsic satisfaction (versus security and pay), such as "If you had a choice, economically, would you choose similar work again?" or "Would you want your son or daughter to do this kind of work?" the majority of professionals surveyed answered yes, but only sixteen to twenty-four percent of blue collar workers did so. That status-response pattern among middle-class and working-class people held true in numerous studies of up to

---

3   "Job satisfaction is the most researched variable in the area of work." Robert L. Kahn, "The Meaning of Work: Interpretation and Proposals for Measurement," in *The Human Meaning of Social Change,* ed. Angus Campbell and Phillip E. Converse (New York: Russell Sage Foundation, 1972), 180.

twenty-three industrialized or semi-industrialized countries.[4] Apparently, then, seventy-six to eighty-four percent of blue-collar workers everywhere were not satisfied with their work, and did not consider that significant enough to register a complaint about unless pressed.[5] We were like that. But if job dissatisfaction didn't generally merit our complaints, then what was the nature of that demoralization that *had* caused us to speak up?

"This is deeper than job dissatisfaction," I had said over the stove a few nights ago to my sociologist friend Laura. We were in the kitchen of her colonial house, with its new teal paint and paisley curtains. Laura and I shared a love of redecorating. We had a friendship consisting of late-night phone calls worrying, alternately, over our kids and the world at large, and also an unspoken agreement to escape activists' worries into frivolous pursuits, like our present task. We were trying out some new *Bon Appétit* recipes for a dinner with friends. She turned to me with characteristic decisiveness, her china doll face and blond curls gleaming under the new track lighting which we'd been admiring. Offering me a spoonful of our seafood sauce concoction, she said, "This is absolutely delicious—here, taste this. Jean, you're talking about classic alienation—re-read Marx!"

"I have!" I testified more or less accurately from memory: "Alienation as the products and social relations of the shop floor capitalized, relations between the workers no longer belonging to them but 'rising up on their hind legs' and confronting them, dominating them as alien objects! I love that monster image from *Capital*.[6] But I need something less abstract, some clue to our distress from modern, everyday experience."

"Then you might like the 1972 Senate Hearings on worker alienation presided over by Ted Kennedy."

4   Robert Kahn, *Work In America*, 15.
5   *Ibid.*
6   Karl Marx, "Results of the Immediate Process of Production," Appendix to *Capital: A Critique of Political Economy*, Volume I, Intr. Ernest Mandel, Trans. Ben Fowkes (New York: Vintage Books, 1977), 1054. ("The Results" was originally planned as Part 7 of Volume I, but was not discovered and published until 1933, and first appeared in English in this 1977 edition of *Capital*.)

The Growing Focus on Work Distress in 1970 to 1990

"In 1970 we revolted!" said Dan Clark, a Lordstown auto worker, before U.S. Senate hearings in 1972. A crisis had prompted Senator Kennedy to hold the hearings. The Lordstown auto workers had staged work slowdowns to protest monotony on the assembly line. Sabotage had occurred with increasing frequency. During the nineteen sixties there had been shootings at the Elden Axel Plant in Detroit, and at other auto plants more than fifty-percent increases in worker absenteeism, turnover and disciplinary lay-offs.[7] "I have come to understand sabotage…as an act of social sanity!" James Wright, the Director of National Policy Affairs for the Center for Urban Ethnic Affairs, testified.[8]

Young workers of the nineteen sixties and seventies, like young students, were rejecting traditional values—in their case the blue-collar values of "the work ethic" and obedience to authority. It was estimated that productivity losses were in the billions. Senator Kennedy opened the third day of hearings with these remarks:

> "We must be concerned that alienation in the workplace is producing a class of angry and discontented workers in factories and plants across this nation. If we are concerned about alienation caused by the war, and by dissatisfaction with government, then surely we should be concerned with the alienation caused by job discontent."[9]

While these absorbing hearings did not help me clarify the differences between alienation, demoralization and job discontent (witnesses tended to refer to those interchangeably), they certainly lent legitimacy to our concerns. Many business and union leaders and several rank and file workers testified to the need for the redesign and "humanization" of work. They talked of symptoms showing up in industry health statistics. People with job stresses and the low self-esteem associated with many industrial jobs, for example, were found to be at higher than average risk for peptic ulcers, smoking, high blood pressure and heart disease.[10] Satisfaction with work,

---

7   Senator Edward Kennedy, opening remarks in *Worker Alienation, 1972*, Senate Hearings Before the Committee on Labor and Public Welfare, Ninety-second Congress, Second Session, S.3916 (Washington: Government Printing Office, 1972), 13, 8. Subsequently to be referred to as Worker Alienation Hearings.
8   *Worker Alienation Hearings,* 20.
9   *Ibid.,* 91.
10   *Work in America,* 81.

they found, was the best predictor of longevity—better than known medical or genetic factors.[11]

The hearings provided persuasive evidence that there was indeed a crisis to be addressed, and Senate Bill 3916 proposed that $20 million of government funding be appropriated for research and practical experiments.[12] "It's shocking that it's only in the last three years that we've had social indicators to measure the quality of working life in the nation," said Dr. John French of the University of Michigan Survey Research Center.[13]

There followed a decade of government and private academic interest in the psychosocial aspects of work. To cite just a few, Melvin Kohn and his colleague Carmi Schooler were beginning to study the impact of job structure on the personality.[14] Daniel Zwerdling, in *Workplace Democracy* (1978), presented experiments with changing the organization of work at industrial sites in the U.S. and Europe. Robert Karasek and Tores Theorell were writing what would become a remarkably comprehensive book, *Healthy Work*, later published in 1990.[15]

In the '80's, however, the Reagan and Bush administrations appear to have put the brakes on exposés and reforms.

The Silence of the Eighties

Back at the plant the next day, I was having coffee with Hildie and Tom, sitting in the sun in the cement yard behind our shop. One picnic table had been placed here for such occasions. We eyed the millwrights coming and going around us, removing or delivering fifty-gallon drums of transformer oil and various chemicals bearing orange "hazardous" labels.

"Look at this!" I said, pulling out my new copy of *Healthy Work*.

Tom put on his reading glasses. "Looks great! A fat one—I hope you're a speed-reader. What are you doing, spending your whole paycheck on books these days?"

---

11   *Work In America, xvii.*
12   *Worker Alienation Hearings,* 7.
13   *Ibid.,* 39.
14   See for example "Reciprocical Effects of Socialization," in *American Journal of Sociology* 84, 1978.
15   Robert Karasek and Tores Theorell, *Healthy Work: Stress, Productivity, and the Reconstruction of Working Life* (New York: Basic Books, 1990).

"Kind of. Actually, I'm a slow reader, but what the heck! I'm on the trail of something related to our types of questions. It looks like a blackout on quality-of-work-life research in the Reagan and Bush administrations. Can I read you a little bit?"

Hildie smiled, tolerant of my bookishness, "Hey, we're all ears!"

"'Part of the hesitancy to address stress at the workplace is obviously political,'" I read aloud from *Healthy Work*. "'During the early 1980's in the United States, the National Institute of Health eliminated the research sections of the National Institute of Mental Health that were studying work stress, and dramatically cut funding for research at the National Institute for Occupational Safety and Health...The U.S. Office of Management and Budget has deleted job stress measurements on some occupational health questionnaires.'[16] Now doesn't that sound like the administration found questions like ours somehow threatening?"

"And you're surprised at that?" Tom was a dyed-in-the-wool Democrat.

Hildie, who had been studying her sneakers, looked up and gave me one of the little bemused smiles she reserved for unenlightened liberal types.

"Now, Jean. Why would you think this is a nice world where if you need information you just get it? This is military thinking. You know, information control, and operating only on a 'need to know' basis. Can't let the public know too much. Reagan was a war hero in his own mind and Bush was head of the CIA. Why would they think different? This place tries to operate in the same way—suppress information—but more like the Keystone Cops! Remember Bobby and those chemical safety data sheets?"

We all laughed. Last year, Bobby the spray painter developed some strange medical symptoms—dizziness, lack of muscle coordination, and hallucinations, as I recall. We persuaded him to make the company give him the Material Safety Data Sheets—a list of the chemicals in the brand-name paint cleaners he used. The state legislature had recently passed a "Right to Know" law mandating that these be made available in all workplaces.

We had wanted to see Bobby's Data Sheets in order to help him because the sheets alone were of little use without detailed explanations of the chemicals' effects on people, which could be obtained from the Mass. Coalition of Occupational Safety and Health (MassCOSH). I had that information, and management knew it. The company health and safety

16   *Ibid.,* 16.

man's job was to provide information. What he said to Bobby was: "What are you fussing about? That rinse is just Oakite, like laundry soap. My wife washes my underwear in it for God's sake!" Something was fishy. Bobby's boss had been told to forbid him to talk to me, and Shaunessy's mission apparently was to guard the pass—to hold the line between Bobby's department and mine. He had stood behind me all morning when the data sheets came out and forbade me to leave my seat. Chained to the chair! But of course they had forgotten to cover the cafeteria, where Bobby reluctantly showed us the sheets at lunch time. Putting our information together we had learned that the cleaner Bobby used was indeed Oakite, but a special kind—"Oakite 56"— with an extra industrial ingredient, Methylene Chloride. It was routinely emptied into the drains in our shop floor and piped on into the nearby river. My health information from MassCOSH revealed that long-term exposure to its fumes was known to cause hallucinations, loss of muscle coordination, liver damage, and cancer in lab animals. A while after Bobby knew what might be causing his symptoms, he was granted an early retirement.

"Hildie's right. It's a lot like the army here," said Tom. "'Don't let the enlisted men have too much information.' Probably those N.I.H. studies were threatening, for the same reason our Oakite data sheets were. The Reagan administration was probably trying to black out evidence that could lead to liability claims on corporations over job stress, or who knows what kind of injury. What kind of injury have we got? That's what we're trying to find out, right, in our seditious little group? Hey, Jeannie, keep on reading. If nothing else, it must be good for the brain cells!"

The buzzer rang and I passed the book to Tom—"Hey, check it out at lunch if you can tear yourself away from *The Wall Street Journal!*"

Work and Human Development

Despite the government information blackouts of the eighties, scholars persisted with inquiries about the human dimensions of work that they had begun in the '70s. Quality of life at work seemed to be coming into its own as an issue.

One afternoon, curled up on my favorite leather couch at the William James Library, I began to understand our problem. I was reading the work of Melvin Kohn, Professor of Sociology at Johns Hopkins University, whom I liked especially because he said that he had held a number of blue-collar jobs before becoming a professor. He said he was troubled that researchers tended to see *job dissatisfaction* as the only psychological ramification of work. "In fact it is only one and far from the most important ramification" he said. "Work affects people beyond the time and place of the job—their values, self-conception, orientation to social reality, even intellectual functioning."[17]

That was it! It wasn't the fact that we didn't enjoy work that bothered us. It was that we sensed it was affecting us in other ways we didn't understand. At the time of the Gulf War, during the hostilities in the shop, I remembered thinking 'something in this work is changing us, as if we were living by Love Canal.'

Our work—work in general—was a *formative* agent. It could alter us, shape the direction of our lives. By 1990, that had become an official position of the American Sociological Association, which said in its annual volume, that year entitled *The Nature of Work:* "We can say with considerable confidence that job conditions really do have an influence on personality, and, moreover, that they do so in strong measure."[18] Apparently work was an important factor in adult growth and development.

The developmental psychologist Jean Piaget established that the need for growth and development in human beings was a primary drive, inherent in the structure of the human brain.[19] For Abraham Maslow, the need for development was among the highest in a hierarchy of human needs, often met in "a task, a vocation or calling, some beloved work."[20] But these and other developmental theories of human stages, including those of Erik Eriksson, were based on interviews with professional people.[21] For people like that, it seemed, development was assumed to be positive, a kind of gentlemen's agreement that work should be a situation where people could

---

17   See "Unresolved Issues in the Relationship between Work and Personality," *The Nature of Work, American Sociological Association's 1991 Presidential Series,* ed. Kai Erikson and Steven Peter Vallas (New Haven: Yale University Press, 1990), 40, 57.

18   From "Introduction," *The Nature of Work,* 2.

19   Jean Piaget, *The Origins of Intelligence in Children* (New York: International Universities Press, 1952), 7-8.

20   Abraham Maslow, *Toward a Psychology of Being* (Princeton: Van Nostrand Company, 1962), 13.

21   Neil J. Smelser and Erik Erikson, ed., *Themes of Work and Love in Adulthood* (Cambridge: Harvard University Press, 1981), 162-3.

expect to come together to grapple with problems and thus grow in competence, wisdom and mutually maturing relations.

But what happened if the inherent need for growth was not being met, or development was negative? What if, in more constricted circumstances, people came to have diminished expectations and a diminished sense of self?

Darkness was falling beyond the two-story windows of William James, so I gathered my belongings. I looked around at the students in Shetland sweaters, who had draped themselves over easy chairs and were challenging each other in intense conversations. I threw a jacket over my shoulders and left, walking along Kirkland and Cambridge Streets in the gathering darkness, staying close to the red brick walls that enclosed Harvard Yard.

These old sheltering walls always reminded me of their twins, similar 18th Century brick structures at the Massachusetts Correctional Institution at Bridgewater, confines I entered every morning some years ago to work as a therapist at the Treatment Center for Sexually Dangerous Persons. It too was quite an awesome institution. The intimacies shared with me there still gripped me painfully. I could imagine the inmates telling me 'We'll give you development. How about seeing your mother murdered in front of your eyes? How about the terror of abandonment in the crib, or getting beat up as a baby?' Together we had traced the development of their crimes in the slow extinguishing of expectations, the hardening of defenses, the smoldering rage, the relief discovered in vengeance. "Life is not a flower garden, you know!" they'd tell me.

It's about time to end this period of study, I thought that night as I laid out my work clothes and set my alarm for 5:00 A.M. I patted my Siamese cat, Dow Jonesy, who always felt entitled to decide lights out time at my house, settling himself authoritatively on my shins. I flicked out the light. But one last passage was haunting me. It wasn't from my sociology or psychology books, but from *A Theology of Liberation* by Gustavo Gutierrez, which lay on my bedside table. I had been touched by these Catholics in Latin America, whose faith-based stands for the poor had recently cost some their lives. I flicked on the light again, finding the passage, one preoccupied, as I was beginning to be, with development and underdevelopment, and gaps that could happen between well-off people and the others. Guiterez was thinking about this on the level of countries:

"The imbalance between developed and underdeveloped countries—caused by the relationships of dependence—becomes more acute…The poor, dominated nations keep falling behind; the gap continues to grow…Should things continue as they are, we will soon be able to speak of two human groups, two kinds of people. Biologists have pointed with alarm to the fact that the incessant widening of the distances between the developed and the underdeveloped countries is producing a marked separation of two human groups; this implies the appearance, in a short time, of a true anthropological differentiation.'"[22]

Under-development leading to alterations in the species? What a modern vision of evil. For the liberation theologians, the perpetuation of sub-human conditions is the essence of sin.[23]

Then what of the growing gaps in development between different *classes* within the dominating industrialized countries? Surely, something as extreme as "anthropological differentiation" would never happen to us? Yet the passage warned that the gradual, imperceptible changes that daily life imposes have unforeseen consequences. That warning has continued to hover, for me, like a ghostly canary in the mines of our explorations.

Working Without A Blue Print

I needed to temper the foreboding I felt about class underdevelopment. As yet we didn't know anything good or bad about our development at work. Next month was approaching—time for the group's second session. I needed to think realistically about how we might proceed. I was hiding in the ladies' room, making some notes at morning break. We could start by using as a framework some of the concerns we had expressed. They had fallen into two categories: first, declining intellectual functioning and mental apathy and second, dysfunctional social relations and symptoms of emotional distress. We might begin by tracing these to our actual work practices or relations. Then we might want to find research to help us explain them, or do our own analysis of what was going on. Beyond that, I had no plan, no logical hypothesis.

I didn't really want to see our discussions limited to some preconceived structure. We wanted our talks to be spontaneous— authentic observations.

---

22   Gustavo Gutierrez, A *Theology of Liberation*, translated and edited by Sister Caridad Inda and John Eagleson (New York: Orbis Books, 1988), 53.
23   *Ibid.*, 103.

In the months that followed they would prove to be just that, but also ka-
leidoscopic, with thoughts tumbling around and forming new patterns, or
no logical pattern, derailed. They would come to be in need of some organization, so between groups I would write out our main insights and give
them to each person. I could see that we were in the habit of discounting
our own thoughts, which seemed to vanish like shadows, so felt that some
evidence of their significance on paper might encourage us.

Later that day I had lunch with Tom in our new cafeteria, which had
appeared like a dream after the recent shutdown. It had comfortable aqua
leather booths, sunny windows and decorative fake plants.

"You know what this is about don't you?" Tom smiled.

"Uh…they're trying to soften us up for some big take-back they plan in
the contract?"

"I'll bet you money they're looking to sell the whole building in a few
years and our jobs with it. What would you do if you wanted to sell your
house, Jean? You'd think ahead and fix it up some, wouldn't you?" (He was
to prove right about that several years later).

"You know, I have to tell you something," I said, picking at my iceberg
lettuce and tomatoes, the "fresh salad" people had been clamoring for the
cafeteria to serve. "I love this group. But I feel kind of nervous about it.
The reading I've done makes me think we're dealing with something quite
complex, with more serious implications than we suspected, and I'm afraid
of messing it up. I don't know for sure where it's going, or how we should
do it. Any advice?"

"Look, Jean," he said, "that's all right. We don't have to be sure. The important thing is that we are doing some thinking. I feel very committed to
this. To tell you the truth, I'm doing it in memory of my grandmother and
something she once told me. She worked all her life in a mill. When she
was quite old she said to me: 'Try never to work in a factory. It's a terrible
thing to work all your life and when you're done, to look behind you and
see no footprints in the sand.'"

IV

The Dinner Party

"You have no friends here, only acquaintances. They'll just stab you in the back in the end." That was the common maxim at the plant, the admonition of workers with thirty years in. "No fraternizing," management said. "With all your different backgrounds, you'll only end up in a fight. Stick to getting the product out."

My vacuum roared. The group was coming to dinner in twenty minutes. "What would be wrong with just socializing some night, before we start the serious stuff?" Suzanne and Hildie had proposed. I wanted that too. I needed to be with the group in the intimacy of home.

I cast a nervous eye over my living room. It was a casual place with secondhand furniture, homemade pink chintz slipcovers, and big red cushions scattered for sitting on the floor. A sociable space, I hoped, where all kinds of people could feel at home and usually did. The walls were covered with family photos of in-laws, parents, kids. Melissa, a little girl of nine, is squealing and jumping into a waterfall on a picnic. A grown-up Marc is smiling patiently, his arms around both frail grandmas. I'd always wanted it to be like anybody else's house—nothing odd that could make people feel uncomfortable. But the kitchen.

I folded my arms, surveying the kitchen. Too late to change it. I thought of it as my personal space where I could feel free to indulge my flaming radical taste. The walls were bright with gaily-colored posters recalling treasured episodes in my life. Red letters dripped: *"No Blood for Oil—End the War in the Gulf!"* Brash black graphics: *"Harvard Parties While South Africa Burns: DIVEST!"* arched over green and red wavy stripes, impressionistic lines of marching Africans. I shook my head.

My favorite was a little print over the toaster, almost a collector's item, beginning to yellow with age and stamped with a red buffalo: *"Washington D.C., July 15, 1978. The Longest Walk: Support Native Americans in their*

Continental Walk to Protest the Seizure of Land and Water Rights!" That
day I had stood in a grassy encampment exclusively for Native Americans,
official guests of the U.S. Government during the protest. I was perhaps the
only non-Indian camping there, invited by the United American Indians
of New England and my Mohawk boyfriend, an organizer of the event and
a founding member of A.I.M., The American Indian Movement.

"The *Landlords* are here, *Duus!*" he had whispered in my ear, grinning
as the demonstration began. *"Duus"* was his Indian word for sweetheart.

A small, straight-backed woman in her eighties, wearing her traditional
dress, long layers of embroidered black velvet skirts in the hot sun, had
stepped to the podium. She was from the Navajo nation and spoke no
English; a young man stood by to translate from her native Diné. The
image still arrests me. This was the first time I witnessed something like a
separate and sovereign nation inside U.S. borders. She hesitated, overcome
at the sight of thousands of Native people, fulfilling the prophecy of the
return of the warriors to protect sacred land. Warm applause encouraged
her to greet us.

"Ho! Brothers and sisters. It is a good day to die!"

A hush fell over the crowd. She had just greeted us with the traditional
warrior's call to battle. But everyone knew these same words were also
the once-in-a-lifetime declaration which traditional elders make when they
believe they have fulfilled their destiny and lived long enough. She was a
sheepherder who had walked all the way from South Dakota.

The doorbell rang. I jumped into my sandals and ran a comb hurriedly
through my hair. A nice looking young man in a sports jacket stood at my
door.

"Hi, Miss Jean!" Dominic smiled shyly. "I got lost. I thought you'd have
to send the team of bloodhounds out to find me. I can see the headlines
now: "pudgy Italian, dazed and confused, taken hostage in the ghetto!"

"*Handsome* Italian!" I smiled. "Hi!" In a sports coat he looked more like
a prizefighter than pudgy. "I've never seen you dressed up!" He handed me
a big warm pan.

"Stuffed shells in my own sauce, with three kinds of meat, simmered for
four hours. Back-breaking work, Miss Jean!"

Suzanne chuckled, just behind him. "Nobody's going to harm a hair of
your little Sicilian head in our neighborhood! Hey, if I survived growing

up the only black girl in an Italian neighborhood, you can make it through the night here!"

Suddenly they were all trooping up my steep steps together. "Jeannie, this is a nice piece of property! What is it, about 1910?" Tom smiled. "Let me carry this wine to the kitchen—it's heavy."

He was dressed up too, wearing a black cable turtleneck sweater with a gray tweed sports jacket. They were *all* dressed up—Sean in a light blue sports jacket and gray shirt open at the neck, and Nora, suddenly a knock-out in heels and a form-fitting black jersey dress. But of course, it was Friday night!

You're more than a little under-dressed! I thought to myself, brushing some flour from my loose blue corduroy cooking shirt.

They filed courteously into the dining room, setting down their offerings. I savored the aroma of Suzanne's jag—rice and beans with sausage—and Jasmine's homemade bread. Nora set out a plate of impeccably designed *hors d'oeuvres*, pumpernickel strips with squares of cucumber, green pepper, radish slashes and tiny shrimp arranged in geometric patterns.

"And this is from *my* people," Sean said matter-of-factly, setting down two six-packs of Guinness and breaking open a couple.

"Hey, welcome everybody!" I said. "You folks don't believe in coming empty-handed, do you! *Thanks!* Come, grab yourselves some wine or beer and sit down in here!"

"*Jesus*, Jean, you better get a chair lift for those steps!" Sean pretended shortness of breath. "This is pretty though. Somebody did a nice paint job!" he said, appraising the living room. "And a jungle for a dining room!"

Hildie grinned. "Very nice. I worked in a greenhouse once. That ficus could use repotting, don't you think?"

"Who's the *babe*?!" Dominic asked, scrutinizing one photo.

"The one balancing a plate of Easter breakfast on her head?" I smiled. "That babe's Melissa, my baby."

"Miss Jean, I could surround her with riches. I could buy her mother a better model of car!" Dominick posed, arching his eyebrows villainously. He'd make a darned good husband for someone, I thought to myself. Everyone knew he was dying to get married, and he wouldn't be a success in his family's eyes until he did. The guys in the shop were always belittling him for having too high standards in girls, and for not sleeping around.

"Well you could at least keep her in stuffed shells, Dommy," Sean said genially. "Look at that pan! I'm starving!" They weren't shy about hustling to the table and digging in.

"I'm a lousy cook myself," Sean continued, "but that's why I married Molly. First I had to get the approval of my grandmother, the matriarch of the family, a very smart woman. She used to be the nursemaid for the Kennedy kids!"

"Are you serious?" We were impressed. "Did you ever meet the Kennedys?"

"Just once, when I was a little kid, she introduced me to some guy I didn't feel like meeting that was campaigning to be senator. She said his name was Jack." Sean smiled. "Anyhow, these days at my house we mostly eat take-out because I'm pushing Molly to keep studying to get her R.N. And I'm out myself half the week nights agitating with the neighbors to keep the school down the block a neighborhood school!"

"You mean, 'neighborhood school' as in South Boston anti-busing type neighborhood school?" said Jasmine, looking uncomfortable. Most of us remembered the national TV cameras panning in on white Irish adults in Southie tossing rocks at school busses bearing little black kids.

"Well," he wrinkled his freckled nose impishly, "let's say same neighborhood schools, different players. There'll be no rock throwing, and my neighbors are black and Spanish. That's how I like it. Woodly's got me trained!" We smiled. Woodly was Sean's work partner, a soft-spoken black guy from the South who was a gospel singer on Sundays. They were inseparable, like Starsky and Hutch. Sean was always confounding my expectations. One minute he would sound like a stone male chauvinist, defending the rude sexual remarks made by his buddies at work, outraged that their free speech was violated when women accused them of harassment. In the next breath he'd be talking about how he was pushing his wife to be "liberated" and study to advance a career of her own, leaving the kids to him at night. He was very committed to this free-thinking group of ours, and also to the camaraderie in his conservative Army Reserve unit. The blue-collar world at the plant was like that. We were filled with contradictions, unpredictable, which was cause for uneasiness among us, and for sudden pleasant surprises. Life there was like the Kandinsky print in my living room, a black factory with an ominous red glare inside, yet yellow and green bushes bursting like spring around it. We spent the evening eating and chatting lightly, exchanging small talk about families.

"How did you meet your present husband, Suzanne?" Tom asked, examining the family photo she'd passed around of a pudgy baby grandson with Asian eyes and Suzanne's tan-gold skin, sitting on his Japanese mama's lap next to her son Michael, and Harry, the step-grandpa in question.

She laughed. "Well, it was twenty years ago and I was just back to Boston from working on submarines at an American division in Virginia. One day I was visiting my dad in the hospital and this guy in the other bed, in *traction*," she chuckled, "had his eye on me. He was white but *all right!* It was love at first sight. I didn't want to get married again but he just wore me down till I said yes!"

Jasmine tended to keep to herself in the shop and now she was doing that here, off in the living room examining my prints. She always dressed like an artist, tonight in an African tunic with brown arcs and squares that emphasized her big eyes and high cheekbones.

"Well, *I'm* not going to get married again!" she said. "I like running my own show. I run a tight ship at home. My two-year-old is well behaved— no 'terrible twos' for him! My own parents were very strict—they hit us a lot. I'm second generation, up from the South." I found it interesting that she always referred to herself as "second generation," as if the predominantly black states in the South were a separate country from which you could be an immigrant.

"I think a lot of people from the South are strict like that," she continued. "It's from the history of slavery and hard times. They had to be. They were determined that the next generation shouldn't stay in that little crummy life. We were supposed to make something of ourselves."

Suddenly there was a streak of fur, jolting us all backward, as Dow Jones landed his Siamese self smugly in the breadbasket.

"God, Jean, that's the worst pet I ever saw!" said Sean, shaking his head and laughing. I swooped Jonesy up to be locked away, knowing his untrainable will to recapture newly seized territory, no matter how many times I'd remove him. "I bet their cats have a little working-class discipline!" I hissed at him as I dumped him in the bathroom and hurried back.

Nora was straightening the place mats and righting the salt shakers that had flown every which way. She helped herself to another tiny serving of my seafood lasagna, not anything that would compromise the fit of that dress.

"Well I'm second generation too, Jasmine. My father was a Russian immigrant who became a physics professor, and he was also strict. My family was very intellectual, but I kicked over the traces and rejected that intellectual life."

"*No* you didn't," I objected. "You're still always reading and raising questions—that's how all of us are, isn't it? We're thinkers! We're asking questions!"

"That's right!" Hildie laughed, "*Intellectuals*. Of course, at the plant they'd call us oddballs."

"I've been a reader all my life. They can call me whatever they want!" Tom said, cleaning up the last of his jag and turning to Ruth, who was cutting a huge sheet cake she'd decorated with yellow roses. "You've been so quiet, Ruth. I know *one* thing about you! If you ever retire, you can sure make your living as a baker!"

"Well, my family is me and my twin girls," she offered. "They're fifteen, and six foot one! They really stand out on the freshman basketball team, let me tell you! These days I only see them at meal times. When *I* retire I plan to go back to the South, or I *did* till the twins started objecting. Yet and still, I'll find a way someday, and when I do, I'm going to invite you all down to visit me on my *plantation*!" We giggled. "For now, I spend all my time after work with my minister, rehabbing a storefront we've rented for a church. My minister, she's not bad with the hammer. But it's a good year's project."

She'd taken me by the storefront, an empty shell with no floor. They were collecting discarded lumber for the floor from streets and construction sites, she said. My own church, the first one I'd set foot in in years, was giving them a little lectern as a starter pulpit. Mine was also a storefront, with a raucous congregation made up of social activists and people from the drug and alcohol recovery movement. Ruth's was to be much more traditional, Southern Baptist. That meant that dissent and social action would be considered wrong in a church, where people should stick to the power of prayer. We were more the "Praise-the-Lord-and-pass-the-ammunition" types. Ruth's gentle quietness was appealing. She had a strength and patience that I suspected came from many years of "making a way out of no way."

"And how about you?" she returned Tom's courtesy.

"Well, my five are all grown up now," he said, reaching for the coffee pot and pouring some all around. "This is my second wife. My first wife died tragically young, of cancer, leaving me with two babies. So I worked hard, took courses, with the help of my family, and went into broadcasting. I never got a college degree, but I began to make some good money. I guess I was on the way to having what was supposed to be the American dream. But it wasn't really money I was chasing. It was freedom—some peace of mind to be able to sit down and say 'this is what I believe.' I'm not sure I'll ever acquire that. I'm still searching. I don't know—it's been a long trip."

There was only the clinking of forks on china for a while.

Tom had about him a combination of sadness and determination I'd always liked and wondered about. There was a solidity in his Korean war veteran's carriage and in what he left unsaid, what he had lived, I guess. While he often talked freely at work to anyone who'd listen about his skeptical views of current events, he usually played it close to the vest about personal life and feelings. I was touched by his openness now.

How cautious we are, though, tonight, I thought—polite, not going too far. We're *trained* to this reticence at American. Maybe we'll always be like this in the group. Or maybe down the road we'll surprise each other. We are like people kept too long in some kind of quarantine, wary of contact, unsure of ourselves. Me too.

"It's been a long trip for a lot of us," Hildie sighed. "It has been for me. Since I didn't get to be in the military police like the men in my family, I did what everybody in the fifties did. Got married, had kids, worked what they used to call 'mothers' hours,' and got divorced. Then I got bogged down at American." She sat back pensively, blowing careful smoke rings. "Jean, I have a question. You have a degree and all. You could have been making some real bucks. Why are you working in a factory?"

Eight pairs of eyes were on me. I was asked that once at work by two old hard-liners at the company who thought I was a foreign agent. I stiffened and gave the same automatic answer now: "It pays more than mental health work did. I had kids in college."

"No, I mean really why." They waited.

I glanced at Nora. I wasn't ready for this. My reasons were very personal, and would make me sound like I came from Mars. But I felt obliged to break my own reticence, take the chance of saying too much.

"Give her another piece of cake," Sean said.

They passed me a slice and I took a few bites, hesitating. "Okay I guess I'm like you, Tom—never really been chasing money either. My dad was an orphan who'd seen tough times, and he always said: 'Money doesn't matter. The only thing that matters in life is the good you see in certain special people.' Maybe that was what inspired me about the Civil Rights and Peace Movements. Thousands of those special people fighting for the good society. How to make a long story short? Well, when I got to know extremely disadvantaged people like my dad had been, through my jobs in prison and in the streets, I wanted to join the fight. I wanted to change the way the decks were stacked against them."

"Redistribute the wealth!" Tom said.

"That's right. And where was the power to force such a thing to happen? The theory among many people in the 1970's was—the power is in the hands of the working people."

Dominick clenched and unclenched his fists, grinning and shaking his head. "I must need to work out more!"

"You and a lot of others got *really* radicalized," Tom said.

"Yes we did. It wasn't just theory then. In France, Italy, Africa, workers were militant, preparing for general strikes. So activists here were full of hope and decided they better get to know U.S. workers a whole lot better. They knew they had plenty to learn and they better go to the source. Stop talking the talk and walk the walk. Go for the gold. Work in factories. It sounded like the life for me. What can I say? Here I am, fourteen years later, like the song says—still crazy after all these years."

Tom smiled. "That's a love song, Jean. What's to love? Maybe that's another question for us."

We were quiet for a few minutes.

"I admired the ideals of the Civil Rights movement too," Tom went on. "But...I don't know about you, but all I see around me now is cynicism."

"I think people are by nature selfish and greedy," Hildie said. "Look at the shop. If people like that took things over, the strong would just trample the weak, like they've always done."

"Hey, Miss Jean, I have an idea!" Dominic giggled. "You've got all those posters in the kitchen—*No Blood for Oil!* Let's paint over them *'No Blood for Missiles!'* We could hold them up and march around the cafeteria! We could borrow a tom-tom and do some war whoops!"

"Yeah!" I could see Sean warming to the subject. "Militant, hell, we could be military! We *are* military! We could make your house a bunker! It's on a frigging hill! We could mount telescopes in the windows trained on American. You've got an instructor in the Reserves here—I could whip you sorry people into shape in no time! I think I could even train that cat for a suicide mission to demolish Heavy Assembly! And if they laid us off in retaliation, we could become a 'Reserve Army of the Unemployed.'" He arched an eyebrow at me.

I shrugged and smiled wryly. At American, I got used to it long ago, this thin line between jokes and ridicule.

"Wait a minute!" Nora said quietly. "You can laugh now but it wasn't long ago that *we* had some dreams too—admit it! In the '84 union election, every one of us took *heat* supporting John Angelino. You tell me why."

"We had a good chance to overthrow machine politics and win democracy," Suzanne said stoutly. "Like we used to say, *The Union is Us!* All of us, black, white or purple. It was the first time that damn union ever saw a slate of officers that had black people and women on it up there with John. Not to mention being willing to strike for the first time in thirty-five years if they shipped out our jobs!"

Nora thought for a moment, smoothing her napkin. "See, I think there was something more. I think we shared a dream of overcoming too. Of overcoming the low, mean relations there. Of creating a new little world— we just *called* it a new union. And we almost had it. Remember how wonderful it felt not to be afraid to go to campaign meetings—no intimidation and ridicule like at union meetings? The old guys told me that even our campaign *parties* felt different. Not like union parties years ago that used to break down inside of half an hour with people insulting each other and getting into drunken fistfights in the men's room. Remember our parties at the Best Western? There'd be hundreds of us blue-shirts from plants all over the state who didn't really know each other. But the atmosphere of respect was awesome."

"It was, wasn't it?" I said. "Because we knew that in the past week every one of us had been under attack and had had to summon up courage and principles we didn't even know we had."

"Yeah." Sean muttered. "We had it. And we lost. We lost it all. Through the union's cheating, lying and fear tactics. And let's not even mention the retaliation afterward, or what happened to John."

John's death was a taboo subject that still sat like a glacier over many of us in American's shops. We weren't about to break the taboo tonight.

"What John did was ask some big questions," Suzanne said, raising her cup. "Let's just say our next round's to John."

We nodded and downed the last of our coffee.

"All right, it's getting late." Hildie stood up, piling on an armload of plates. "Time for a little K.P. Come on all you rebel troops—seize the kitchen! March!"

V

Work and the Mind

The Couch Potato

Tom pushed open the pristine paneled door of our meeting room, trailing in yellow October leaves wet and clinging to his New Hampshire work boots. He swung a hefty red Coleman cooler down with a thud and announced:

"You know what my Jewish grandfather used to say about the mind? He'd say, 'If you have brains, you have everything. With knowledge you can be a King!'" He smiled at us. "That's what he used to tell me when I was a little kid riding around on his shoulders!"

"Don't know about your brains, but the brawn's not bad—for a grandfather." Sean lifted the top of the cooler a crack. "What did you bring us, some Buds?"

"Hell no, this is a *church*, man! I bought a couple rounds of cokes for the house. Hey, where's Jasmine and Dominic?"

"Laid off to second shift. You didn't hear?" said Nora. "We're like the leaves, aren't we? You never know when the next one will fly."

"Like bowling balls!" said Hildie, dragging a chair to the window. "Bam! Another two down!"

"Seven left standing!" Suzanne chuckled. She had the kind of smile that's meant by "radiant"—it immediately lit up situations and sparkled her tan-gold face, making her look, today, like a plump autumn Mrs. America in her magenta silk slacks and shirt.

"Okay, everybody," Tom called us to order, pushing up the sleeves of his white sweatshirt. Although he worked in Test, which was considered middle-class, semi-professional work within American's hierarchy, he usually saw no compelling reason to dress the part. "Listen. To start things off, I have a question I've been thinking about: has anyone in this room ever had a job that they really loved? What does one need, to really feel that way about a job? To say wow, and really look forward to getting up in the morning?"

Everyone was silent. Then Hildie said she knew somebody like that once. Was I the only one who had ever had a job I loved?

"I had one," Sean said. "It was my job at Boston University, in the Dissertation Library. I had fifteen girls working under me!" We laughed and made a few smart remarks.

"The pay was lousy, but I really enjoyed the work. No one was saying 'Well, we need a thousand parts out by the end of the month for shipping date.' The responsibility I had was to sort out theses to be rebound or destroyed. What I still can't get over is how the people who used the library would come in because they actually *wanted* to hear other peoples' ideas and read other people's material. They were open-minded enough to accept a different premise. It didn't matter if you had a degree, if you were working in there you could argue a point and everybody listened."

"Oh, just like American?" Tom raised an eyebrow.

Sean scowled. "Don't get me started! How aggravating it is to look from side to side on the shop floor and see people so dormant, with no opinions. To know that they accept life with no goals, no insight, no viable responses to criticism, never wanting to do anything."

"Joe Six-pack" Tom said. "The guy that goes home and just slumps in front of the TV. The stereotype. Trouble is, sometimes it's true."

"What I would like to know," I said, "is what is the anatomy of Joe Six-Pack? What causes the dormancy?"

"I have developed a theory about that," Hildie said hesitantly. "It's called 'The Evolution of the Couch Potato.'"

"Hey, let's hear it!" Tom said. "Come on out of that corner. What are you doing hiding over there?"

"Sneaking a cigarette," she grinned sheepishly. She let it hiss out in a cup of water and ambled over to join us.

"This is my theory," she said. "You're glad to have the job at first, then you find out you won't get ahead, that it's all politics. So you get depressed, then you accept it, then you are hit by the repetitiousness and boredom. You want out and you know you can't leave. Then comes resignation and lost hope—'I'm so bored I don't care'—but you probably *do* care. You're just so depressed again that you lose energy and creativeness and start being a couch potato. If you look around you at work you'll see people in various stages of this evolution. The company doesn't care—there's always someone else to take your place." She paused, then said firmly, "I think most blue-collar workers are in this place."

"So underneath the couch potato is depression," I said.

"I've got a theory that goes along with the couch potato and depression," Nora said. "It's from this book I've been reading. Can I tell you about it?" She held up a book that said *Helplessness: On Depression, Development and Death* by Martin E.P. Seligman.[1]

"Now there's a catchy title!" Tom frowned. "What the heck. Tell us about it."

Learned Helplessness

Nora took some notes from the pocket of her trim black down vest and grabbed a coke. "Okay, Seligman's main theory[2] here is that adults get depressed from being raised with too little control over their lives as kids, that is, with over-controlling parents. But my question to you is: do you think we could get depressed from having too little control at *work*?'"

"Hmm," said Hildie.

"This is a little bit hard because we have to abstract what we can learn from some experiments Seligman did and try to apply it to our situation," Nora went on. "Let me describe the experiments. They're about helplessness, and they're mean. He gave a group of dogs electric shocks but they were restrained in harnesses and couldn't do anything about it. Then he tried it with other dogs that had a button they could press to stop the shocks. He wanted to know if feeling helpless affected their ability to learn. So he did it all over again, but this time they weren't helpless anymore—all of them had buttons they could learn to press to stop the shocks." She paused for a swig of coke. "To make a long story short, the ones that had the button *before* were able to learn fast how to stop the shocks. But the ones who had no control the first time took two hundred tries to learn to stop the shocks. They seem to have learned, all too well, that they were helpless."

Suzanne shook her head, "Where were the Animal Rights people?"

"I know!" Nora continued. "Anyhow, I need to tell you just one more. Seligman also wanted to know if lack of control could cause depression. So

1   (New York: Scribner, 1975).

2   *Ibid.*, 111.

he put some monkeys in a cage with a button they could press to get food and air conditioning. Afterward he put them in a second cage where they had no control button. Pretty soon they became listless, uninterested in their surroundings and depressed. So do you think this could be the reason for the apathy of the couch potato? Lack of control and depression?"

"But those are animals," Hildie objected. "They have no control over their situations. We do."

Sean tapped his pencil and frowned. "I agree! We're not that helpless, are we? Then again, I could see it applying to life in the ghetto—the subliminal derogatory messages people get."

"Whether it's the ghetto or American, I think it does apply." Suzanne agreed with Nora. "We *feel* we have no control, that we can't leave or get another job."

Ruth raised her hand hesitantly. "I imagined myself being one of these animals and I said to myself, 'Well, Ruth, it's not like you're in a cage and can't even bark!' But still I felt like that dog. He must have said, 'Well, what can you do? This is how it's gonna be the rest of your life.'"

We were silent for a moment.

"See," Nora said. "I think I feel helpless and depressed like that when management keeps making me do my job in a way I know is wrong, so the unit's going to fail, but they force me because they're in a hurry to meet production."

"There you go—that's learned helplessness!" Tom was clearly enjoying the intellectual exercise.

Hildegaard took out her cigarettes. "I still think we have the choice of leaving, so we're not helpless. Myself, though, I choose not to lose my house. So I'm locked in here and I have to adjust to it. I have to admit I have gotten severely depressed every January since I've been at American."

I was getting the feeling that Hildie and Sean were threatened by the idea of having no control, but I didn't understand why.

Sean was frowning, lost in thought, and then he said very quietly. "The dog experiment made me remember what that control feels like—the ultimate in breaking you down. I was in a situation once where they constrained us—in the army. To break us down they locked us in on a military reservation and punished us. We really had no choice but AWOL. I saw a guy jump out of a third floor window, and two others try to shoot themselves."

We were quiet, taken aback. I was struck by the fact that Sean had experienced a whole different magnitude of control than I had ever been subjected to; perhaps that was why he had more of a sense of urgency than I did about maintaining what personal control you could. Maybe Hildegaard, in her military family, had been subjected to some kind of coercive control too. I looked up.

"How frightening—being captives like that. It's true American doesn't use that kind of control, deadly force. Maybe eventually we'll figure out what they do use."

Ruth folded and refolded her napkin, smoothing it carefully with her long fingers. "About learned helplessness and growing up—we were always told as kids 'white kids are fragile, they can't do anything for themselves. But *you're* going to learn.' So I was taught at home not to be helpless like the white girls, but outside, with all the prejudices toward black people, I learned 'you're not good enough for this and that,' and so I learned helplessness there, I guess. I was living in New York City with my great aunt. What kind of authority figure could I tell you she was? An Adolph Hitler figure! She used to make me be quiet when she hit me so the neighbors wouldn't hear. So of course I was helpless, till I got out with other people, other races.

"You have to give up what you learned as a child or it will hold you back. Then in the '60's so much was exploding. It seemed as if we could do anything we wanted! Working at American in the model shop, with its specialized work, I had more say over what I did. But now, laid off from the model shop to this machine, it's so stressful and demeaning I do feel helpless again. But don't we have to remember there's life at home? That this is only eight hours?"

"But it's tragic to lose eight hours every day," Nora objected. "Why can't we just be normal?"

"Why couldn't we unlearn our helplessness and organize to change these conditions?" I said, apparently feeling the need to assert some control myself. Their raised eyebrows made me remember I'd broken the cardinal rule of the group: these were to be only discussion groups, not organizing. I always hoped that they would change their minds.

Hildegaard laughed. "Oh right! Yeah, sure! You've got about a snowball's chance in hell of doing that!" she said. "Let's take a break!"

Ruth stretched her long legs and yanked hard on the flaming orange seal of the barbecued chips. She offered them to each of us as we stood up, walked about and watched Nora do some stretching exercises.

"Hey, Ruth," Tom grinned, opening the cooler and motioning for people to help themselves, "You're tall! Did you ever play basketball yourself as a teenager?"

"Oh no, my aunt wouldn't let me. She was more into coaching me to be a maid."

"How did you get out of there, anyhow?" Hildie asked from across the room.

"Well, my aunt's brother—my great uncle—took me aside one day and said 'You shouldn't stay and take the way she's treating you!' He helped me get an application for the Job Corps—that was my escape." She turned to Nora. "So how's the new house coming?"

"Oops!" Nora caught a blob of yogurt dip that was about to fall on the damask chair. "It's really beautiful out in the country these days. I watch the tree colors and want to paint. But we're still knocking down walls. There's this little barn up in back with seventy years of junk in it. When I get that cleared, some day, I will have a great studio. Meanwhile all I'm doing is making a few sketches."

"When I'm not working, I spend all my time wallpapering!" Suzanne laughed ruefully. "I told Harry if he keeps putting it on crooked he's gonna make me turn gray overnight. I'll be an old lady before that damn house gets done!"

"Well I've got just what you girls need!" Sean stood up, hooking his thumbs under his green plaid shirt and throwing his shoulders back. "Me! A cheap, experienced contractor!"

"Oh right, that's all I need! You and Harry!" Suzanne grinned. "I think I'd run away to Aruba!"

"Come on, you people, get back to business," Hildie said, closing the window as people settled around the table again. "Who else has a theory about apathy or dormancy?"

"Me," said Sean and I, at the same time. "You first!" I said to him. He held up a dog-eared book.

The Army, Swedish Workers and Apathy

"Okay," said Sean. "Jean gave me this book to check out, because it's by the U.S. Army, right?" I nodded. The title was *The Manipulation of Human Behavior.*

"All right, let me give you people a little food for thought here. It seems that, in the '60's when this was written, the army was having to figure out what would happen to people isolated in space or at radar stations. They found people would get what they called 'sensory deprivation.' Now could that apply to you guys who do repetitive work? A little sensory deprivation on the job? Listen to this." He opened the book to a marked page, put some reading glasses on his nose and read slowly and deliberately:

> "Deprived of meaningful sensory input, the brain does not function normally. The skill most impaired is that of general reasoning and problem solving. Perception is disrupted, with interest giving way to boredom, attention giving way to distractibility.... Subjects tend to develop tension, headaches, irritability, seclusiveness and tend to become easily confused or—apathetic."[3]

"Bingo," said Tom. "Sensory deprivation. I'd say that's twenty- four-seven at American."

"And what I have," I said, bringing out some notes, "talks about the chemical side of the sensory deprivation and the apathy. It's an experiment by two Swedish 'socio-physiologists' they're called. They measured the urine of six hundred Swedish saw mill workers!" (Groans and giggles)

"Pisser!" Sean said. "Swedes, huh?"

"Hey, what can I say? What they were trying to do with the urine was to measure peoples' level of adrenaline and cortisol while they worked. What they found was that fast-paced machine work like yours, Ruth, left the workers with high adrenaline, in overdrive, even for hours after work. But slow, passive, unstimulating work like the rest of us do (they called it work with "a low level of arousal") slows down the cortical processes in the brain, leaving the person inactive and bored.[4] Think about it! That would mean our apathy gets locked in by what are known as "autonomic" chemical processes in the brain. So if we feel like our jobs are numbing us, we just might be right!"

3   *The Manipulation of Human Behavior*, eds. Bidderman and Zimmer (New York: John Wiley and Sons, 1961), 87, 72, 90.

4   Marianne Frankenhaeuser, Ph.D. and Bertil Gardell, Ph.D., "Underload and Overload in Working Life: Outline of a Multi-disciplinary Approach," *Journal of Human Stress #3,* September, 1976, 36.

"I do have a lot of trouble getting started at home," Suzanne said, frowning. "You're in such a state of stagnation that you can't climb out of it by yourself."

Ruth leaned forward and said softly, "I feel like they say too! You all don't know what it feels like to work at those fast machines all day. I get so stressed I used to run back and forth to the bathroom and make little drawings just to do something that was mine!"

"What a lovely vegetable garden we are!" Sean said, signalling that the tape was about to end. I held up my hand to stop the flow so we wouldn't miss anything, and quickly inserted a fresh cassette as he leaned back in his chair.

"Okay," he continued. "So it's a problem of no stimulation. But maybe it's our own fault. When I first came to American I went to night school in electronics. I used to read. But now I'm so aggravated and useless, I don't read. So I don't stimulate myself and I do regress to an animal state! The beautiful part about something Tom said the other day was it made me think. I said to myself, 'I'm worthless. Here I am forty years old and all I do is sit around home and watch cartoons with the kids, swearing and regressing. I'm too bright of a person for this!'"

"I have a question," Hildie said, heading back from the window.

"Oh, oh!" Sean said. "Heads up! Hildie has another one of her questions!"

"My question is this." She said. "Let's say this couch potato-mental shutdown thing does happen, whether it's from brain chemistry or learned helplessness. Then what happens to our IQs over time? As I said before, I used to have a fairly high IQ, but now I doubt I could function on the outside. Does something really happen to our IQs? Can they change?"

"Well," I said, "There's good news and bad news. Let me give you some reports from my reading."

Changes in IQ in Aging and at Work

I handed out copies of a graph shaped like a hill, with the peak marked at age twenty five. "You'll notice that our expert here, Paul Baltes, made his graph of a lifetime's intellectual functioning peak at age twenty-five. From twenty-five years old it's gradually down-hill into age ninety, as you can see here. But see this dotted line above it? The much higher hill? That represents the IQs of people whose minds are used, as he says, 'optimally'— they're exercised more."[5]

"Oh!" Sean said. "So some of you guys are over the hill, but over a better hill if you keep the brain cells peddling!"

"Right. And you're not far behind us," I said. "So it looks like the bad news is if we don't exercise our minds, they deteriorate more. But if we do, we can alleviate that. Another guy, K.W. Shaie, came up with similar conclusions after giving IQ tests to five hundred people repeatedly over twenty-one years. They kept or increased their IQs if they kept their lives complex and stimulating. If they didn't, their IQs decreased."[6]

"Use it or lose it. I always said that," Suzanne chuckled, "but I wasn't talking about IQs!"

"Hey," Tom grinned at her. "I guess you're not *that* gray yet!"

"Well," Nora said. "If we extract from these studies, I can see they could also apply to our work. They could be telling us that we're not using it, so we could lose it! But are there any studies directly about IQ and *work*?"

"Very few," I said. "Melvin Kohn, who I like because he used to work in a factory before he became a researcher, studied three thousand men and their jobs over a ten-year period. He found that what he called their 'mental flexibility' increased by twenty-five percent when they had little supervision and needed to do thinking and judging for themselves. But in the case of the men who did routine work and had what Kohn called 'excess supervision,' the men's mental flexibility stayed the same or declined."[7]

"Men again!" Nora said. "How come they never study women?!"

---

5   Baltes, Reese and Lipsitt, "Life-span Developmental Psychology," originally in *American Review of Psychology* #31, 1980, 65-110.

6   See K.W. Shaie, "The optimization of cognitive functioning in old age: Predictions based on cohort-sequential and longitudinal data," in P. B. Baltes & M. M. Baltes (Eds.), *Successful aging: Perspectives from the behavioral sciences* (Cambridge: Cambridge University Press, 1990), 94-117.

7   Melvin Kohn, "Unresolved Issues in Work/Personality," *The Nature of Work: Sociological Perspectives* (New Haven: Yale University Press, 1990), 40.

"As a matter of fact, Kohn and his colleagues Joanne Miller, Carmi Schooler and Karen Miller had established, in 1979, that the results were about the same for women."[8]

Nora pushed a strand of hair behind her ear. "See, I think the question of having less mental flexibility might apply to my work. Can I explain what happened to me this week?"

She paused to collect her thoughts. She liked to be well organized and attentive to details in her thinking.

"I've been thinking about this between sessions. I feel like it's a real struggle for me to use my mind now." She leaned forward, looking at us. "This week I'm on downtime, expected to just sit there with my hands folded, because we've been out of parts for several days. So I asked a couple of the guys in sheet metal—their knowledge is in a different area from mine—to teach me what they do. It's really complicated stuff. I'll understand the concept of how to figure things out. I'll say, well okay, let me put that theory into use as far as holding metal and bending metal. But even though I understand the concept, it's such a struggle for me to put the formula into action. You know, it's like my brain is in a fog and those theories are floating around and I just can't really do it. A few years ago when I was in art school it was different. I used to be able to pick up ideas and put them into use much more quickly because I used them every day."

"I've only just recently started thinking how the lack of stimulation affects me too," I said. I had been avoiding the question of altered mental functioning for thirteen years here, telling myself that having no stimulation went with the territory. "To tell you the truth, I've always said to myself about the boredom, 'Hey, put up with it. You have a college degree and you chose this work. What did you expect, a daily break for seminars?'"

People smiled without saying anything.

"But being in the group showed me that you all are troubled by this too," I continued. "So I've let myself face it more. And I've been noticing that I've changed in a very basic way after years in this place."

"What do you mean?" Suzanne asked.

"Well, see, now when I go home, I always head for the concrete, practical tasks, like we do at work. At first I liked that. In the past, when I had thinking-type jobs, I used to put off physical tasks at home because, truthfully, I was no good at them and they made me feel helpless. I used to really

---

8   *Ibid.*, 42.

admire a working class friend I had—his name was Renny. He could fix anything because, as he said, he had a 'real job.' He used to tease me, 'when are you gonna get a *real* job?'"

"Yeah, right!" Suzanne grinned. "Well you've got one now!"

"Yeah! Well now I've gotten a little more like him—good at practical work. I was proud of this at first. But I've gotten to a point where I avoid reading and thinking tasks. It's like I've gained ability to do concrete work, but lost ability to deal with conceptual work. And you know why I avoid it? I think it's because now it's become discouraging for me, almost threatening."

"And you with that *Hahvahd* degree in your closet!" Sean wouldn't let me forget that. I should never have told him.

"Is that where it is? I haven't seen it in years!" I said, not kidding.

Hildie sat back, thinking. "This stuff is not good news for us, is it, if I get the drift," she said. "It suggests we may have suffered some real damage to our IQs over the years without even knowing it."

I nodded slowly. For me, that was just beginning to sink in. The years we'd put in, perhaps debilitating years, had drifted like smoke into the past, beyond our reach. There was no changing them now. And we never suspected. They were just everyday experience, nothing out of the ordinary. I didn't want to tell them the rest of what I knew. I looked at the clock, saying nothing.

Tom looked uncomfortable, shifting in his chair. "You haven't told us the whole thing, have you, Jeannie? Come on."

"All right," I said, searching my notes. "This is my last report. A lot of the sociologists I was reading kept referring to one key study on IQ and work. It was by Rolf Von Schleicher and it was only available in German. So I got it copied at Widener and asked a certain German immigrant here at American, who asked to remain anonymous to protect the innocent, to translate it, which she did very well and which was very nice of her." They all nodded, knowing just who I meant. "Von Schleicher divided the workers he tested into three age groups—the 20's, the 30's and the over 40's. He then divided each age group according to the type of jobs they had—complex jobs needing a college degree, skilled trades needing training also, or jobs that you could learn as you worked or that needed no learning at all."

"Oh, oh, bad news for the unskilled jobs, right?" Tom said.

"I'm afraid so." I looked around hesitantly. "The workers with complex jobs and college training showed no loss of IQ difference between the younger and older people in their job group. There was a little loss of IQ, but not too much, between young skilled tradesmen and older ones. But people in simple jobs like ours that took little training showed the most loss of IQ over time. Von Schleicher didn't beat around the bush. He concluded"— I took out our friend's translation and read: "The development of the intelligence efficiency in the adult depends on the intellectual employment of the individual. Steady intellectual usage promotes, lack of or deficient intelligence stimulation hinders or inhibits development of intelligence."[9]

Now the group went quiet. Tom shuffled his papers, looked over his notes again and wrote something down. Nobody said anything for a long time. I brushed crumbs from the table and picked up our used paper plates, watching their faces for a reaction, waiting for them to express the anger I was feeling. I finally asked, "What do you think?"

One by one, instead of commenting on the material or their feelings, everybody very solemnly presented their intentions to leave American as soon as possible. Nora would try to sell sculpture. Ruth might start an Amway business. Sean had been looking into hazardous waste removal. Suzanne thought about learning tax consulting. Tom sighed "I guess I could go back to advertising. And you, Hildie?"

"Well, you people are the first ones I'm telling," she replied. "Just this week, I've been investigating becoming my own boss by re-mortgaging my house to buy a corner grocery store down the street."

Sean offered free help with remodeling.

"I've always said, your house is just a bank account with a roof on it!" said Tom. "But I hope you won't have a bad boss! That's fourteen hours a day seven days a week with her! Remember too, you have the right to fail if you want to." (He had undoubtedly read in *The Wall Street Journal* about the high failure rates of small businesses.)

"Lots of pessimism here! We'll drag Tom down to help us remodel for a little mental therapy!" said Sean.

---

9   "The Intellectual Development in Relationship to the Level of Work Activity," ["Die Intelligenzleistung Erwachsener in Abhangigkeit vom Bniveau der beruflichen Tatigkeit,"] *Probleme und Ergbnisse der Psychologie*, Heft 44/1973, Seite 25 bis 55, Aus Der Bezirksnervenklinik Schwerin, 25-55. I am in fact indebted to a fellow worker at "American Missile" for the translation of this article from the German.

We grew quiet again, sipping coffee for a while in silence and watching the yellow leaves on the birch outside the window turning up silver sides in the late October wind. Sean said in a low voice:

"Are the effects of the workplace reversible?"

"While you were talking," Tom said quietly, "I wrote on this scrap of paper, *'What would be the method for stopping this lobotomizing?'*"

"They've used up my strength and my mental abilities!" Suzanne said gruffly. "Don't they owe me something?"

Workers, Change Your Minds!

It was later in the year, 3:45 on a January afternoon. I could see my breath as I started to warm up my car. First shift workers, hard to recognize behind fur trimmed parkas, were hurrying to their cars, every man for himself, so to speak, in the rush to get to the narrow exit first and head home. I let the crowd go, turned on some music, and let the car really warm up, content to have a little time to think before I made my regular trip to the William James. Some questions I had were beginning to feel urgent.

Social policy makers were claiming a need for drastic changes in American workplaces and workers. President George H. W. Bush's 1990 Bipartisan Commission on the Skills of the American Workforce warned:

> "America is headed toward an economic cliff. If basic changes are not made...the gap between the economic 'haves' and 'have-nots' will continue to widen still further and social tensions will deepen!"[10]

The gist of the report was that it was necessary to alter U.S. workers' development in order to win the next round of global competition in manufacturing. Standard manufacturing would be done in other countries at lower wages, and the American products of the future would be specialized products filling a niche market. For this, we workers would be required to become inventive, take initiative, work collaboratively on projects instead of taking orders from bosses.

---

10   The Executive Summary of the findings of the Bi-Partisan Commission's *America's Choice: High Skills or low wages!* was kindly provided to me by the Boston Office of Senator Edward M. Kennedy. Hereafter referred to as E.S., 8, 3, 7.

That's nice, I thought to myself. You manufacturers have set us up in work that has been fragmented and repetitive, designed by Frederick Taylor and Henry Ford. You've split off thinking to the engineering and management level, and emphasized unquestioning obedience as our most important character trait.

Now it's all different. Robert Reich says U.S. corporations need to adapt to training us for flexible production and failure to do so will "rend the social fabric irreparably."[11] *The Economist* magazine says only 5% of companies are moving in the direction of being collaborative and non-hierarchical.

This policy consensus seems to me like a high-speed train, oblivious to everything but its destination. Oblivious to any input from workers about what in our development—let's face it, *underdevelopment*—might need to be addressed.

The blast of a horn behind me signaled it was my turn to get in line for the exit. Soon I was on the open road and passing The Ground Round where young workers who had no family obligations were slamming car doors and teasing each other, on their way in for a few rounds of beers.

They don't have a clue, I thought. They're so carefree about the future.

A red Cutlass swerved on a patch of ice, so I slowed down and snapped off the radio, knowing that thinking and driving was about as far as my multi-tasking abilities might stretch. I was headed now toward Cambridge.

Where are the unions on these changes, I thought as I drove down Main Street. People are going to need broader education than the unions back—not just upgrading practical skills![12] They are going to need more self-esteem, more practice with independent thinking on the job, and more human development than the military-industrial management model permits now.

11   *The Next American Frontier: A Provocative Program for Economic Renewal* (New York: Penguin Books, 1984), 21.

12   An exception is SEIU, the Service Employees International Union. In hearings arising from the findings of the Bipartisan Commission, John Sweeney, president of the International, testified in favor of the High Skills, Competitive Workforce Act of 1991 and noted "All workers, both young and experienced, both employed and unemployed, should have guaranteed access to broad-based academic education and training as well as occupational training." From *Hearings before the Committee on Labor and Human Resources United States Senate 102nd Congress, Second Session, on S.1790* (Washington: U.S. Government Printing Office, 1992), 28. The same record of Hearings contains a document, "AFL-CIO Reviews the Issues," June, 1990, in which it is noted that plant closings and layoffs cause personal stress and disillusionment that should be addressed by union counseling and emotional support, *Ibid*, 48.

I tried to pay extra attention to the road because I could feel myself getting furious at the constraints we would have to fight both from the company and the union. Human development! In the old, male-dominated unions like ours, human development is not a fit subject for labor-management discussions—I can hear them saying it's 'something that belongs at home with the women and children.' Well they may think it doesn't belong in the union hall, but these days it belongs in the boardroom. An article I read the other day said that two thousand business executives responded to a survey that the main requirement for economic progress was "improved human capital."[13] The same article quoted a headline from a recent *New York Times* series that complained: "Impending U.S. Jobs Disaster: Workers Unqualified to Work!"[14]

Bread and roses! I thought to myself as I eased onto Storrow Drive. What we're doing in our discussion group is considering issues that break with bread and butter unionism. We're talking about quality of life, making a life as well as making a living. We're thinking like those women in the 1912 textile mills in Lawrence. I thought of the antique sepia-toned photos of those women, which I'd once seen, the women filing past in the streets while businessmen in bowler hats stood watching. Their demands must have stunned you! I thought. How the cigars must have dropped from your mouths. For those little ladies, those upstarts, to walk off the job, not just for money, yet, but for all the life shut down in making a living. And to have the audacity to demand more than men did—to yell in your faces "and roses!"

As I crawled along in a long line of commuter traffic beside the Charles River, it struck me for the first time that my grandmother had died in 1915, which was just after the Lawrence strikes. "You're just like her—quiet," Dad used to say over and over, when I was little. I never knew what I was supposed to say. Then she had faded from family stories.

A cold wind off the Charles River blew a gust of snow across the windshield, obscuring my view. She worked in the Amoskeag Mills of Manchester, New Hampshire, not far from Lawrence, and died of brown lung disease. Could she have known of the strikes? 'Grandmother, I never knew you. Could it be that you too stood at a dusty loom, just a young girl, and held out hope for roses? A rose to you and a prayer for our understanding.'

13   *Human Capital and America's Future*, ed. David W. Hornbook and Lester M. Salamon (Baltimore: Johns Hopkins University Press, 1991), 1-2.
14   *Ibid.*

The Anatomy of Class

I parked near the William James Library. These thoughts, and the gray, slushy winter afternoon in the city were sobering. In this fast global race to the top, here I was, still back searching the libraries, the slow person, the tortoise who never had won races. My reading and thinking abilities were not what they once were. The theories I read seemed, as Nora had said, "to float around in a fog in my brain." Here I was, in 1992, in the dawning information age, not very computer literate and so still relying on a fairly random search of books and bibliographies.

I sat in the lamp light at a polished mahogany library table, and surrounded myself with recent journals filled with articles on the effects of environment on the mind. I wondered if someone would object to this outsider monopolizing graduate student texts. Just let me have a little more time, I thought, as I skimmed summaries in journals. A number referred to work by Marian Cleves Diamond, who established that environment can alter the anatomy of the mammalian brain, and particularly the cerebral cortex, which affects learning ability.

I located *Enriching Heredity: The Impact of the Environment on the Anatomy of the Human Brain*[15] in which Diamond, a neuroanatomist, published the results of two decades of research on changes in rats' brains in relation to environmental stimulation. I took it to a comfortable leather chair and poured over it, fascinated.

Diamond and her colleagues at the University of California at Berkeley exposed one group of rats to eighty-day vacations in very stimulating environments. The rats had challenging mazes, varied toys, and plenty of glucose pellets as rewards for problem-solving, water and "all the food you can eat" whenever they wanted it. A second group was placed in solitary confinement in a deprived environment without toys, mazes or problems, but still given food, water and glucose pellets as often as the "enriched" rats. *Those in stimulating environments showed measurable increases in brain chemistry and brain weight from growth of the cerebral cortex.* In other experiments some of the vacationers were put in the deprived setting. The decreased stimulation diminished their nerve cells and cortical thickness in their brains and "at times the effects of impoverishment [were] greater than

---

15   (New York: Free Press, 1988).

those brought about by a comparable period of enrichment."[16] At every age, from newborn to elderly rats, the research showed these effects took place.

Diamond, who conducted her research with human aging in mind, commented that "the results from enriched animals provide a degree of optimism about the potential of the brain in elderly human beings, just as the effects of impoverishment warn us of the deleterious consequences of inactivity."[17] But sitting in the library I was struck by the enormity of the implications for us: *the cerebral cortex grows with increased stimulation and is diminished by deprived stimulation.*

I went outside and, intensely distressed, I bought cigarettes for the first time in years and paced around the block, thinking. It seemed all too clear that there might be physiological consequences to being underemployed, to being in a chronically deprived work environment.

This was the 90's. No longer did anyone tolerate brown lung disease like my grandmother's, or the loss of an eye or a limb due to dangerous, negligent working conditions. Occupational health and safety laws had been passed and companies were liable for harm at work. How, then, were we to view the harm to the brain in the form of "diminished nerve cells, decreased brain chemistry and cortical thickness affecting learning ability"[18] that might well result from the deprived conditions of long-term rote work? Who had even considered it? No one, I later learned from a friend who was a worker's compensation attorney.

Two decades of research on brain chemistry and physiology had altered the understanding of human development. Why had so little of this research been applied to the effects of work, especially to the kind of work that two thirds of the population, the working people, do? Too much opposition from corporate funders of private academic research? Were scholars at private institutions afraid of losing their jobs just like we were? Then where was the public funding for research, the public will to address this fundamental question of equality? I stood alone for a while, my thoughts with my friends back at the plant, loyal workers, putting in extra long hours these days. And with the memory of John Angelino. I longed for one of our nightly campaign conversations. His fine mind would have grappled with a problem like this. It was growing dark. Two young women passed me on the library steps, turning up fur collars in the wind and frowning

16   *Ibid.*, 53-4, 156-7.
17   *Ibid.*, 157.
18   *Ibid.*, 1.

at my unenlightened smoking habit. I headed back up the steps, across the luxurious granite concourse surrounding the entrance, and inside to gather my books and notes and to go home. A warm light glowed on the teak bookcases and green marble floors. A professor in Harris tweed, waiting to check-out books for morning classes, struck a casual pose and perused *The New York Times*.

What is this place? I thought. In what text here, in whose face can I read the life I am living now? But of course, I too was here once, I remember: it doesn't exist. Except, perhaps, in occasional headlines considered "intriguing" like "U.S. Workers Unqualified to Work!"

Are we, now? Do you captains of industry find us losing contenders for the next round? After exposing our minds for ninety years to your broken, sawed-off work, are you shocked at our diminished capacity, are you feeling, frankly, rather betrayed? Well, 'the chickens have come home to roost!' as Malcolm X said in another era of social violence.

I turned my back and hurried out across the bare concourse. Malcolm! I thought. You also used to say that people with skin like mine would never learn. But don't be too sure. I've learned a hand-me-down thing or two. Questions might be here, but not the answers. Answers are where they always were. Answers are in the raised fist and the moving feet. Answers are in the street.

From these discoveries about the relation between our minds and our work, we turned next to another question. What was happening to our human relations—our social interactions and expectations within the constraints of military-industrial culture?

VI

Relations of Production

Kidding Around

"This place is fantasy-land!" Dominic frowned disapprovingly. "People would never have the freedom on the outside to do the crazy things they do in here. It's like they click their heels together and they're in Oz!"

The bosses were at their morning meeting and we were watching the back bench and Rob's latest prank. Rob was thirty-one and had curly gray hair. He was one of the popular jocks who played on the company softball team. I first saw him in a First Aid class before he had come to work in our department, a stranger then, with most of his head completely wrapped in white gauze 'Wow!' I'd thought, 'He looks like a Greek statue!'

"I look just like Tom Selleck!" he often reminded us now. But it had soon become apparent that what he really took pride in were not his classic good looks but his ability to act like a nut.

"Watch this!" Rob whispered to Dom and me. He had found a gleaming new black enameled toolbox and had glued it to a bench. One by one several enterprising people, glancing around to be sure they weren't watched, tried unsuccessfully to appropriate it. I smiled to myself as I went back to my seat in the first row.

"Now," Rob announced, "I have to tell you that I have been assigned by the company to do inspection of the first row!"

Methodically, he stopped in front of each of us older women and looked down our blouses. What kind of feminist am I? I thought, shrieking and laughing like the rest. But I knew a lot about sexual harassment and this was something different. It was pure outrageousness, Rob's specialty, performed to lift us out of the grim day of rules and propriety. In fact we all played these games. We broke conventional and feminist rules, boasted of our looks and sexual prowess. We flirted elaborately with each other—young and old, black and white, gay and straight, popular and not so popular—with no intent of conquest or control. Flirting was our favorite kind of joke or pleasantry, a nod to special individual value in an alienating day. Rob was always looking to include under his outrageous wing the newest, shyest, most outcast in the department, looking to "bring them out," he said.

"Rob, you're just like a mother hen!" Joseph laughed (he was the shyest). Like Joseph, having some residue of shyness myself, I enjoyed being brought out.

"Now Juanita," Julio said to me, "you still owe me more coffee if you're going to be my pet!"

"Let's make coffee," said his countryman Eduardo, who wore camouflage shirts left over from his U. S. Army training days in Central American jungles. "The coffee here tastes like horse piss! I've got some El Pico. How are we going to make it?" I had lived in Spain and knew the promise of the flannel filters used to make strong coffee there.

"A sock!" I said. "We need a sock! Could you make it a clean one, please?" Someone produced one from a gym bag and soon the rich aroma reached the nostrils of the surrounding gringos, who were pronounced not tough enough to take this brew.

"But now my pet has to do the cleaning up!" said Julio. "That is because I am the boss, the king, and you couldn't get anyone else to do it, Juanita." Along came Fred, an electrician and member in good standing of the local chapter of the John Birch Society, who, it was widely known, was quite taken with talking with me every morning, his private commie conquest. I enjoyed knowing him too.

"Fred!" I said. "You're an electrician and get around everywhere but I can't leave the bench. Would you do me a favor? Would you wash this coffee sock out for us?" He did.

"Juanita!" said Julio. "I am shocked! Aren't you ashamed of tricking someone into being your pet like that? I didn't think you could do such a thing!" I was a little shocked at myself. Shaunessy suddenly stood over us, shaking his head and laughing at these children in his charge. It was true that, especially when expert workers like Julio and Eduardo were involved, play was one freedom he enjoyed slipping us on the sly.

Many of my memories of our work relations are of this kind of fun, but this lightheartedness came to have an edge. There was one thing about Never-never Land, I realized. Even if we tired of play, like the boys in Peter Pan, this was a place where we were not to grow up. There was no call for our maturity. Management's consensus that we were child-like was perhaps a useful rationale for their control. Like all play, our play had significant content. Stanley Aronowitz describes the street games of his working-class childhood—Johnny on the Pony, Knucks, Kick the Can—as games that rehearse a role, conditioning working-class kids to endure pain, frustration, and to suffer punishment without showing emotion.[1] Our games, though different, also hinted at our circumstances. They were about triumphant individual egos or unsuspecting fools. They mimicked the liberty to do and say whatever came to mind, to be free spirits, teasing children in the face of grim adult necessity. They were games about freedom and coercion, valuing and devaluing, domination and subordination.

Knowing Your Place

Shaunessy, standing by the time clock, pounced. "You know the rules. You're five minutes late from lunch, Alonso. This is a verbal warning. If you're late again this month you get a written warning. Two written warnings and you get suspended, with possible loss of job."

"I know the rules," I mumbled, vowing to someday get revenge for all the mothers with kids here. I was late because Cynthia, a young mother, had stopped me in the hall for help figuring out how to get permission to leave early for a conference at her daughter's school. Should I bother to explain to him? Hardly. Here, parenting problems were irrelevant. In another building last week a woman had lost custody of her child because she was afraid to ask for time off to appear in court at the hearing. Several years ago I'd presented Cynthia's kind of problem to my Assistant Business Agent as a union issue.

"You know what I think?" he'd said. "I think all you women should stay at home with your kids." I slid into my seat in silence and sent clouds of acrid smoke wafting up as I wielded an oversized soldering iron on wires

---

1   *False Promises: The Shaping of American Working Class Consciousness* (New York: McGraw Hill, 1973), 65.

as thick as size-ten knitting needles. An hour later I met Nora in the lady's room.

"I was five minutes late!" I said. "Did you hear Shaunessy?"

"I heard him. Unbelievable!" Nora leaned against the stone sink. Management had removed the chairs overnight as a method for improving production.

"I still can't get used to these rules. I wish I could figure out why they feel entitled to order us free citizens around like this!" I shook my head, tipping my box of wheat thins in her direction. "It would never happen in middle class jobs!"

Nora raised an eyebrow, "Are you kidding? Those jobs and ours, they're like night and day!"

"My friend Susan was talking about that difference just the other day," I said. "She worked at G. E. for years, straight out of high school, like all her family had, then eventually got a job as an industrial health teacher. 'I love it. It's not a job,' she told me, 'because I can do anything I want in it. Even after teaching for eight years I still get nervous whenever I'm in Lynn. I feel like I have to hurry and get out of town before The G. E. notices I'm gone and reaches out and snatches me back inside!'" We laughed.

"I remember what it was like when I made that kind of switch in the other direction—from the middle class to a job in a shipyard," Nora said.

"Tell me!" I said, grinning and pulling out my pen and pad. That we were conducting an ongoing investigation, any place, any time was by now a given for us group members.

"Well," she began, pausing. She had a way of stopping to select her thoughts with a precision I could imagine her using when she selected the tiny semiprecious stones she strung inside her miniature sculptures. "Well. When I first went to work in manufacturing, in a shipyard, I had certain personal rules I never violated—like honesty. I wouldn't pretend I wasn't doing something normal when the bosses came around, like talking to someone or getting a coffee or reading the headlines or whatever I happened to be doing. I was amazed to find that these normal things were against the rules. I'd never been treated without respect—the respect an adult gives another adult. But of course I was making a constant spectacle of myself, acting normal. So I gradually changed. I entered their rules, which are usually senseless and dishonest. But I lost my self-respect. I'm angry at them, but also at myself, so it gets turned inward."

The buzzer rang and we went back to work in our respective departments, just in time, as Ahern, the general foreman, Shaunessy's boss, came by.

"Damn it!" he yelled at Joseph. "We needed that unit out yesterday!" He strode to the back of the room in a huff. Joseph was the most uncomplaining, compliant worker of us all. A Portuguese immigrant, he had wavy black hair, kept as carefully in place as his emotions. We all respected his quiet, religious, conscientious ways, and we felt protective of him.

"That really does it!" I muttered. "I can't believe this! Yelling at Joseph, of all people! We'd never get yelled at like this in most jobs! They'd never get away with it!" People at the surrounding benches shook their heads at me.

"That's ridiculous, Jean. All jobs are like this—every one I've ever had," Rudy chided me. "He's the boss. He can do whatever he wants. You have to accept it."

I did have to accept it. The personal judgment and autonomy taken for granted elsewhere were abnormal here, just as Nora had said, violable at any time. My friends' innocence of this difference always filled me with anguish. On the other hand, my innocence had them constantly engaged in a re-education campaign—"Explain to Jean Life in the Real World."

"Hey, Miss Jean," Joseph said, "you think this is bad, you should have seen life in the old country!"

Angie, the widow of a foreman, spent much of the workday lecturing me, the truant from the established order, for my own good, as she said. She shook her blonde bouffant head disapprovingly.

"He's right. Listen, I remember doing exercises with Mussolini's Youth Brigades when I was little. Then later when the Nazis occupied Italy my whole family had to go on the run because my father supported Mussolini. *Madon'!* We lived in barns, in the snow, without shoes. It was my job to beg bread from the soldiers."

"In my town in Portugal, you grew up knowing your place," Joseph said. "You weren't supposed to even talk to upper-class people. In the churches they had two kinds of pews—cushioned mahogany ones for the upper class, and wooden benches for the rest of us who worked on farms."

I reached elbow-deep into the oil-filled unit in front of me to retrieve a dropped lock washer and nut, paying attention this time to tightening them more carefully around the screw holding my magnetized coils in place. If Nora had learned her place, "entering their rules" and turning her anger inward, had these folks, who had long ago had to internalize subordination, also internalized the anger? Perhaps the subordination and the anger had come to be housed in all of us as normal, like long-embedded splinters to which the flesh adjusts, irritants beneath the surface.

But what force intimidated us now, ensuring our subordination? There were no Nazi troops here, no semi-feudal European class system, no use of deadly force. This was only a workplace. It was as Sean had said: "The company, which everyone hides behind, is a non-person. What are you going to hate?" And what was it we feared? There was some kind of coercive control that we couldn't find. It was as if there were a heavy veil over the place, which our eyes penetrated only gradually.

One source of intimidation, of course, was obvious. To be subordinate was an official requirement for keeping our jobs. Rule number fifteen of twenty-nine prohibited acts stated: Refusal to accept or follow orders or directions from proper authority, or any other form of insubordination. The twenty-eight other rules ended with the proviso: these are not all-inclusive. In other words, as everyone said, "They can fire you for anything they want to." Or "They'll lay off five people with less seniority just to get to one bad apple."

"They treat the people kind of like a plantation," Ruth commented in group. "You're not supposed to question what the master says or be an intellectual. If you do, you get fifty lashes. Just walk along, do as they say. If you go over the fence, you lose your job."

Losing your job here was like falling off the edge of the world. In this company town where whole families worked for several generations at the plant and kept stern watch over their young, your relatives probably had worked long and hard to get you into American. So getting fired for insubordination would be a frightening and shameful prospect, almost like taking your life. It was impulsive waste that was stupid, a sin and a disgrace—being a loser. Nearly all other jobs around were half this pay scale, if there were any to be found. Wages of $25-$60,000 a year, home ownership, college for kids, middle-class status—it was a short, fast fall from this life to the other one, etched in everyone's minds.

Long-term poverty and unemployment were well known to most families. Forty percent of U. S. workers experience them at least once each decade.[2] The Depression was not just in history. It was around the corner, in some impoverished neighboring family. And beyond that was the outer darkness everyone had been raised to fear and scorn—"the underclass," with its vulnerability to drug abuse, crime, jail. It lurked on the working-class streets of this town, and in most families, a constant reminder of failure—the shameful, irredeemable relative, talked of in hushed tones.

People often said that the basic instruction of their working-class parents, the bottom-line obligation, was 'Just go to work every day and stay out of jail.' In some unexamined recess of the mind, that was what life boiled down to here—be the decent kind of person who works, or the kind in jail. And for the many people raised in strict, patriarchal families, to lose your job for insubordination probably carried an additional stigma— the internal curse of making an assault on the authority of the father.

And what about me? Was I so immune? I had learned to tread carefully because I knew the company used petty rule violations as a pretext to get rid of activists and I didn't want to waste the years I had invested here. But more importantly, following the rules was a tricky situation for me. If I broke them too often, I would become, in their eyes, just another fool who couldn't be re-educated, a loose cannon on the deck. Take them too seriously and I would be disrespecting the adult rights and dignity that I tried to stand up for. So I broke them when it seemed important, and fell into the habit of following them most days.

In conforming, did I also internalize the subordination? Since I didn't feel inferior to the bosses, I thought not. But I was wrong. I still find in myself heavy doses of that subordination, like a toxin in the blood. It lingered in the way I shrank from taking leadership in activities outside work, though that had come naturally to me since grade school. It has lingered in a certain passivity and tendency to fatalism in off moments, and in a sense of helplessness and lack of agency.

It was rare that people were threatened with job loss for insubordination, but it happened to two of my friends. One day Crystal talked back to Shaunessy and found herself instantly suspended. She fell on the ice in her

---

2   Michael Zweig, "Class and Poverty in the U. S. Economy," in *Religion and Economic Justice* (Philadelphia: Temple University Press, 1991), 211. Bertram Gross points out that "Hidden unemployment at all levels, while unreflected in official statistics, is nonetheless widely sensed by the employed. The unemployment of the underclass, while never large enough to threaten the system, is large enough to enhance the lower and middle-income employees' appreciation of their own stake in the system." "Incentives for System Acceptance," *Friendly Fascism: The New Face of Power in America* (Boston: South End Press, 1980), 284.

fury as she headed for the parking lot, and so sued the company for both compensation and racial discrimination. She won, apparently. She sent us a picture of herself next to her new SUV while on a trip to Hawaii.

"Dolly isn't keeping up on the news this week like she's used to" began a *Boston Herald* article. Dolly, a friend from our women's committee, was a welder in a nearby building. She had been threatened with suspension for reading *The Herald* at her bench on her lunch break.

"What do the government and the company think? That we're robots, not people?" she said to me. "That we don't do human things like read the paper and have families that we want to keep pictures of on our desks like other workplaces? What do they think we're here and working for anyway? Because we like it?"

The union had sided with management against her. They denied receiving the host of grievances on the right to read at lunch break, even in departments that banned reading matter during work hours. Dolly leaked this matter to the newspaper. Several weeks later she was one of four people fired for allegedly not meeting government welding standards, something she had done satisfactorily for twelve years. She was well known at the plant as one of the state's first female welders trained through C.E.T.A. (Comprehensive Employment Training Act of 1973), and was once interviewed on television. She organized eighty coworkers to go down to the union hall and make the union fight for her job.

It only took a few examples or rumors of job loss for insubordination each year to keep us running scared and compliant. Coercive control doesn't have to be asserted continually to have a chilling effect. Sometimes the pressure we felt had frightening consequences: accidents happened.

Leroy was a young fellow who had been trained as a machinist by the Job Corps and was still in a trial period at American. One morning he ran to make it on time, fell the length of the stairs to the concrete basement and broke his back. The last we saw of him was on a stretcher, being carried to an ambulance.

Another worker, Jimmy, was scarred terribly by burns sustained one afternoon when he rushed his move-cart full of chemicals for a "hot job," overturned it, and splashed himself with acid. Also, word had reached us of the death of an electrician ordered to "get a move on" and skip standard procedures in repairing a high voltage box. He took a lethal jolt.

Obedience Training

'You don't get paid to think!' that guy had the nerve to say to me!" Hildie said out of the corner of her mouth, heading for the front row with a tub of tested units.

"It isn't just that we don't get paid to think," Jasmine replied. (She was in early for second shift) "We get paid to obey, even if it's wrong. Like the time I got in trouble for using the downstairs bathroom. Human Relations said I could use it, but my boss said no. So I had to be called in before a whole lot of men to explain that I had my period and needed some privacy and that's why I used the downstairs bathroom."

"You have no right to tell me how long I can take to go to the bathroom!"

I looked to the back of the room, startled. It was Nina, stamping a high heel at Ahern.

"You think I don't have a right to monitor the time you spend in the bathroom?" he yelled. "I can make you pee in a paper cup if I want to! I can make you move your bench to the hallway! You'll do exactly as I say!" She sat down, bowing her head over her work. He strode out.

"*Va f'a in culo'!*" she mumbled after him in Italian, not her native language nor mine, but that of the department, and finished it off with our common Italian non-verbal translation of the phrase, a flip of the back of the fingers out from under the chin.

"Whoa!" we murmured.

"They want to keep us so intimidated that if they say jump, we'll say how high!" Emma grumbled. She was a very thin person—nerves, she told me.

"What seems to be the problem here?!" Billy was pushing a cart with a hot job from the model shop. He looked kind of like a blonde Robert de Niro with a crew cut, and always carried himself stiff and erect as if he were still a soldier in the Vietnam War. His clothes were ironed to perfection, his shoes meticulously polished. His face was always tense. "You people should stop complaining like babies. You think too much. Just do your work. What do you want, to close this place down? We're a month behind on some orders ya know, and I have certain sources that tell me that the brass in Washington are thinking of giving this contract to Tennessee."

People don't get by in this command-and-control culture without developing character traits to cope with it, I thought to myself, frowning at Billy and shooting a loud blast from my air hose across the deck of my unit, scattering bits of wire and solder debris around his feet. He was sometimes quite a nice person, but his personality was typical of a fairly large minority of people here. They coped with the tension and need for obedience by identifying with the power structure, sometimes giving orders and being authoritarian themselves. They were offended by anyone who didn't hold in awe the authorities and obedience. Of course I was one of the culprits. Billy didn't go so far as to report on his fellow union members, which would have violated a fundamental union principle, but some did. These people were the "eyes all around us," the enraged gatekeepers of conformity. They set the tone. Their influence on the rest of us was like background contamination. We were all exposed to it regularly, but some of us were more susceptible to it than others.

The buzzer rang for our ten-minute break. The green monster machine in the oil room roared as it circulated oil through units, and the afternoon air was thick with the gray fog of solder smoke as we poured coffee from our thermoses and congregated around the front row.

Suzanne, Hildegard, Tom and Nora ambled over, and Al came by from the Mold Department. Suzanne frowned, warming her hands around her cup of coffee.

"American is like the Navy ship I worked on when I was a repair technician for the company down south. They want all you little soldiers marching in a row for eight hours. In the service there's no excuses for anything. If you were sick, you worked anyway. We even asked permission to go to the head."

"All of us little soldiers," I said. "Did I miss something? Do Ahern and Shaunessy and Billy think we're in the armed forces here, and they're our commanding officers? Is this place like the real military?"

Tom laughed. "Sure! When I first came here it struck me that this place was exactly like being in the military. Even to the policy of no fraternizing between the officer class and enlisted personnel. Why should the foremen treat us as if we were servants in the field, with zero intellect and no sensitivity or feelings? They don't even answer you when you say good morning. 'Hey, Asshole! Did you hear me say good morning?' I'm thinking, and Ahern's looking at me like 'what the hell's the matter with him that he said good morning?'"

"Not *exactly* like being in the military," Hildegard said. "Because the military makes sense—it's set up for life and death conditions, and it gives people discipline and pride. The military does have a rule, though, where you can be disciplined (even the wives) for failure to conform to military life".

"You have to remember," Tom said, "that most of the foremen in here were officers in some branch of the armed forces once. I've been told that's what American looks for when they hire managers—military background. The Right Stuff by the Pentagon's standards. And some of them are still gung-ho officers in the Reserves."

"Yeah, I think it's like the military in the way they treat us like their property," Al put in, blushing a little. He was a shy, very quiet, tall Navy vet who worked heating up plastics and epoxies to fill completed units. He rode his bike fifteen miles to work every day to keep healthy. "I resent the way the company withholds information from us. Like not telling us we're going to be laid off till the day it happens. That reminds me of the service. We were moved around like baggage, and not told about transfers till an hour before we shipped out."

"The idea in basic training," Sam said, "is to completely destroy your ego and make it subject to their command. They make you believe you can trust no one, are completely isolated and dependent on them. There, there's no one who cares—it's all male, all macho. Men are cold and uncaring anyway. I've never felt so alone in my life as I did there. Here, at least you go home to your family at night."

"It's the same in domestic violence situations," Nora put in. "The perpetrator breaks the woman's ego down and makes her feel isolated and completely dependent on him."

The buzzer sounded and we shrugged and went back to our benches. I checked a spec to see where to solder the little turquoise bead-like diodes I was holding. The military culture must be all around us, I thought. Why is it invisible to me? This is a defense plant—-it should be obvious. But it's not. Because we're also civilian workers with the right not to be discriminated against plastered on the walls just because we do work under government contracts. That's what Nina was trying to say to Ahern—we have some rights here. But we don't in his mind. It's confusing. I wish I knew more about military culture.

Basic Training

The next day I was sitting in a red booth at The Wicked Wolf after work. The Wolf was the watering hole across from the plant. It was a pretty ordinary place, with worn leather booths, candles flickering under milk glass globes, and couples huddled in dark corners in back, whispering over beers. Sean had told me to meet him here because he had something he wanted to give me.

"Hi, Jean, how are ya?" he slid into a seat opposite me and ordered a Guinness. "Look, I heard about your little military briefing in the shop yesterday," he grinned, tickled at my naiveté, "and since I know you learn by reading I decided you should have this, which a marine friend gave me." He handed me a dog-eared copy of a book entitled *Guidebook for Marines*. I took it eagerly and flipped through the first pages. Apparently it was written well before the end of the Cold War, but it had no date or place of publication.[3]

"God, Sean, what a timeless document! Thanks!"

"And just to get you into the spirit of it I wanted you to have this too." He held out a combat fatigue jacket.

"Thanks," I said, really pleased. "Nobody's ever given me one of these before! Hey, I can't wait to read this! I just don't get the military way of thinking very well. I wasn't brought up with it like everybody else was. My Dad was kept out of World War II because he was a County Agricultural Agent, necessary to food production at home and all that. Do you think we're leading a military life here?"

"In a way, sure we are," he said. "Jean, there's something important for you to understand. I was taught it as an instructor in the Reserves: in the military people are technically designated as *non-personas*. Officially, they are government property. Think about it."

That night, doing dishes absentmindedly, I thought about how the military was a normal component of family life for most of my friends in the shop. Crystal used to brag that her three brothers, all organizers in the meat packers' union, were decorated vets.

---

3   It appears that this *Guidebook* was the 5th Revised Edition, January, 1956, which is described as having an "aqua green" cover like my copy, and 50's cars and styles pictured. (Washington: U. S. Government Printing Office, 1956). The era would be about when our managers would have enlisted.

"Hey, Jeannie," she announced to me one day. "I'm going to teach you black history, long as we're sitting together here. We're going to make you a white chick with a black hip!" Her first lesson was about her aunt, a WAC (member of the Women's Army Corps) in World War II, who had been made to tuck her hair up under her cap to look like a man so she could go out and join the black soldiers on the front lines. "And my aunt told me the white WACS never got any order to go to the front like that!"

That night I settled into my pink chintz chair with the *Guidebook for Marines* and looked up at my only link to military family bonding—a photo of my late Auntie Phil, here a young girl in a Navy uniform, with the rank of Ensign Junior Grade. I'd painstakingly attached the medals she'd bequeathed me to the picture frame. She had run away in 1942 to be one of the first U. S. Waves (Women Accepted for Volunteer Emergency Service, the Women's Reserve of the U. S. Naval Reserve). Our bonding hadn't really been about the military but about a woman using her head. She used to tell me worldly stories from her best drinking buddy in the service, the Catholic chaplain, and, when I was thinking mainly about prom dresses, she had made me a birthday present of my first Thesaurus. I smiled at her.

"What would you think of me now, A.P., your wimpy niece with this book in my lap, trying to acquire a military mind?"

The *Guidebook* was fascinating. It was like a searchlight beam into hidden recesses of shop life. It explained, for example, Shaunessy's habit of pacing about doing surveillance, especially when a known activist like Chelsea visited me. It would be as if he'd at last spotted enemy troops in the area, and he would spring into action, calling her boss. That always seemed bizarre to me. Why did he need to pace around and watch us, when he often told us he considered us excellent workers? But the surveillance wasn't about work. It was about a higher order of responsibility, as he must have conceived it. Shaunessy had been a Navy man, but my guess was that the Navy's sentry practices must have been similar to those laid out by the *Guidebook*. It required everyone on guard duty to memorize the general orders for sentries, among which were:

1. To take charge of the post and all government property in view. You report immediately to the corporal of the guard, by telephone or other means, every unusual or suspicious occurrence. You apprehend and turn over to the corporal all suspicious persons, all parties involved in a disorder on or near your post, and all parties who try to enter your post without authority.

2. To walk the post in a military manner, keeping always on the alert, and observing everything that takes place within sight or hearing.

3. To report all violations of the orders I am instructed to enforce.[4]

Once Shaunessy had banned Ed Bearfinder, a big Native American tester who was the token male on our Women's Action Committee, from talking with me. "I won't have them discussing Indian affairs in my area!" he had said. This apprehending of suspicious persons and Shaunessy's frequent phone calls about us to his superiors made sense from the perspective of military leadership.

I had always been a little embarrassed to admit to myself that it bothered me that Shaunessy seemed to truly dislike me. At times I kind of liked him, and I wasn't used to somebody hating me for no reason. I hadn't really done anything bad, I thought, besides the occasional shop-floor mouthing off that everyone else did. Yet what felt like stigmatizing on the part of all managers toward people like Chelsea, Ed and me must really have been that they were judging us, as Martin Luther King hoped, on "the content of our characters." We had "stand-up attitudes," the kind of fighting spirit praised by workers in some unions. But good character in military ideology was nothing of the sort. It involved acquiescing to those in power, carrying out their orders and stifling dissent. The *Guidebook* gave some historic examples:

A note-worthy incident at the beginning of the Civil War period was the participation of Marines in the capture of John Brown and the suppression of the uprising and riot at Harper's Ferry. In peacetime they aided the civil authorities in suppressing labor riots in Baltimore and Philadelphia and enforcing the revenue laws in New York...For more than a decade after the first World War the Marines were continually acting as the strong arm for carrying out the Nation's foreign policy. In three countries [Haiti, the Dominican Republic and Nicaragua] they carried on extensive campaigns against disorderly elements, assisting the governments of those countries to put down armed insurrection, and to organize efficient native constabularies to maintain order after they withdrew.[5]

4   *Guidebook For Marines*, 60.
5   *Ibid.*, 6.

The stigmatizing Ed, Chelsea, and I experienced was a normal, patriotic reaction from this military perspective. We activists were all "suspicious persons," potential labor rioters, uprisers, disorderly elements. And worse still, I was a socialist in their midst, someone who had opposed the strong arm that carried out the nation's foreign policy in the war in the Gulf.

I grinned, recalling some episodes worthy of M*A*S*H. There was the day, ten years ago, when we heard reveille in the office of Gildersleeve, the General Foreman at the time. Later we learned that he was playing a record of reveille loudly on an old phonograph to wake up an engineer who was afflicted with sleeping sickness. And there was the time a plant division manager, a former Navy Admiral, had commanded all foremen to wear roller skates all day to emphasize the need for faster productivity. I very much regretted being out sick that day. People told me that, while other foremen whizzed by with red faces, Shaunessy had disappeared abruptly, spending the rest of the day tossing down a few in a back room at the Wolf.

Good character for a military man meant having a deeper than average understanding of "our American way of life" according to the *Guidebook*. It went on to say: "Through your family, teachers, friends, and church you have acquired an understanding of loyalty, patriotism, and devotion to your country. The Marine Corps will give you every opportunity to fortify your personal beliefs so that you may better serve your Corps and your country."[6]

American Missile also promoted fortification of beliefs. It was not like those workplaces where management's practices were pragmatic and based on what worked best to motivate workers to get the product out. This company, like the military, relied on ideology as the cement to reinforce its authority. And, as in the military, the fundamental components of the ideology were machismo and patriotism.

Machismo

"Everybody's getting super-masculine here!" Dominic observed. " 'Hey baby, I got a big one for ya!' If they're so macho what are they wasting their time for here? They should go for the big money—be a male stripper or a warden beating up people in a women's prison!"

6   *Ibid.*, 53.

I laughed. He had a point about the escalation of machismo.[7] Twenty minutes later I was quoting him to Ruth, Suzanne, Jasmine and Nora.

"He's right. But why do you think machismo's on the rise?" Nora asked. "Could they be acting tough because underneath they're nervous about the economy, and the possibility of layoffs?"

"Maybe," I said. "Gloria Steinem says that where you have low self-esteem, you are apt to see exaggerated gender roles in both men and women."[8]

"See, I think that's very interesting," Nora said, sipping her tea. "And I think you would see it more working in a factory, because working in a factory almost forces you to have a lack of self-esteem. The company demeans you, like asking why you spent so much time in the bathroom, so then you feel, if I have to answer that kind of question, and this person has the right to ask it and demean me like this, I guess it's okay. You get to accept it. I think it's true at American for both genders."

"But it's worse for us women," Suzanne countered, "because of seeing almost no women in the upper echelons of the union jobs here, or in management, or in the union officers. I think in management they're afraid of letting women in—they're afraid they'll take over because a woman will work three times as hard as a man and is quick of mind."

"Right," I said, "and maybe it's worse for us too because especially in the high echelons the men think along old-fashioned military lines, including that women don't belong there."

"It was like that for me working on board the navy ship in Virginia Beach," Suzanne said. "When I first went there, the men were gross. They sang little dirty songs about 'Mary had a little lamb.' The men told me, 'You've got to expect that when you come into a man's world.' But I said if they did it one more time I was going to the captain, because I knew that men in uniform are supposed to respect women."

"That's like the mostly male departments here," I said, "the gross jokes, the hostility and superiority."

"Right," Ruth said, "like the electricians and other guys in the skilled trades. Most of them do private contracting on the side, so they consider themselves small businessmen, and above us."

---

7   *Random House Webster's Unabridged Dictionary, Second Edition,* 2001, 1152, defines machismo in its current usage as "1. a strong or exaggerated sense of manliness; an assumptive attitude that virility, courage, strength, and entitlement to dominate are attributes or concomitants of masculinity; 2. a strong or exaggerated sense of power or the right to dominate."

8   *Revolution from Within: A Book of Self-Esteem* (Boston: Little, Brown and Company, 1992), 258.

"Yeah," I said. "Some of them also hang out with management at lunch or on the golf course, and are gung-ho company guys. I always felt like the two groups share the same upward ambitions and their shared chauvinism is like a route to class mobility. Their exclusive male in-group is like a prized beachhead they've won together, and they really defend it."

"But, I think there's a group of men that are even worse than this." Jasmine objected. "They're really sadistic and obscene. They want to humiliate others."

"I agree," I said. "It's a dark side of chauvinism, that lurks in the background and surfaces when there's a threat to male power. I call this type 'male supremacy.' It's not acceptable to the majority of men here. You usually see it in all-male areas, like what happened to Anna. Remember when Action started, when Dolly first called us together to help her?"

Our Women's Action Committee was born as a response to supremacist threats to women.

Hard Core

It was October 1988. Chelsea, Nora, Meg, Suzanne and I had driven to the Best Western Hotel after work for a hastily called meeting. Three women from another division had put out an S. O. S. to Nora, who used to work with them. We sat around a big walnut table in a darkened corner, ordering drinks and pretzels and watching the door, waiting. In came Dolly, looking very different from the tough, scrappy welder we'd heard about. She was a small, pretty Irish woman with a big cascade of blonde curls like Dolly Parton, and white boots.

"I grew up in Dorchester myself," she nodded at us as Nora introduced us. "In the black housing projects on the Point. My mother had nine kids. Until I was six years old I thought we were black too. Cause we all had the same thing in that project— nothing!"

"Well I grew up in an Italian neighborhood and I thought I was Italian," Suzanne laughed. Dolly grinned at her.

"It was bad those days in the projects though," Dolly continued. "I used to escape and go climbing over the broken glass and bricks out back at night to look at the moonlight. I'd look up and think, 'I know there's something else out there somewhere and I have to find it.' So now I'm a

welder in this frigging place making the big bucks!" We all laughed. She
went on while we awaited the arrival of her friends. "I was the first woman
welder in the Sheet Metal Shop," she said. "The men used to hold back
jobs from me so I couldn't learn my trade. Then more women came and
there were eight of us out of a hundred and twenty people in the department. Now we're down again to three. I wish we'd had some women to get
together with for support then—maybe more would have stayed."

"A lot of the departments I've been in were about eighty-five percent
women, but the men controlled everything!" Suzanne said.

"Here comes somebody." Dolly stood up, waved and pointed to our table.
Margie O'Sullivan bustled in. She was cute, tiny and perky with curly
upswept hair. She chirped vivaciously, like a little chickadee, telling us she
was from Charlestown, a tough white section of Boston, where she'd raised
six kids alone.

"I'm saving up to buy a trailer for one now, thank you! It's great to meet
you girls! Nora's told us all about you. I'm a Labor Grade Four Inspector
and I've had to fight for it all the way. You feel like you're alone out there
in the dark. You don't realize there are some sisters out here! Look Dolly—
here's Anna." A slim, beautiful young woman with long dark hair and a
black leather vest over her white carpenter's pants hung back by the door,
looking undecided about whether to join us or leave. We patted a chair
and encouraged her to come over, like a bunch of cheery mothers, which
we were. When Margie told the waitress we were meeting about women's
problems at work, she brought Anna some tea, and free refills all around.
Dolly looked at Anna.

"Go ahead. Tell them. Just tell it like it happened."

"Okay," she began, shifting uncomfortably in her seat. She had olive skin
and big soft brown eyes. "I'm an assembler of finished units, a Labor Grade
Three. I got special training for it in the Army. I'm the only woman in the
department. They've made my life hell in there. Every day the obscene gestures, the rude remarks, the hostility, so thick. I always try to just ignore
it. But yesterday I was standing on a tall ladder that I have to use in order
to bend over and down into the body of the missile. All of a sudden this
gang of guys was behind me, looking at my bum, taunting and shouting
'Look at that, blood all over her ass. That's what you get when you get a
bitch doing work she shouldn't. ' They kept it up till, I couldn't help it, I

ran out of the room crying. My pants were clean—these same pants. They made it up."

Margie sputtered, "And Dolly and I marched her right over to the union steward, which she didn't want to do, and made him write out a harassment complaint against his buddies. And you know what he said?"

"Yeah," Dolly broke in. "That bastard said it was her own fault for having a 'different lifestyle'!" We knew that was the union's code word for lesbian. We didn't know or care whether she was gay or straight. We knew the allusion to it was a form of sexual aggression, probably because she hadn't yielded to anyone's seduction and she was in male territory.

"That's the union for you!" Chelsea shook her head.

"The hell with them! They're all the same!" Suzanne's eyes flashed. "I used to get that shit when I worked with all guys in Virginia Beach!"

"That's disgusting! We'll back you any way we can!" I said, looking around the table for agreement. "What would you like to do?"

"I don't want anybody fired," Anna said. "We all need the job. I just want it stopped. No, I want more. I want to make the union forbid sexual harassment. I want them to do training of union guys about it like the company supposedly trains managers. When I was in the Army they showed some really good training films to the guys, and they actually changed after that. My sister's still in the Army. I could have her find out the name of the films."

This was the first meeting of what we came to call our "guerilla" women's committee, so named because the union refused to permit an official union women's committee.

The next day we accompanied Anna to meet with the union Business Agent and his Assistants. They grudgingly agreed to look over examples of contractual sexual harassment policies from other unions. They didn't like taking suggestions from these smaller, service-sector women's unions. They were used to lording it over them in the state AFL-CIO. And they were not about to insult their skilled trades power base with films or corrective education. So a few months later we organized a program of education about harassment ourselves. The union made us rent our own union hall for it, tore up our leaflets and put out the word through the steward system that people better not show up. About twenty-nine women came anyway.

We continued meeting every month.

"Let's call ourselves Action!" Dolly grinned. "The union won't have any idea what that means!" As women approached us with more sexual harassment cases, we began to see a pattern. This kind of harassment always happened to women new to top Labor Grade jobs—Labor Grades One, Two, Three and Four— male territory. In each instance, the harassment was carried out by groups of men, and was of a crude, sadistic and degrading nature.

A black Caribbean woman was named Group Leader of the janitors (typically a black and Hispanic male domain). The men smeared feces on her workbench. They hung voodoo signs around it. She got anonymous threatening phone calls at home, and suffered paranoia and such severe anxiety that she gave up the job. Unfortunately, we learned of this after the fact.

A white woman in another plant, a new Labor Grade Three Inspector, came to work one night to find photos of penises on her bench, and a huge sign saying "Woman Haters' Club" in her work area. Her fellow workers were watching pornographic films in pajamas in an adjoining room. They made repeated threats against her and her husband, a worker on an earlier shift. The foreman tolerated this behavior from his key workers, and the union said, "Boys will be boys." She became so anxious she had to go out on leave, and was too frightened and upset to trust anyone, including us, with more than her initial story.

I was struck by the eerie similarity between these acts and the profile of the type of sex offenders who had been considered the most dangerous in my prison job. They were the rapists in whom sex and aggression were fused and interchangeable—aggression in the service of sexuality—that is, being sadistic was what excited them. I was shocked that, although violent crimes weren't committed at American, similar behavior was tolerated.

Apparently here sexuality served aggression—sex used as an attack. This fusion must have been familiar to the men in charge, from their military experience. I heard reports, for example, that pilots in the Gulf War were frequently shown pornographic films just before they were to set out on bombing missions.[9] Perhaps here too, sometimes managers viewed sexual aggression as a useful tool, though of course they would disavow association

---

9   A student in a class at University of Massachusetts Boston, in which I was a guest speaker, reported this to me. She had learned it from a friend who was at that time a bomber pilot in the Gulf War.

with it. It reminded me of public officials in the South denying involvement with Ku Klux Klan violence, while secretly promoting it.

We put a temporary stop to this behavior. We had a pro bono adviser, a prominent Boston African American attorney and former judge. At our request she would write us curt letters advising that cases like these had merit for a lawsuit. All we had to do was drop a few copies judiciously in the right union and management hands and the harassment would cease, at least temporarily.

Since I never had a high level job, I never experienced threatening harassment like that myself. But I did experience this kind of gross hostility once. It was in the Sheet Metal Shop. As their union steward, I'd intervened when the men, for sport, had been tormenting another union member for weeks, a young fellow who seemed to them a little odd. Finally he'd come to me for help. These same sheet metal guys had spearheaded my campaign for steward, so I went to them and urged them to back off from their prey and to show a little union solidarity. Their sudden obscenity toward me was chilling. Apparently by intruding on their hunting ground, interfering with their sport, I'd gone too far with my power, also trespassing on male territory. "Hey, Alonso, we do what we want in here, understand? And if you don't like it you can come over here and put your mouth around this," said one man, unzipping his fly and exposing himself.

Machismo was a strong element in the ideological cement reinforcing military-industrial authority. It was part of our official culture. The other ideological element was patriotism.

Patriotism

"Patriotism is the last refuge of a scoundrel!"[10] Tom whispered, to me, gesturing toward the stars and stripes flying from most toolboxes as he passed my bench carrying a bucket of units to test. It was the time of the Gulf War, when the patriotism in the shop was intense.

"What's the matter with *us*? Where are our flags?" I asked him. "I find it kind of scary."

"I'm glad I only have a few more years here," he said.

I carried a bucket of small coils with magnets banded into them, put them on the outgoing wagon for testing, and picked up more coils and magnets. We were working pretty conscientiously these days, trying to hurry production for the war effort.

I thought of Tolstoy's definition as I soldered missile parts: *Patriotism is the principle that will justify the training of wholesale murderers.*[11] But when my friends here buy these dime store flags, it's because they're hungry for community bonds and personal significance, I thought. The fact is, patriotism is very important to consciousness here. I can't just dismiss it. I need to try to understand it.

It was break time, so I went looking for Tom. He put away his Wall Street Journal and grinned. "So have you bought extra company stock, Jeannie? Now's the time!"

"No disposable income right now," I said. "Have you?" He shook his head.

"You know," I continued, "I'm dealing with the super-patriotism here by trying to understand it, since I can't escape it. Can I ask you something? When I was a kid I remember our home-town parades on Memorial Day with their warm kind of patriotism. But the patriotism I hear expressed here seems to have an element of tension or fear in it."

"And an unspoken order to conform," Tom said, putting away his *Wall Street Journal* and offering me a coke. "You have to remember the history of this plant. Older workers saw with their own eyes the company and the government together coming down on anybody not considered 100% loyal. During the Cold War the company fired even loyal employees if they had relatives behind the iron curtain. Angie told me there used to be a prison

10   Boswell tells us that Samuel Johnson made this pronouncement that "patriotism is the last refuge of a scoundrel" on the evening of April 7, 1775, and says that Johnson was not indicting patriotism in general, only false patriotism.

11   Quoted in Wikiquotes from Tolstoy, but without attribution to one of his works.

camp on or adjoining company grounds during World War II. She and the girls would go out and watch the Italian prisoners of war peer at them from behind barbed wire. Scary. And we still have to sign a loyalty oath to work here, right?"

"That was enough to make me tense!" I said. "I would think the immigrants here must feel the need to sound extra loyal, above suspicion."

That night I went home, heated up the Italian spaghetti sauce Angie had taught me to make, and pulled out some books to read during supper. I opened an old favorite, *The Roots of American Loyalty* by Merle Curti, to a chapter on immigrants. Hans Mattson, a Swedish immigrant, probably speaking for many immigrants of the 1850's, was quoted as saying: "I have not missed Sweden much. I was long aware of the smooth way in which less favored citizens were oppressed, of the too great power of the higher estates…A free country, where all had the right to advantages which the Creator had given then, this was all I sought, and also found."[12]

Maybe, I thought, the immigrants at American are like that. Maybe they wrap themselves in the flag not just because they fear getting fired for lack of loyalty. Maybe they too feel grateful to leave behind class oppression in the old country.

After several hours of reading and thinking, it occurred to me that there were at least two or three different kinds of patriotism at American. One was the vitriolic, conservative patriotism that demonized Saddam Hussein. I found a good definition of this in an article by John Sklaar in *The Nation* magazine: "the worship of national power, of national greatness, nearly always expressed as power over other peoples and qualities, and as power that acknowledges no limits on its own assertion."[13]

This conservative patriotism was the plant's official ideology—military ideology, similar to that of the *Guidebook for Marines*. The requirement that employees sign a Loyalty Oath was not out of line in this culture. In *The Roots of American Loyalty*, Merle Curti traced this type back to the Nativist movement of the mid-Nineteenth Century, which was supported by business and military organizations. They denounced "class interests," such as farmer and labor demands, as unpatriotic, and recommended the

---

12   *The Roots of American Loyalty* (New York: Columbia University Press, 1946), 82.
13   *The Nation*, July 1-22, 1991, 7.

use of the National Guard to put down labor unrest and strikes.[14] This was the patriotism of Teddy Roosevelt, who emphasized male and military prowess as its necessary elements. Its later supporters, according to Curti, were the American Legion, the Ku Klux Klan, the leadership of the Boy Scouts of America, and certain large corporations, which provided much of the financial backing for its propaganda. In wartime its adherents persecuted German and Japanese Americans, pacifists, liberals and socialists under the Sedition Act[15].

Back at my bench the next day, I wanted to do some shop floor research.

I turned around to face Rudy. "What does it mean to be patriotic?" I asked him, putting down my soldering iron to signify the seriousness of my question.

"Well, Jean, no offense, but you wouldn't be patriotic because you don't feel loyal to the company," Rudi replied.

"I don't think I'm patriotic either because I'm not loyal to the company," Suzanne put in.

"Did you say the country or the company?" I asked. They assured me they meant the company.

I thought they were confusing loyalty to company with loyalty to country. But as I did some more reading that evening, I realized that this was not confusion but a second, and very common strain of patriotism: patriarchal patriotism. In *The Nation's* issue on patriotism, Monsignor William Shannon discussed this, which he said people expressed as humility, loyalty and sense of indebtedness to authority. He explained that it was the patriotism upheld by traditional Catholicism, and came from St. Thomas Aquinas's idea of patriotism as piety, "the virtue that moves us to offer honor and respect to those to whom we are indebted (God, our parents, our homeland and fellow citizens)."[16]

---

14   Curti, 77-9.
15   *Ibid.*, 236, 240.
16   *The Nation*, July 15-22, 119. Monsignor Shannon goes on to point out that in the tradition of Aquinas, patriotism was seen as part of and governed by "the virtue of justice." Therefore "support for country when we are convinced its actions are unjust is no patriotism at all, or bogus patriotism." He criticized the patriotism of the Gulf War as "immature" and "neurotic obedience."

For many workers at American, the majority of whom, incidentally, were Catholic, such piety included indebtedness to the company. To lack this apparently seemed to them almost unnatural or a sin. Really, appreciation and loyalty were important working-class character traits. No wonder Rudy had apologized to me for saying I lacked them.

I was beginning to realize that patriotism was much more than just a management ideology used to keep people in line. A 19th Century preacher, Alexander Crummel, had observed "The state is part of one's personal self."[17] For many, the pious devotion to country was internalized like that. The country was a part of them, a part of the family. Here at this workplace, our industrial relations also included a relationship with the country. What was the relationship between me and my country, then, I asked myself. Dysfunctional! was my first thought. I would be thinking more about this in the future.

There was paternalism in our industrial relations too, like that of 19th Century factory founders.[18] I remembered Shaunessy recently saying to us, "You do a good job and get the product out fast, for the war, and we'll take care of you—see that you get overtime and protect you from interference by the company higher-ups. Don't I always take care of you?"

This had the ring of feudalism about it, which I didn't really know much about. I found an article on feudal dynamics in the marriage relationship.

According to Muriel Nazzari, in the feudal lord-and-serf relationship, as well as the husband-as-provider and stay-at-home- housewife one, there was mutual dependency, but it was unequal dependency. Lord, and husband, had more power.[19] That was true of company paternalism too, I mused. Our loyalty came from dependency experienced as a family bond, and the company was also dependent on us to get the product out.

"It's in the dependency that they've got you!" Hildegard had once commented. But it too was an unequal dependency. The company relied on us to produce profits, but our very subsistence depended on them.

The inequality of this dependency was soon to show up in a striking example. President Bush was to deliver a speech at one of American's plants

17   Curti, 88.

18   See, for example, Judy Lown, "Not So Much a Factory as a Family," in *Gender, Class and Work* ed. Eva Gamarnikow, David Morgan, June Purvis, Daphne Taylorson (London: Heinemann, 1983), 29-30.

19   A point made by Muriel Nazzari in her essay on the similarities of old-fashioned support-service marriages and feudal relations. See "The Significance of Present-Day Changes in the Institution of Marriage," *The Review of Radical Political Economics 12:2* (Summer, 1980), 67.

about the nation's debt to American's workers for producing an essential missile during the Gulf War. The workers at that plant applauded and waved paper flags to affirm their mutual loyalty. But soon enough, the workers were to get the short end of this loyalty. When the war ended, the company laid off many of them because they had completed an entire year's production for the war effort in just a few months, and were no longer needed.

Big Game

"You know what I just saw in Personnel?" I ran to catch up with Hildie and Suzanne on their lunchtime walk. Our boots crunched the new snow.

"A replacement for Shaunessy?" Hildie grinned.

"Hell no!" I laughed. "It was a new, huge, colored poster of a four-way card game between a Russian bear, a Chinese panda, an Arab tiger, and an American eagle, each in uniform and looking fierce. It said: 'New players. Same Old Game. Play it close to the vest!' A security warning. What are they afraid of now?"

"Well it just shows you," Hildie said, "that this place may be funny at times, but you have to remember, we're involved in a high stakes game here. We're not just making vacuum cleaners for household consumers. Our jobs depend on what country does enough favors to be allowed to buy our missiles, what country might get uppity and give us a chance to try out our missiles on them. And which defense contractor keeps or loses the government bidding war to make the missiles in the first place."

"Yeah," I added, "and one ace they like to hold in that bidding war is having the most docile workforce and docile union, right?"

"Sure. Why do you think nobody rocks the boat?" Hildie went on. "It would be like rocking the ship of state. We are in the bottom of that ship. This is the military industrial complex. Look at how fast they got rid of even bit players like Tawana in Mold, and the other guys in Missile Division, for selling pot."

"Yeah, right." I said. "Didn't I tell you those two 'new hires' in Mold were FBI agents? Didn't I tell you that the first day? They weren't hard to spot—they looked just like black and white Ken dolls, remember? Extra tall, extra clean cut, extra good looking and well dressed in somebody's fancy idea of 'work clothes.' After just a couple weeks they get 'laid off' and the drug bust happens, based on the conversations the black guy seduced Tawana into. I tried to warn her to cool it with the pot. I have to say, I'm really against drinking and getting high at work. I think it's dangerous to be high around the machinery and chemicals."

We turned the corner into the building, hurrying to punch in. I sat down and started assembling coils for transformers, applying epoxy to the columns and roof of the transformer holders, which looked like little aqua Greek temples. Hildie was right. I felt so at odds with the unseen coercion gripping us that I tried to ignore what she and others seemed to know instinctively. The authority here was structural, and institutional, backed by the huge deadly force of the military industrial complex, in which we were as powerless and vulnerable as gnats.

I thought of a remark Sean had made—"Because of our fears, which we can't express in the workplace, it's like the company and the union have us held hostage."

I took a small awl and swirled a drop of white epoxy on the pencil-sized columns. I'm not afraid here, I thought, but I do feel the atmosphere of fear. Even people I know who left the plant several years ago still remember it.

I want to get to the bottom of this. I glanced at the clock to see how much time remained for this project. We can't express our fears, I think, because they don't make sense. The coercion that engenders fear doesn't exist in our ordinary American society, in our backyard barbecues and TV sitcoms. So we kind of deny our fears and hope they will go away because they can't be real. Like episodes of domestic violence, they're too outside normal experience for polite conversation. 'So what's wrong with me?' we think, 'I must be abnormal to be having any fears, or maybe I'm wrong'.

But we are not wrong. We are leading a kind of double life. I thought of an observation by Andre Gorz: "On the margin of civil society, with its formal liberties, there persists behind the gates of factories a despotic, authoritarian society with a military discipline and hierarchy."[20] So it's as if we're in one of those movies about early fascist Italy, where people go cheerfully

---

20   *Strategy for Labor: A Radical Proposal*, trans. from the French by Martin A. Nicolaus and Victoria Ortiz (Boston: Beacon Press, 1964), 36.

about their normal life until some sudden round-up happens, and you find out about the ominous forces lurking in the background.

Yet, what are the manifestations of coercion here? I have read of police manuals' descriptions of population control measures for states of emergency: require identification of every individual, require permits to travel, establish checkpoints, and prevent people from assembling.[21] Those very police techniques are routine at American: our identification security badges; the checkpoints in each department; the restriction of our travel from department to department without special permission; forbidding union members to assemble on the shop floor in groups larger than two.

I've been accepting these as normal, and likewise American's dossier keeping and surveillance. Now I read that Dr. Benjamin Gross, formerly an official of the Lyndon Johnson administration, sees surveillance and the keeping of dossiers on certain individuals as institutional tactics that are hallmarks of a fascist trend. He also comments that "old-time red-baiting, the kind that identifies opponents as the agents of Moscow or Peking, would be difficult to bring back in full-blooded form now."[22] Not at American! I thought.

The McCarthy-era tactics, which had served well for years at the plant, continued into the late 80's. I remember that in my bones. The shouting about "commies in our midst" in union meetings when anyone brought up a question, which made my knees shake when I got up to speak. Hundreds of very moderate rank and file members of the Angelino campaign also got redbaited, which was disconcerting to all of us but downright frightening for most workers. It left no doubt about the union's and the company's reserves of power.

The union leadership used to warn new workers about me: "stay away from her, she's a communist." I love to remember how Crystal handled this on her first day at work, when she was warned about me. She said she didn't know what a communist was, but replied saucily "how do you know I'm not a *commonist too*? Don't you tell me who to associate with!"

The redbaiting, which is only name-calling, wasn't as disturbing as its menacing tone. The implied secret power and dire but unknown

<hr>

21   An instructor at the U.S. Army College, writing in the law enforcement journal *The Police Chief*, gives this information. See Christian Parenti in "The 'New' Criminal Justice System: State Repression from 1968 to 2001," *Monthly Review*, New York, July-August, 2001.

22   *Friendly Fascism: The New Face of Power in America* (Montreal: Black Rose Books, 1985), 299.

consequences were unnerving. It was the technique of the bully. I'll never forget meeting it close-up one weekend on Cape Cod—the mandatory union retreat for steward training. There were only three of us out of a hundred stewards who were known to support Angelino and the union reform movement and we figured they'd be out to get us when they got us down there. First the Business agent got me alone in a dark corner with someone he said used to be in the secret service and now worked on American's top secret projects. They both started yelling at me that, with my pro-peace beliefs, just by working at the company I represented a threat to U.S. security. I denied it and excused myself to go into the dining room where dinner was being served. I chose a table at random, started to sit down and one of the B.A.'s henchmen yelled "I won't have Alonso the red, Alonso the Angelino supporter, at my table" and tipped the table over toward me, sending china and food flying.

In industries such as the auto industry, government surveillance is not permitted by the union. But at American the machinery of state power entered at will in the name of national security. Periodically we would get reliable information that the phones, including our pay phones, were being monitored, that cameras were installed in the ceilings, and that F. B. I. agents were around. It was also commonly said that dossiers were kept on dissenters.

It was late afternoon, and I was glad for the typical end-of-shift quiet because I was beginning to see my experience in a new light. It was like watching the details in a photo emerge in a tray of chemicals in my father's dark room. What about those "pre-fascist" hallmarks mentioned by Dr. Gross, the dossier-building and surveillance? I glanced at Angie, whose blonde beehive hairdo was bent over her work. Her brother-in-law worked for the C.I.A. She knew secrets. She and a few other relatives or wives of bosses would be the first to let it be known that our pay phones were tapped, or cameras were hidden over head, or that records were being kept on "troublemakers." I always thought these were just false rumors put out from management to scare us. "You," she kept saying to me, "I hear you have friends in high places, or you would have been kicked out of here long ago." I didn't know what she meant, and assumed she meant all the lawyers I knew from the social justice movement. It didn't hurt to have that fact out there on the grapevine, so I would just shrug mysteriously. Later I was to find out that she was right. A friend told me that a mutual friend from our days as young marrieds, now a Vice President in charge of Personnel at American, had told him that my dossier of "dissident activities" had crossed his desk, but he had chosen to take no action on it.

A case can be made for surveillance of weapons production, but I found this spying on U.S. citizens in the workplace surprising and maddening. After all, a few years before, a Senate subcommittee had censured the FBI's COINTELPRO covert activities against dissenting citizens. People in the know like Angie, with relatives in management, knew more than I did about American's ties to the Secret Service, the CIA and other institutions in the broader community. They didn't talk about it, only alluded to it.

"If you just do your work and mind your business you'll be okay," they said. But what if you didn't?

The Long Arm of American

A co-worker, Wally, suffered from ill health, asthma and ulcers. He'd always wanted to go to Las Vegas, and for his thirty-seventh birthday in the early 1980's, he did. Upon his return, he died very suddenly from a ruptured colon. He had come to work at American right after high school, and had held a special job: because he was small, he was sent down to sit all day inside huge units, where he soldered Beryllium parts. Hearing of this later, I was horrified—"They don't let people do that unprotected any more, Wally. Didn't you worry about working with a radioactive material?"

"Not really," he had laughed. "Hey, I'm alive and here to tell you about it." Years afterward, in April 2000, the Department of Energy began to offer compensation of $150,000 to defense workers injured by past work with beryllium.[23]

I had a growing apprehension about the two thousand chemicals used at American, many hazardous ones with effects unknown to us or even to O.S.H.A. I was beginning to suspect that more people at American than in other companies died rather young—in their early sixties or before—of heart disease and cancers. But what did I know? My impressions at the

---

23   Jon L. Gelman, "Chronic Beryllium Disease Sufferers Get Recognition" at http://www. gelmans. com/Focus/2_/_/vbecoldnjij. pdf or www. berylliumcentral. com. The author refers to increased public attention to the problem due to a 1999 Pulitzer Prize winning Toledo Blade series entitled "Deadly Alliance: How the government chose weapons over workers."

plant were hardly scientific. The only data available found workers in good health. I went to the company nurse about that data, and she acknowledged it was from the records of employees who took part in the company's annual physical exam program—predominantly management, engineers and clerical workers, most of whom were not exposed to chemicals. In one of our nightly conversations during the union reform campaign, I told John Angelino I was worried about this, and that I had a novel idea to benefit the members. He liked my idea, and within the week we went on a short trip to explore its implementation.

Blue-shirt Mission

"John! That big bad boy with the front wheel angled way out like that looks like it's going to collapse!" I said. "The last time I rode on a Harley was with my Uncle Norm when I was ten." John laughed, helping me on, and jumped the starter.

The sky was blue like a cornflower—a perfect May afternoon, as we dipped and swayed through the back streets of Boston. Life is good, I thought. We were deep in the reform campaign and it was rocking American. I had grown to like John a lot, him and his whole family—his petite wife Tina, who had a great throaty voice for yelling campaign slogans, and her sister Jo who was taking heat, like I was, for being a pro-Angelino union steward. John and I were headed for a meeting nobody knew about but us.

I relaxed as we rode along, and thought about my first encounter with John. It was November and about sixty union members had gathered in a darkened room at the Sons of Italy Club to meet the guy about to take on the union machine. He was the first serious opposition candidate for Business Agent in thirty-five years. I remember how we sat around tables with red, green and white checkered cloths, nervously sipping beer. Someone had spotted a car parked outside with a union official in it, watching the door. The incumbents put a premium on loyalty, second only to that of the mob.

Sure doesn't look like a working class hero, I remember thinking, checking out Angelino. Late forties, plain round face, coke-bottle glasses, 1950's haircut. And wearing a tie with one of those navy blue baseball-type union jackets that hung unworn in my closet.

"What are you going to say that's different?" A beefy guy, with shoulder-length hair and brown plaid shirttails flapping, had taken a long swig and stood up to challenge him cockily. "You've been one of them—the union treasurer—for fifteen years, for gods sake!"

"That's true," John said evenly. "I've always thought of myself as a team player. But I've had enough of a team ruled with an iron-hand that despises the members." I had raised my eyebrows and nodded.

"I will start with a slate that reflects the members," he continued, "with a woman named as my top running mate, and for the first time ever, some black members up on the stage as officers. I will not allow any more intimidation and attacks at union meetings. We will no longer constantly play ball with the company. Strikes are hard, but sometimes necessary. And I will institute a policy of electing instead of appointing Chief Stewards. Since the International's Constitution requires appointed officers, I will simply hold a special election and then appoint the peoples' choices."

We had burst into applause in spite of ourselves. The machine's Chief Stewards, who stood guard for the company, had scorned us and refused to process many of our grievances for years. This was not business as usual. At the end of the meeting I had taken a chance and signed a list of people interested in supporting John and his slate.

"I would say this is one of our better ideas, wouldn't you?" John shouted to me over the noise of the Harley, as he rounded a corner with characteristic deliberateness.

"I would say so," I smiled, remembering his first telephone call. It was Thanksgiving morning.

"Hellooo…" an unfamiliar voice had said slowly. "This is John Angelino, Jean. I'm calling to ask you to get actively involved in my campaign. I want your ideas." The aroma of sage filled the kitchen; my turkey was browning nicely. The kids and their college buddies were on their way. Cradling the phone on my shoulder, I wiped greasy hands on my apron and sat down, surprised.

"Well, thank you, John. Happy Holidays. I certainly liked the things you had to say at the Sons! But you should consider that if I'm involved, you'll get redbaited. I'm not the agent from Moscow our current leader enjoys implying, but it's no secret that I am a socialist."

"I know that. I'm from Lynn. My father and uncles all worked at G.E., where socialists founded the union. The union I have in mind will respect everyone's ideas. I don't agree with your philosophy, by the way—I'm more conservative, and a Catholic— but I'd like to discuss it sometime. You've stood up to the union's abuse for years. I've watched you. I respect you and I want you on my team." It was the first of our daily phone chats.

His supporters became known as "The Blue Shirts." At first, just a few of us wore them, emblazoned with "John Angelino—The Union is Us!" We dreamed of democracy, each in our own way, the John Birch Society members, the moderates and me. Since this didn't exist, it was ours to create according to our own imaginations. Soon American's plants all over the state had rising tides of blue, which made us sitting duck targets. The incumbents' supporters growled threats in our faces and the company wrote us up for trivial matters and switched our jobs to isolated areas.

The union and the company had joined forces to put me, as a renegade shop steward, into "receivership" (suspension of my steward status) for "spending too much time on members' grievances." Senior Italian ladies had cornered the Chief Steward, yelling: "We voted for her! What the hell have *you* done for us? We thought we left Mussolini back in the old country!"

The more the attacks came down, the more campaigners' telephone wires, crisscrossing the state, hummed. We strangers were becoming comrades, laughing, reporting the latest outrages, and emboldening each other. We attributed each attack to our growing power.

The Harley swayed sideways, ducking beneath May green boughs hanging low, and came to a smooth stop in a parking lot adjoining the brick building that was home to many progressive advocacy groups.

"Thank you for trying a new mode of transportation!" John said politely. "Did you like it?"

"Loved it!" I said gaily. "And thank you for trying something way off the union charts!"

We made our way up soft, blue-carpeted stairs to the office of the Massachusetts State Cancer Registry. I cast a sidelong glance at John, wondering how he was doing away from his usual turf. He *was* conservative. He'd turned out to be one of the smartest people I knew, a true intellectual with a very open mind, just now realizing his dream of attending a Jesuit college at night. In the new freedom of this campaign, I was opening my mind too, letting myself imagine what a real union could do. What needs beyond bread and butter issues could we address?

Jim, the Registry Director, had welcomed us in. He was in his mid-forties, tall, blonde and slightly balding, his blue work shirt open at the neck. I knew him to be a radical scientist, one of those folks who'd slipped through the system's cracks and was trying to make some real changes—probably not long for his job, I thought to myself.

"Jim," I said, "John and I have a project in mind for the new union leadership we think will soon be elected. Remember that MassCOSH workshop I attended, where you superimposed a map of clusters of increased cancer cases over a map of the eastern part of the state, and they coincided with industrial cities?" He nodded and smiled. "Well, I began to imagine a map like that of cancer cases among our membership, matched up to departments where they worked, then researched for the chemicals used in those departments. We would have to send illness and mortality questionnaires to all ten thousand of our members and also to retirees, or their families. Is that feasible? Is it something you could help us with?"

"It's a great idea!" he said, raising a questioning eyebrow at John. "So you're the challenger at American! A lot of people I know are wishing you well. But that's off the record. On the record is this: I think your membership, one of the largest work forces in the state, would be, in an epidemiological sense, very significant. I would certainly be interested. But the problem is that, since this is at present an internal union campaign, it would be improper, illegal in fact, to use state funds for the survey. If you could find other funding for the mailing and processing for now, once you were in office, John, I could legitimately analyze any data you presented me with. I'd love to help."

John, the only treasurer who had ever increased the union funds by judicious investment in the stock market, had made a quick calculation. "That would take at least $5000, wouldn't you say?"

Jim sat back, pursed his lips a minute then nodded. "At least."

"The campaign is in debt. Many of us have re-mortgaged our homes and used up our savings. I don't see how we could do that."

Jim tapped his pencil, rubbed his chin a bit, and closed his eyes, thinking. I smiled at John, gesturing with my head toward a pink and gray poster, a painting of manacled industrial hands turning into a flight of doves.

"I'll tell you what!" said Jim. "I don't see why the American Cancer Society shouldn't help with that funding. Once the data is in, my office could work with it. Here's their number. I'm very happy you came to see me. Get back to me, will you?"

He pressed a piece of paper into my hand and we thanked him as we headed out into the dappled light of late afternoon.

"What do you think?" I said, doing my best to straddle the Harley gracefully. "Will it bring too much heat, or should we go for it?"

"I think he's a nice man. I think we are talking about the possibility of saving lives. What better service can we offer the members? We should go forward if we get the money. Now, may I give you a real ride home? You're comfortable with a little speed? I'd like to get back to Lynn before my family's suppertime."

The next afternoon I made the call. A Cancer Society aide took my detailed message outlining our idea, and asking for the Society's help. I hung up, lingering by the phone, noting my frayed linoleum floor needed washing again. My thoughts wandered.

Since we worked in plants so far apart, it was the after-hours phone calls between us that were weaving a circle of new acquaintances in this campaign. They excited us. Yet, we talked with our old guarded habits, half-cautious, never completely certain which one of us might prove to be a union plant, which one might cave in to the company's influence, as many had, what reversal of hope lay in wait around the hairpin turns we were navigating. I smiled at the thought of our owl-eyed, droll candidate and his little idiosyncrasy—his secret life as a biker.

I liked these new friends a lot. Liked? It was hard to love at American, it struck me. There was always the distance. A teacher once told me about a dog she had, who came to her as a beaten stray and stayed. He liked to sit with her, but always at a distance, just beyond arm's reach. It was hard to love at American, each of us keeping ourselves just beyond harm's reach. But I loved John, in the way that all of us did. Inside our widening circle, with danger hovering, we loved this good thing happening, loved the rectitude of it all, the shared laughs and the intrigue, the tricks to out-fox the enemy. And, though we sat at a careful distance from it, we loved in ourselves the dignity.

A week later the phone rang, rousing me out of a sound sleep. The kids? A campaign emergency? I stumbled, barefoot, to the phone, shaking my-self awake. My watch said midnight.

"Hello?"

"Hello. This is…(I don't remember his name. It was the director of the local Cancer Society). I am sorry to call so late, but I'm going out of town tomorrow and it was important for me to speak with you before I leave."

I held my breath—was it finally going to happen?

"Thanks for calling me back. I've been anxious to talk with you."

"You must not pursue this project. Everyone knows that the only proven causes of industrial cancer are asbestos and benzene. Anything else would be speculation. You should drop this idea immediately. Good night."

I sat down, shocked at the crater that seemed to open before me. He didn't say, "I'm sorry, we can't provide you with funds." He called at mid-night to tell me not to pursue the project. I was shaken by the implications. I could only assume that what I'd just heard was evidence, not provable as usual, of American's sinister reach.

John had not been entirely surprised. "I would imagine that American and the Cancer Society share members of the Board of Directors, wouldn't you? And of course there are the generous donations we union members make every year to the conventional recipients of The United Way, includ-ing the Cancer Society, for which American takes complete credit. I'm sure a phone call was made to the company. It's all right. When we win, we will submit the project to the membership for approval. I can assure you there is ample money in the union treasury to fund several surveys!"

Two and a half years later Suzanne and I rode in my car in stunned si-lence. We were part of a funeral procession slowly winding its way through Lynn, past its working-class triple-decker houses, pelted with rain, as the casket, in the Italian tradition, was driven by the home of the deceased for a last goodbye on the way to the grave.

John had lost the election by only a few hundred votes. He had decided not to contest the union's many violations of federal laws governing union elections, knowing that everyone, even management and the incumbent's supporters, expected him to win the next election by a landslide.

Two and a half years later, in January, when it was time to launch the new campaign, John had developed some flu-like symptoms. I received a call from Tim Coughlin, like me one of John's confidantes. He was calling from John's hospital room.

"He doesn't want to see anyone, Jean, because his face and body are grossly swollen and so are all his internal organs. It doesn't look good. He's here at Mass General Hospital with the best doctors in the country and they have no idea of the cause."

In three weeks John was dead.

The union forbade its officers to attend the funeral, putting out the rumor that John died of AIDS. Tim and several other leading campaigners and friends quit their jobs at American two weeks later and disappeared. They were all Vietnam veterans who knew very well the intricacies of war. John had no equal. The campaign collapsed in frightened silence.

This was the nature of our industrial relations. Our work was strategic to the power of the State, supplying the deadly force that underwrote it. Therefore, like certain oil-producing regions, we had to be kept under strict surveillance and control. The union too was strategic, the guarantor of a no-strike, stable and compliant workforce. A reformed union, subject to the uncertainties of strikes, independent investigations and participatory democracy, must have been judged to have an unacceptable level of risk. The company was virtually an extension of the military, an appendage to its customer, the Department of Defense. And in the military, a commanding officer can be removed for losing control of his men; perhaps these imperatives also influenced those in command in the defense industry. Or perhaps it was a given that any individual who stood in the way of national security must be rendered expendable.

We were under the control of this culture for a very long time—thirty-five to forty-five years for the average person. How did it affect us? What vestiges of control and subordination had become lodged in our relations and in our characters?

♠

VII

Some Consequences of Command and Control

Not long ago I was on vacation in a European city and at a dinner party, seated opposite a man I didn't know. He was a handsome, world-weary man of fifty, a friend of a friend, and a self-described "rightist." He probably had been told I wasn't. Prospects for conversation looked dim until he told me he had decided to take time off to reflect on changing his career.

"These big corporations are all the same—ruthless!" he said. "I've just quit my job as a Human Resources consultant at the European office of a major U. S. defense company, American Missile. I knew I had to quit when I was asked to observe their standard management training program. The required reading was *Patton*, for god's sake!"

"No!" I said.

"Are you familiar with Patton?" he asked. "His motto was *'I'm the best damn ass-kicker in the whole U.S. Army!'* His rule was 'It's eat or be eaten, kill or be killed. My men won't win if I ask them *kindly!'*[1] Survival of the fittest. The idea is, you know, you only get results if you put people under extreme pressure."

"I do know." I smiled. "I worked on the shop floor at American for fifteen years and now I'm trying to write about it."

"No kidding!" He grinned and handed me his card. "Call me!"

This fortunate coincidence reassured me: we had not been mistaken to sense that our work relations were militarized. They were: it was no accident but a company requirement. And here was a conservative human resources expert who found that management model outrageous just as we had. This verification was important to me because in 1992 and later, when

---

1   Alan Axelrod, *Patton on Leadership: Strategic Lessons for Corporate Warfare* (Paramus, N.J.: Prentis Hall Press, 1999), 184 and 32.

we set about to analyze our harsh relations, we had come to some troubling conclusions.

Shop Floor Analysis

It was September, 1992, and we were ready to clarify our findings. What were the symptoms we experienced? Some of them were obvious to any reasonable person on the shop floor. They were: excessive anger, depression, anxiety and fearfulness. I was sure they were unusually prevalent here. Still, to check my own perceptions, I opted, once again, for my favorite research method—the clandestine shop-floor survey.

Shaunessy had stepped out for a smoke so I picked up a box of diodes to carry in order to appear, to his informants, gainfully employed, and hustled over to see Dominic. He was in earlier than his second shift, working some over-time. He was dressed in immaculate white carpenters' pants and a white izod sports jersey.

"Hey, look at the Energizer Bunny!" Rob yelled at him.

Dom gave him a dirty look and continued hunting through his bench drawer.

"Hi Miss Jean! Somebody took my custom-made angle wrench. I hate people going in my drawers! Even though the tools are all American's, it's my *space*. I think I'll trot around it twice a day and urinate in the corners to mark my territory!"

I giggled. "Listen, Dommy, could I ask you a question?"

"Shoot, Miss Jean."

"What do you think is the main mood around here? How would you describe us if you had to use one word?"

"How about *angry*? I can feel the anger from the assholes in here because their lives suck so bad. They have to take it out somewhere so they get super macho."

"Super macho?"

"Sure. To cover the fact they have no self-esteem, no self-confidence. There's no esprit de corps in here, no unwritten rules of conduct. Professionals, they have a *code*. If they act badly toward each other, they say 'that's unprofessional.' What have we got in here? It's 'un*factory*?' There's no holds barred here—everything and everybody is fair game. 'Oh, you hit him? You shoulda killed him.' The factory code, *really,* is 'be obnoxious, be a jerk.' We're not allowed to have a conscience or an opinion. Why? Because we're just peasants. Management is the brains and we're the arms and legs." He snickered: "Or the intestines!" He motioned with his head to alert me that the boss was rounding the corner.

I slid back into my seat just as Shaunessy began striding around. I cast a side-long glance at Julio, who was bent over a spec trying to figure out the best way to do a new job. New jobs were entrusted to him because he was skilled and experienced from working in American's Carlisle Research and Development Labs before he got bumped back here in a lay-off.

"I *hate* to interrupt you, especially to ask you a serious question," I said in a stage whisper, "but I *have* to. Listen, Julio, what would you say the difference in atmosphere is between the Carlisle labs and here?" I took a paint brush and pushed down the plunger on my red solvent can, which produced a cascade of chloroethene to wet the brush.

"Juanita, what are you doing cleaning that same unit again? Oh *I* see, *I* see. You can do it to look busy while we talk, without messing anything up like you usually do. I can read you like a book, Juanita." I gave him a menacing look.

"Okay, okay." He was grinning, pleased with himself. "The biggest difference is the anger. Here you hear four-letter words all the time, people shouting at each other and ordering each other around. People see the bosses yelling for nothing so they do it too."

I whipped out a pamphlet—a great find I'd picked up that week from an Army Recruiting office—and looked at him slyly.

"Listen to this army pamphlet, *hombre,* and you'll find out why they yell. It says here: '*In basic training you'll think the sergeant does an unusual amount of shouting. But it's his job to turn you into a good soldier within a few short weeks. The shouting and toughness are all part of the process.*' So now I bet you're going to turn into a good soldier too any day, *Julito!*"

He shook his head. "No me, Jean. No me!" He spoke English perfectly like most people from Puerto Rico, but he liked to put on an "I no speak English" act to give people a hard time.

"Okay. Let me 'splain to you, Juanita," he said, pleased with his fake accent. "At the Carlisle labs the engineers gave us respect—adult treatment. There was no anger and no pressure. We were treated like colleagues. I loved it! When people from the other divisions, like this one, were bumped up there with us, they were nervous wrecks! When my wife worked up there, one day she broke a PC board so she started crying. The engineer didn't care—he just said 'That's Okay. Get another one.' The people from here were so intimidated they would get very nervous when we took 20 minute breaks, and very nervous anytime the managing engineers were around. We used to have to spend quite a few weeks reassuring them that this wasn't like the other plants at American."

"Like frightened pups! It took them that long to unlearn what they expected from here?" I said, scrubbing off some congealed brown flux I'd missed on a solder joint.

"Yeah. Like that. A bunch of *perritos!* Even Lillian *mi esposa!* But Juanita you shouldn't be calling my wife a dog! She's not a dog—she's very pretty. Anyway, finally after we reassured them about a hundred times, for weeks, they would change and realize they could expect respect. Here, you're just a number."

The buzzer sounded for break. I spotted Sam and Nora chatting over cokes in the hallway. It was unusual to catch them together so I hurried over to seize on this good interview op.

"Hi guys," I said. "Am I interrupting anything? I wanted to ask you something."

Sam made room for me along the wall. "Sure, Jeannie, what's on your mind?"

"What I'd like to know is, in your opinion, what's the main mood here? What would you say is the main characteristic of this place?"

"That it's *dehumanizing* and *oppressive!*" Nora said promptly, stealing a glance at Sam to see if he thought she was being too radical. "I feel the people that run the plant put a lot of effort into making us feel this way. It's the old idea—if you *browbeat* people they won't think and they'll be better workers. See, Jean, I think the angry patriotism in here during the Gulf War was also related to the oppression. People feel oppressed and angry but they also feel—I don't know—maybe the authoritarian system is comforting to them. Then they had someone like Saddam Hussein who became a symbol of the oppressor for them, and they wanted to see him crushed. They feel so helpless, so angry that it was comforting to them to think that America, at least, could be strong and right."

Sam raised his eyebrows, interested, and thought a moment.

"The main thing I sense here is the feeling we have that we're incompetent," he said. "We all know we can do more than this. And the lack of stimulation too. *Years* will go by and there's no stimulation whatsoever. So people end up squirting water at each other—anything to break the boredom. And we are angry. I've noticed I'm very cranky when I get home, and I tell my wife the job is driving me nuts. The other main mood here is depression, no question! But what *I* think happened during the Gulf War—why people were especially angry at *you*, Miss Jean, for protesting it, was that after day in and day out of doing a boring job with no meaning, at last they felt that what they did meant something. But you in effect said it didn't. Myself, I don't express my opinions much because of the people here. You can't trust them. They're very gossipy, nasty, get things wrong."

Back at my bench after break, I chose the simplest task on my current project—tinning leads—so I could think some more. I turned on one of the little plastic fans the company had given us when we complained about inhaling the solder fumes. But all it did was blow the spirals of smoke into somebody else's face, so I turned it off.

They see what I see. I nodded decisively to my own thoughts. People here are either down in the dumps or like high tension wires that can spark anger any minute. We're very unpredictable—friendly one day, hostile the next.

The anger is always there. It can go off like a land mine, or it can take the form of unexpected coldness and cynicism that appears out of nowhere and snaps down on you like a steel trap. We try to keep it underground, but it can leak out in sneaky moves and provocations, petty jealousies. What was it Dominic said the other day? I got out a pink three by five card and read: "It's not so much the *job* I hate. It's the petty stuff, union people trying to screw each other, using personal information against you, be better than you, berate you, outdo you for overtime, at your throat for stupid things. Miss Jean, if you ever wanted to get ahead here you'd have to *claw* your way to the top!"

I looked up as Julio came back, arms across his stomach, covering the *Yankee Stadium* on his white T-shirt. His black moustache drooped at the corners and he frowned.

"Where have you been, Julio?" I said. "Did you go and eat an ice cream sandwich like you do every day?" He nodded. "And now you have cramps, right? Cause you won't listen to me and try skipping lactose!" I knew if I let him know I felt bad for him he'd make fun of me.

He settled into his seat and examined some delicate wires in the supply tub in front of him, with raised eyebrows. "Juanita. You're right. That I won't listen to a woman who's just my pet and does what I tell her. But I might try skipping it tomorrow because *I* already thought of that. And how come you're talking to yourself again?"

"Well, because I'm thinking about the atmosphere. If you don't know when people will be nice or nasty, you have to guard your trust, right?"

"Sure. And if you came in with it, like *you* did, Juanita, you better get over it!"

I nodded. If you were a slow learner on that score, like I was, the old timers would set you straight. I could still hear Eleanor: "Don't be so nice! She'll only end up stabbing you in the back!" Or, Angie: "Miss Jean, how many times have I told you, you watch what you say to him. He runs to the boss with everything!" After a while we new hires would get the message and develop a distrusting and cynical attitude of our own, like Archie Bunkers.

I put on some heavy blue rubber gloves before I sloshed chloroethene on my freshly tinned leads because, as I had told everybody who would listen, chloroethene has caused cancer in lab animals. First I touched the lead gingerly with one bare finger. You had to be careful to let the leads cool before you washed them, or you would get a dull, pock-marked surface—what we called "cold solder," which didn't conduct right and would fail in test. Then again, I thought to myself, a lot of people don't want any part of the hostilities, so what they do is sink into withdrawal, which seems like the more dignified thing to do. But that can turn into depression.

"Gina!" Eleanor grinned when I jumped. "You're staring into space! Now let's get to work here! Push those 755's out the door!" She was known as a person who "does beautiful work" (the top accolade here) and also as "a good worker" (an efficient producer), but she didn't take the pressures of production as seriously as she pretended. Hadn't she and Angie been the ones to show me the old timers' trick of completing an extra hour's worth of units fast in the morning and hiding them in a drawer? That way you could take it easy and chat in the afternoon, they said, and still have work to turn in.

"Now, Gina Lollobrigida, what's on your mind dear? What's the matter?"

"Nothing's the matter, Eleanora. I'm thinking about depression. Do you think a lot of people are depressed in here?" She was the wrong person to ask. She was always so cheery and stout-hearted. She often made me think of Mrs. Yarrington, a portly lady with a rosy face and army uniform who had commanded the Rocky Hill American Legion Post in parades when I was a kid.

"Well, that depends," she said, "on what you mean. To me, most people have down days now and then—it's just part of life. You could call anything depression, couldn't you? You could get depressed if you couldn't get that new car you wanted."

"True. But with serious depression, the kind you need a doctor for, it's different. Then you get into a low mood for a long time and you can't climb out of it. You feel paralyzed, so you don't do any of the things you used to enjoy doing. You feel fatigued and helpless and hopeless. Everything looks negative to you. You're irritable, and sometimes you cry. You feel very incompetent, and in a way you really *are* incompetent, because the depression affects your memory and concentration and your IQ actually goes down. It changes you. And sometimes it can make you have thoughts of suicide."

"Oh well, that's *different*. I can see quite a few people who look down like *that*—you haven't heard them say much in years. But then, how would you know? People don't let on how they feel around here."

"You've got *that* right!" I said and went back to work. It struck me that the clinical description of depression that I'd just recited fit to a 'T' how people had said they felt in our first group session. I remembered it by heart:

"I used to go camping and do a lot of things after work. Now I just sit in front of the TV, no drive anymore. I feel like a retarded dog." "I used to like to do ceramics, go out dancing, but I have no energy for any of that anymore." "I used to like knitting, crocheting—and motorcycle riding, just so you don't think I'm a deadhead! Now I don't think I could function on the outside. I wonder does my brain still function, or am I on automatic pilot? You know you're not stupid, and yet in a certain way you *are*." "I used to do all kinds of mechanical work but now I have to force myself to do anything at home. I just go home and drop and my kids say, 'Mommy, what's *wrong* with you? Why are you always so *tired*?'"

"Miss Jean, you think too much. Take my advice and relax a little. Now listen to me." She leaned over and whispered the rest. "When we get this dozen done, I'll go to the lady's room. You wait a few minutes after I leave, then follow me. Look here." She opened a big package wrapped in tinfoil just wide enough for a quick peak inside. "I want you to try some of this nice gumdrop cake my sister-in-law made."

Eleanor and Julio were my buddies. It was quite a while before I understood the significance of the buddy relationships that abounded here. They were not like friendships I'd seen anywhere else. People would choose one person they felt they could trust for warnings, advanced information and personal support in hostile territory. My buddies had a special characteristic that I noticed was true of nearly all the buddy relationships at American. We chose as buddies people who were very different from ourselves. I, for example, had never known anybody from Puerto Rico this well before, or been close to a conservative person like Eleanor. Many buddies here were opposites of each other—white and black, gay and straight, young and old. I think we chose opposites as a way of treating ourselves to an adventure during the monotony of the work day—a novel relationship with a kind of person that might not be so accessible to us in our outside lives.

I was fond of both Julio and Eleanor, yet in time I understood that having them as buddies had a negative aspect: the *need* for buddies here implied a perceived threat in our environment. A friend told me that he had also observed buddy relationships at the tough and dangerous navy shipyard where he worked—"Tom and Jerry relationships" they were called there. Sociologist Erving Goffman, in *Asylums*, says that "buddy formations" are hallmarks of "total institutions"—prisons, mental hospitals, convents and the army.[2] Judith Herman says that they were characteristic of Nazi concentration camps, known in that context as "stable pairs."[3]

There was another phenomenon which, like the buddy relationships, on the surface seemed fairly ordinary, but which I suspected was also a product of our harsh relations. It was a slow shutting down of altruism. I had watched it recently.

2   *Asylums: Essays on the social situation of mental patients and other inmates* (New York: Anchor Books, 1961), 59.
3   *Trauma And Recovery: The aftermath of violence—from domestic abuse to political terror* (New York: Basic Books, 1992), 91.

"Okay, everybody—get ready to cough it up!" Rob stood up and raised his voice behind us to call us to attention, ready for duty. "This is a collection to put in a sympathy card for Bill's family, from our department."

Bill had been one of our two elder group leaders, Williamson being the other. Group leaders were hybrids of a sort. They were in the union but served as assistants to management, organizing the work flow and giving us workers technical guidance. Two days ago, only six months into his retirement, Bill had died of a heart attack.

"He's another one!" Angie shook her head. "See that? Forty years at the plant and he hardly gets to enjoy his retirement, like a lotta people here."

"I'm sending around this piece of paper," Rob went on. "Write your name down if you want to go to the funeral together. That way I can get permission from Shaunessy for all of us to get an hour off."

The 8" by 8" gray cardboard diode box we always used for collections had a slot in the top just the width of several dollar bills, the expected donation. Rob was carefully printing "Family of Bill" with a large black felt-tip marker so nobody would accuse him of collecting the money for himself.

Angie and Eleanor and I, like Rob and several others including Shaunessy, were community-spirited types when it came to collections. We had a dollar ready for just about any request. This time, given the importance of the occasion, we stuffed fives in the slot and then turned around to watch the old timers, Bill's contemporaries.

"What did I tell you?" Angie muttered out of the side of her mouth. A lot of the back row people were suddenly too busy to look up from their work. They just shook their heads when Rob came around. We exchanged glances. This happened time and again, but it never failed to shock the rest of us. Collections were one of the few approved ways we had of expressing sympathy and good will together. Sometimes the old refusers would start to join in, then think better of their altruism, as if they couldn't afford it, or the dollar, or the hour off from work. Sooner or later one of them would grumble: "You're just a number here anyway. So I have to look out for number one."

This renunciation of personal involvement and failure of altruism were so frequent and inappropriate, given our long association and fairly good pay, that I think it represented a deterioration of ordinary social instincts and courtesy—a kind of de-socialization.

I wrote to the group a week before the January session: "Sociologists Sam Bowles and Herb Gintis say that the workplace is 'a school where individuals become who they are.'[4] Next meeting, could we focus on who we've learned to be in this place?"

At quarter of four on the day of that session, we arrived together, unwinding mufflers and peeling off outer layers—damp coats and snow-encrusted boots—which we left outside our blue meeting room, padding in, comfortable together in stocking feet. We looked novel to each other encased in layers against the cold. Ruth could have been an ad for a ski lodge, striking in her homemade red cable sweater. Sean was wearing four layers of sweatshirts—a male fashion statement that said 'I'm too tough to need a coat.' I'd seen him dressed like this at 7:00 that morning shoveling off the loading dock. I buttoned up the delphinium mohair cardigan my mother had knit for me, which made me look like a fat blue bear. Hildie and Suzanne grinned and reached out to pat me. People always did that when I had this sweater on. I rather liked it.

Tom took his place at the head of the table and with palms extended in a pastoral gesture, invited us to take the seats around him and get started.

"Oh oh, he's calling us into formation!" Sean slouched down into his seat.

"I've been thinking a lot about American since our last session," Tom began. "I've come to the conclusion that sometimes our fellow workers are worse than the bosses. Maybe some people wage war on their colleagues to make themselves feel better at the bottom of the totem pole. But it's amazing to me that they do it in *groups!*"

Sean lowered his mouth to take a careful swig of the mulled cider I'd made, which had seeds and sticks floating in it, raised his eyebrows at me as if to say 'not as bad as it looks,' and said "Such as?"

Tom shook his head slowly, "Well…I worked in one American division where there were the usual cliques and backbiting. But those cliques got their kicks out of setting somebody up to fail. They targeted my group leader, a very nice older lady, and really ground her down. I came to see that they were tripping her up on just a few things she didn't know, so I taught them to her. Then what did they do? They attacked *me* for helping her! I asked myself, is this human nature in its worst condition?"

<hr>

4   "The Economy Produces People: An Introduction to Post-Liberal Democracy," in Michael Zweig, ed. *Ibid.*, 222.

"I've seen plenty of that!" Suzanne's voice had a rough edge when she was disgusted. "Bosses and cliques getting together and creating a problem for somebody, then standing back to watch the fireworks."

"It's the same in my department," Ruth nodded. "Old ladies fighting and acting like kids, dog-eat-dog. We get our heads so filled with garbage from all the gossip, and we have to watch people kicking somebody when they're down. It makes me want to bring in the uzi!"

Nora leaned forward. "See, what you're talking about is just what I *don't* like to think about *at all*—all the hostility around us at work. And what alarms me even *more* and what I *really* don't like dealing with is my *own* hostility. So I put my face shield down and stay in my little work booth. I don't want to be disturbed. It's comforting. There's no outside agitation."

"Me too," Ruth said. "I get into my own little world."

"I play my own games with reality," Tom nodded. "I create mental vignettes with the cast of characters out there, and my own private jokes and double talk."

"Yeah," Sean said. "I rant and rave about what an unsafe environment we work in then, when people don't want to hear it, I withdraw too. I get very bitter and angry."

At that point I withdrew to think, with the excuse of going over to the stove, which was a convenience of our conference room, to heat some more cider. Maybe peaceful withdrawal isn't such a bad strategy at work, I was thinking. But it has an insidious way of becoming an ingrained habit. Like that constant response to discussions on the shop floor—"I don't get involved"—that's supposed to be such a badge of moral superiority. Well, people don't get involved in controversy to avoid getting themselves in trouble and that's understandable, I thought as I crushed a few more cardamom seeds into the cider. But I'm willing to bet that this non-involvement becomes a way of life for some people. And to them, people like me who do "get involved" are very puzzling. How many times have I heard "It might be a good cause, Jean, but why would you do that after work when nobody's even paying you to do it?!"

"Ouch!" I'd left the metal spoon too long in the pot.

"That's what you get for thinking during production again!" Hildie laughed. I dropped in more pieces of cinnamon stick and sat back down.

"Okay," I said, "This is what I was thinking. I was wondering if withdrawal has some down sides, if it can become a habit and kind of follow us home? Let me ask you a question. How many people at work do you know who are involved in any community activities? You know, the Elks or Eastern Star or the VFW•or *anything*?" They shook their heads.

"Hardly anybody except a few of us in black churches," Ruth said. "Everybody's welcome in church."

"Charity begins at home," Hildie said. "Any time I have I'd rather spend with my family."

"Me too," Tom nodded. "But you're right, Jean. I can count on one hand the people in there who are involved in their communities—or for that matter in the union." He grabbed a handful of popcorn, passed the bag around and turned to Ruth. "See, I think you hit on something just now. You said everybody feels welcome at church. In my opinion, after working at American all day, people don't expect to feel welcome elsewhere. Why would they? Think about it."

"I see what you're saying," I said. "You get no experience doing anything but following orders at work, so why would you feel competent to take initiative in outside projects? You've come to expect people will attack you and ridicule you, so you figure, why should outsiders be any different? Why would you want to expose yourself to *that* after work?"

"Exactly," Tom said. "Your home is your castle. There you can count on mattering and being respected."

"But having to withdraw from the hostility *costs* us," I said. "People *need* some friends at work. I read a study that said the best buffer against stress at work is not your family but support from your co-workers."

No one said anything. I noticed a blue damask curtain ripple by an open window. It was snowing lightly outside. Then people began to speak up, one by one, very quietly.

"It's as if we feel so assaulted at work, "Nora said, "that we go home and kind of lick our wounds, and curl up into a fetal position—cuddle up into our little homes like a cocoon—instead of being able to interact with people. The downside of withdrawal is isolation. We shut down our contact with human beings. We are *isolating* ourselves in preference for *depression*, instead of making ourselves feel better as we do in this group! Yet I still would rather be in my own little world. It's unhealthy. Why can't we just be normal?" She looked at the floor in the silence that followed.

"You know," Tom said slowly, "it *pains* me that there are not more people in this group, that more people don't want to get involved."

I had the feeling that something deeper was saddening him, so I asked, "Are you feeling pained by our loneliness at work?"

He grimaced and nodded. "I am."

Ruth put her hand on the back of his chair. "No man owes no man anything but love and the word of God," she said to him gently. "You share a spiritual love. Like here. We trust each other. We all trust each other."

Tom nodded without saying anything for a while.

"We're trying to get at this *thing* together," he said quietly, looking around at each one of us. "We don't know what it is really, or what paths we're taking. We're trying to discover something. Of course you can't go to all five hundred or five thousand people in the plant, but if we could enlarge this group to twenty, even, maybe the effects would reach others. I know you *differently* now, it's a different relationship."

I kept silent and listened as we entered into a kind of meditation on our alienation.

"In the plant, we come from different worlds," Sean began. "We *do* have common bonds and we *want* to reach out. But it's hard. It used to be that at work everyone was the same as in my neighborhood—Irish Catholic or Italian Catholic. It was easy to deal with someone you didn't like because you had the whole social structure behind you. But now we have no cushions to fall back on. We work in a society that is not defined for us by our social background. We have people coming from Asia, India, Africa. You could be sitting next to somebody from Alaska. In my culture, to break the ice, you'd say 'Hey, kid, would you like to go out and have a beer?' But maybe in another culture that's not acceptable. Maybe for most ladies it's all right to go out bowling together after work but in another society maybe you got married at seventeen and what's acceptable is to go right home and be with your husband. In my neighborhood, if somebody said 'that's a real weird shirt!' I'd figure maybe he'd had a bad day, but"—he grinned at Nora—"if *you* say it to me maybe it's a compliment. In this group we really have extended the courtesy to each other, and the trust, to break down those barriers."

"No." Hildegarde had been shaking her head. "No," she said. "*Outside* this group, I think it's more a matter of you can't *trust* people enough to be open with each other. If you see someone's having a hard time you say 'Gee, is something wrong? Can I help?' But most of the time they say 'oh nothing,' because if they really open up to most people in here, chances are it's all over the plant. And then the person becomes segregated. There's always the fear, 'if I open up, they'll hold it over me.' It's too bad."

We looked at our laps and said nothing for a while.

"It *is* too bad," Tom said. "I'm *decent*, not out to do you in. I *admire* other people's talents. I want others to enjoy them too. Everyone wants to feel necessary. It's peace of mind."

Sean turned to him. "The other day I watched a segment on TV about a guy who was raised as a kid by a commune with good values—you know, living off the land, having close relationships with an extended family of people that aren't your blood relatives. Money didn't matter to them—only quality of life did. He's an architect now and he knows he has to work and earn a living but he tries to bring the values he was raised with into his workplace." He studied his hands for a minute, then looked up and said slowly, "I know that I'm very angry at work most of the time because I really can't see… I have a conflict with what I was brought up with, and what I see as the *brutalizing* that goes on at work. I can't seem to see a way to reconcile them."

"Once I had a job where I was put on a *misfits* line," Hildegard said. "It was a production line of dissatisfied people. The boss took a gamble that if he treated us with respect and let us talk and read when there was no work, we would change. And we did. We *did* develop trust and closeness, and after a while we out-produced all the other departments."

"Or maybe it's like being in a foxhole." Sean looked into his cup and downed the last of his cider. "There, like at work, you were with someone you thought you'd never care to talk to. But when you were alone there the shield would drop. Or like a detox where I once worked as a second job. We learned that for a person to let their guard down and give back to you, you had to open up and give them something of yourself too."

We sat in silence. There was darkness now behind the icy streaks on the window panes, but no one got up to leave.

"You know," Tom said, looking around at us, "coming together can either split people apart like it does at work, or it can bring them closer together. Sometimes you can get a phoenix out of the ashes."

The snow-covered bridge over the Charles was dangerous as I swerved toward Boston and home. My mind was not on driving, so I slowed down, turning the knob of the windshield wipers to high speed until they rushed back and forth, clearing a few seconds of visibility that disappeared and cleared again. Driving was often my time for seeing into things, for understanding. Someone told me it's because driving is a right-side-of-the-brain activity, relying on primitive reactions and intuitions, and so opening up those faculties. My understanding of the group today was coming to me like that now. It cleared and disappeared then cleared a little more, like the visibility on the road ahead.

The brutalizing that goes on at work. Did he mean "becoming brutes" or "getting brutalized"? I guess we're supposed to reconcile ourselves to both, to fit in. But some part of us does not fit in.

I continued on down Massachusetts Avenue, which was deserted in the storm. The discussion felt like being at a wake, sharing loss and memories. It was as if the missing persons hovering around our first session came trooping back today. The good people, raised to trust, not out to do you in. The people, in from the foxholes and the misfits' lines, who once knew how to banish alienation. Our former selves, the innocents, sent to some other country long ago like children cloistered from the ravages of war.

I came to a stop inside the towering square white walls I had shovelled around myself at five a.m., climbed out, hung my bag over my shoulder and pulled myself up my steep steps by their homely iron pipe railing. Some Yankee owner ninety years ago had imbedded it in cement, undoubtedly muttering to himself, "There. That should last a while." My old house often felt to me like a repository of ninety years of seasoned, overarching perspectives on all difficulties. It was comforting. I need perspective now, I thought. We have sustained losses. I need to look at them dispassionately and write them down.

The heat and lights were on low, as I'd left them this morning, welcome as I took off my damp coat and boots. I boiled some macaroni for Mom's 1950's tuna casserole recipe, collected a blue pad and silver pen, and soon sat down to supper, serving myself some noodles gooey with stretching strands of cheese. Jones settled himself on my lap, the compromise he and I had reached about who belonged at or on the dining room table. I began to write, too preoccupied at first to notice the sleek beige paw closing in on its prey, the largest chunk of tuna on my plate.

"Jones! Get down! I haven't got time for an argument!" I said, easing him off my lap.

There was no question that we exhibited clinical symptoms: sudden anger, free-floating anxiety—what Sean described as "fears that hold us hostage that we can't express in the work place." Jumpiness and nervousness. Depression. Low self-esteem, apathy and withdrawal. Giving up on social or community participation. Loss of altruism, a de-socialization.

I got up and made myself a cup of tea, dipping the Jasmine and the Earl Grey tea bags up and down, up and down in an old blue-willow Woolworth's cup until the spreading darkness and aroma gave the water a weak identity, then settled into my living room rocker with it.

I knew the clinical terms to describe these symptoms well enough, but there were existential conditions—altered states of our existence—that did not have convenient names. What would be the word for having to make yourself into someone other than the person you had meant to be? What syndrome was having to be a guarded person with humane tendencies suppressed?

I took a sip of tea and sat thinking. Symptoms can be reversed. But what about more general changes in us? What about the one I prefer not to name, because it can become such a disability that respect requires turning away from it. I'm talking about the dulling down and narrowing of life that happens gradually. I've felt its pull myself. It's there in the days emptied of personal content when we are nothing but parts in and parts out, pre-authorized motions. Those primitive motions, all the same, so easy and familiar, have lulled me until thoughts are nothing but discomfort, a disturbance of my dormancy, and wishes are more bother than they're worth. The emptiness falls down around us like that, a dark and comforting blanket, and reinforces itself with every day it recurs. How would we measure its consequences?

I'm not imagining this. Someone else observed it too. I stood up and pulled down a pile of books from the bookcase, leafing through them until I came to Arthur Kornhauser's study of auto workers, and read its troubling conclusion:

"The unsatisfactory mental health of working people consists in no small measure of their dwarfed desires and deadened initiative, reduction of their goals and restriction of their efforts to a point where life is relatively empty and only half meaningful."[5]

I closed the book and sat back down. I know this happens to people at American because they told me so: "Work makes me feel empty, like a robot. There's no learning here, no hope for the future."

I shifted in my chair. Maybe it is the shutting down of hope and initiative in years of daily routine that causes our fatalism—"Hey, you can't fight city hall!" as everyone tells me. Melvin Kohn's research is about this. He says that "highly routinized jobs restrict possibility for exercising initiative, thought and judgment."[6] That kind of routine work, together with close supervision that dictates how it is to be done, gives working people, he says, very little experience that their activities can have any consequence, and therefore little reason to feel in control of fate.[7] He found conformity leading to fatalism to be characteristic of working-class people in most industrialized countries.[8]

I was filled with regret as I thought about Kohn's conclusion, after a lifetime of studying working people, that resigned acceptance of low expectations and obedience got generalized from work to family values. That's the wisdom working people instill in their children, both as principle and as preparation for the work life that awaits them.[9] Basic training, I sighed. Reproduction of oppression—kids tailor-made and ready for work—trained at no cost to the manufacturer. Discouraged, I turned out the light and went to bed.

---

5   *Work in America*, 85.
6   *The Nature of Work*, 42.
7   Melvin Kohn, *Class and Conformity: A Study in Values* (Chicago: University of Chicago Press, 1977), 189.
8   *Ibid.*, 163.
9   *Ibid.*, 201.

Putting Two and Two Together

It was a year or so later, in the course of my writing, that all the clinical symptoms and traits we had borne witness to began to make sense. I was on a trip at the time.

We were thirty minutes out of Logan Airport and the American Airlines flight attendant was dispensing coffee and pretzels. The man in the seat next to mine held them while I struggled to release my tray from the upright position.

"What do you do?" he smiled politely as he took care not to spill my coffee. "Are you travelling on business?"

"No, I'm going to Florida for a vacation. What I do for a living is make missile parts at an American Missile plant near Boston."

I assumed he would find that boring enough to return to his book, which was what I was anxious to do myself. I had reserved for this flight a book Nora had urged me to read. "I think it relates to us," she said, though it was now 1993, and our group had finished a year ago. I peered discretely out the window at the green and brown patches of Connecticut farmland below.

"Well isn't that interesting!" he said. "I work for Weapons Procurement at the Pentagon."

"Do you really? What a coincidence!" I said, taken aback. I knew this called for a lot of discretion, much as I would have liked to tell him all about certain careless, slipshod work we had sometimes been made to ship out. *Loose lips sink ships!* I smiled to myself. One phone call from him and I'd be out of a job. And if I asked him too many questions I would scare him away like a frightened deer, who was at this moment approaching.

"Well, tell me," I said by way of amiable conversation, "do you think some day both of our jobs could become obsolete? Do you think we might some day have lasting peace?"

He raised his eyebrows. "Oh, we can't have that. No, no!"

"Why?" He could hardly imagine how interested I was.

"Why, because then we wouldn't have winners and losers, and we *have* to have winners and losers!"

At that he appeared to think better of random plane conversations with wrong-thinking people, and returned to his book, *The Real Anita Hill,* until he disembarked in D.C.

By the end of the plane ride I knew a great deal about winners and losers, or rather, about tyrants and captives. My book had a disturbing cover painting with slashes of red and black across it, and was entitled *Trauma and Recovery: The aftermath of violence—from domestic abuse to political terror.*[10] In it, psychiatrist Judith Herman described the after-effects of trauma suffered by war veterans and survivors of rape, domestic violence, sexual abuse and captivity. There was one arresting fact that made clear why Nora was anxious for me to read it: these survivors' symptoms, though more acute, were similar to our own.

This seemed a serious discovery. If we had symptoms like those of trauma survivors, perhaps it meant that we had in fact been subject to some kind of trauma ourselves. I wanted to be very careful here. I had never heard of anyone linking post-traumatic stress with the stress of factory work. Such a comparison seemed on the surface far-fetched and disrespectful of the severe damage and suffering sustained by survivors of atrocities. Furthermore, we had none of the *acute* symptoms of people who have undergone violent, life-threatening events—the flashbacks, amnesia, dissociation, for example, now known to be common to Vietnam vets and rape victims. We did not fit the definition of post-traumatic stress in the standard *Diagnostic and Statistical Manual of the American Psychiatric Association III,* which says that "the essential feature of this disorder is the development of characteristic symptoms following a psychologically distressing event that is outside the range of usual human experience."[11] But our symptoms were similar to many of those suffered by people with something slightly different, what Dr. Herman proposed to call "complex chronic post-traumatic stress syndrome." People who have this have "a history of subjection to totalitarian control over a prolonged period (months to years),"[12] and suffer from apathy, depression, fearfulness, diminished self-esteem, inconsistent relationships alternating between closeness and hostility or withdrawal, among many other possible symptoms. Hallmarks of such survivors, she said, are shattered trust and a shattered sense of connection between one's self and the community. They also sometimes have an impaired capacity

10   Judith Lewis Herman, M.D. (New York: Basic Books, 1992).
11   Published by the American Psychiatric Association, Washington, DC, 1987, 247.
12   Herman, *Ibid.,* 121.

for altruism, and feelings of helplessness, isolation and disempowerment. In those who have suffered long-term exposure to coercive control, such as those in captivity, there is "an avoidance or constriction, a narrowing that applies to every aspect of life."[13]

We were dropping altitude for a landing in Miami and soon touched down with two big bumps and glided to a stop. We were safely on the ground. I generally liked to let most of my fellow travelers be on their way before I struggled with my luggage, so I settled back in my seat and waited.

Suppose our experience *did* bear the marks of post-traumatic stress, even if our symptoms were more low-grade and on-going than most. Why was there this similarity? We had not been subjected to violence or forced captivity. But, Judith Herman said that some people, like domestic abuse survivors, are constrained by barriers to escape that are invisible—economic, social, psychological or emotional—yet are still very powerful.[14] Our barriers to escape were like that. Herman's book was called "a stunning achievement" because she was the first to make the connection between survivors of trauma in war or prison camps, and survivors of domestic abuse. The thing they had in common, she said, was the *psychological impact of subordination to coercive control.*[15] That was, of course, what linked us too: the command-and-control practices of the military were surely an exemplary version of coercive control. The sobering fact was that for many years we were subject to a control which, while not directly violent, was hugely powerful and was embedded in a culture that often displayed among its features a fusion of sex, aggression and the mores of war.

The cabin was clearing, so I stowed these thoughts in the back of my mind until the return trip. I tugged at my overstuffed carry-on, let it drop to the aisle with a lurch, and tried to steer it without bumping the last of the motley assortment of vacationers like me as we found our way to Baggage Claim.

I looked out the door where people milled about in summer shorts, just as our luggage began to tumble onto the carousel. A tall handsome tanned man was coming toward me with arms outstretched! I ran over to him and held him tight, my big boy who had long ago shed his waist-length teenage locks. He grabbed my mammoth black suitcase with its frayed red and green Christmas bow, now passing us a second time, and ushered me

13   *Ibid.,* 52, 55, 87.
14   *Ibid.,* 74.
15   *Ibid.,* 75.

outside. This was the interlude I always savored—the shock of finding myself on a movie set, among surreal palm trees and enveloped by the scent of bougainvilleas and the warmth of a soft Southern evening. I had grown to love like family this exotic peninsula, South Florida, that masqueraded as part of the United States.

I could see Marcus's aging silver-blue Lincoln Town Car in the first row of the garage. While he lifted my luggage into the trunk I slid into the front seat with Marcus's little dog, Shug Avery. She was named for the charismatic character in *The Color Purple*. My only grandchild was as charismatic as her namesake. She remembered me and leapt into my lap, wiggling her fat Schipperke body uncontrollably. When I stopped patting her for a moment, she pushed her head under my hand and slid it down the length of my fingers, demonstrating a pat, since the technique had obviously slipped my mind. I giggled, let my hand go limp, and she repeated this six times. "She's *very* beautiful!" I said. "A regular black beauty, aren't you!"

"Mom. Get a grip. Yesterday a man asked me if she was a pig or a warthog!" Marcus grinned as he pulled out onto Route 195 heading east toward Miami Beach.

We spent the evening catching up and exchanging opinions about the welfare of sister Melissa, who was now living in Paris, and looking at websites Marcus had designed. Then we relaxed and watched two of our favorite movies, *The Last Picture Show,* and Marlon Brando in *A Streetcar Named Desire.* Having kids who shared my taste in movies seemed like one of the great benefits of reproduction.

The next day Marcus prepared a vegetarian lunch—salad and mozzarella and avocado sandwiches on Cuban bread. He was beginning to win me over to vegetarianism with his motto "I don't eat anything with a face." We discussed Elizabeth George's mysteries that we'd shared, but my mind drifted a bit as we talked.

"Mom, you seem preoccupied."

"It's nothing really. I've been thinking about stress and our work, and trying not to! I'm on vacation!"

"Come on, Mom, you know I'm interested in that stuff. Anyhow I already skimmed the trauma book you left on the couch last night." He passed me a tong-full of curly frisée lettuce and grapefruit salad.

I could count on Marcus to pour over books as he had been doing since he was a year and a half. I would come to his crib in the morning and find him sitting up flipping over the cardboard pages of animal books I'd left for him and making little baa-baa noises to himself.

"So why are you reading it?"

"Because my friend Nora from work urged me to. She thinks the trauma symptoms it describes are like those we uncovered in our discussion group. I think she's right, but it seems wrong to compare our troubles with war or domestic abuse—too radical."

"*No,* Mom!" he feigned surprise. Last Christmas he'd given me a framed clock with his own computer graphic picture on the face. It was a a 1950's June Cleaver-type mom in a red housedress. It was captioned: *Miss Jean says armed revolt is still an option.* "Explain to me why it's radical. Wait a minute while I get some ketchup for the sandwiches."

I slipped the ever-attentive Shug Avery a morsel of sandwich while Marcus was in the kitchen. "It's radical because it's stretching the clinical definitions of trauma and PTSD, as if I were talking pop psychology."

He returned with the ketchup bottle. "Shug! Stop bothering Nana! You know you never get food at the table!" I looked down at her primly, and ran down the list of common symptoms for him. "But trauma generally involves an exposure to a situation beyond the usual realm of human experience. That's hardly factory work."

"True, but maybe people haven't been willing to think beyond established categories." He sat back, hesitating about something. "My friends and I developed a lot of those symptoms after we'd been taking care of friends dying of AIDS. As I've said before, it felt like we were in a war zone, with destruction going on all around us that was completely invisible to the average passer-by."

"I know," I said. We ate in silence for a few minutes. He'd been living in Boston then. It was before the medicines had been developed for people with AIDS, and he had been there for friends felled by the disease. He used to tell me about receiving midnight calls from boys whose suicide attempts had failed. He'd served as medical proxy for friends whose infections had spread to their brains. He'd closed the eyes of the dead. I had feared he would contract the virus. Bereaved family members called him an angel. My heart had ached then to see him become a veteran of such devastation at his young age. They are all so young, I was thinking now. The victims of

AIDS, rape and war, the seventeen-year-olds we send away so carelessly—"our boys." I had known the long uncertainty of mothers waiting.

"Mom, why don't you get out of there? Aren't fifteen years enough?"

"I'm not ready to leave."

"You don't want to leave your friends there with the destructiveness, do you?"

I didn't answer.

I retired to my room after lunch while Marcus made some phone calls.

I can't do this, I thought. I can't compare the state of mind of someone devastated by an exploding shell to our anxieties in defense production. But why do we have similar stress symptoms?

I went to Marcus's computer and googled "P.T.S.D." An hour later I had some clues.

"Mommy, come out on the balcony. I want to show you something," Marc called, sliding the heavy hurricane doors aside and collecting bench cushions. The sky was suddenly blackening and what looked like a tornado was funneling over the ocean.

"Let's go for a ride and track it!"

"Oh fun!" I said "Chasing tornados!" Marcus always had The Weather Channel on down here. He loved the weather of Miami with its aura of violent change and the unexpected lying in wait.

We took the Lincoln and headed north into driving rain. Palm trees whipped in the gales and people were reaching with hooked metal poles to pull down hurricane shutters on the little Cuban restaurants that lined Collins Avenue. It wasn't far from here that Hurricane Andrew had destroyed thousands of homes several years ago. I tried to suppress my apprehension and be a sport. I looked at him for some indication of what to expect.

"It's okay, Mom. There's no hurricane warning out. Those funnels aren't really tornadoes, they're water spouts caused by converging warm and cold fronts. I was scared the first time I saw one—'Auntie Em! Auntie Em! It's a twister!' Down here you never know for sure what will happen in a storm, though. We always have to be ready for evacuation, like last year when they made everybody on Collins Avenue move inland for a couple days. I've put together a survivors' kit."

"Have you now?" I smiled. "What's in it?"

"Here it is in the back seat. Look! It's got a map of South Florida, a gallon of gas, a bag of dog food, batteries, rice and beans, a first aid kit, four gallons of spring water, twenty Lindt chocolate bars, those five books you see there, and one of those gadgets for breaking out of a car that's underwater and the vacuum inside won't let you escape. Do you have one, Mom? You should get one."

"Not yet." I lived on a hill, not right next to the Atlantic, but I didn't want to indicate in any way that I wouldn't consider his suggestion. I glanced at one of the five books, Hannah Arendt's *The Origins of Totalitarianism*.

"Wow! You're ready to survive *any* eventuality here in South Florida aren't you!"

"In these times, you never know, Mom."

"I used your computer this afternoon," I said. "And I learned that you were quite right in suggesting that people may not have been willing to think beyond established categories of trauma. But it seems that in the U.K. and Scandinavia they have had such discussions for several years now. They've found similar symptoms to PTSD in people suffering long-term distress who have not sustained a single trauma, but rather a series of small ones, such as hospitalizations, EMT work or bullying at work. The U.K. has a National Workplace Bullying Advice Line which notes that this type of PTSD might be better referred to as 'PDSD' or Prolonged Duress Stress Disorder. A Dr. Heinz Leymann of Sweden brought sixty-five victims of extreme social stress at work to a clinic specializing in the treatment of PTSD in returning war veterans and fifty-nine of them were diagnosed with full-blown PTSD symptoms."[16]

"Mom, I think you should read my book there on totalitarianism by Hannah Arendt," Marcus said, with one hand on the wheel and the other groping in the back seat. I grabbed the book for him quickly.

"I'd love to. I'd like to see what she says about methods of control used by totalitarian regimes because I just read in Judith Herman about how Amnesty International has made a list of the methods of coercion, as told

16   Article written in 1984 has appeared in *European Journal of Work and Organizational Psychology* (EJWOP), 1996, 5, 2.

to them by released captives. Apparently they are much the same the world over."

We were passing by Aventura, an upscale shopping mall with rows of palm trees wrapped in strings of lights.

"So what was the list? A handy guide to torture?" Marcus asked, going his usual 20 miles over my speed comfort level, possibly a universal form of maternal intimidation.

"No," I said. "By the way, down here do people slow down on wet roads?"

"What do you want me to do, drive like all the seniors down here and cause an accident? Mom, sit back, close your eyes, breathe deeply and answer my question."

"Okay, no. The coercion methods weren't like torture. The abusive coercion was achieved by keeping people in a constant state of fear through sudden outbursts of rage, unpredictable enforcement of petty rules, then, to undermine peoples' resistance, occasional granting of petty favors. The captors demand not just obedience but complete devotion and loyalty. Wife-batterers do that too."

"And they do that stuff at your work?"

"Oh, big time. All of it. And demanding loyalty? That used to come in the form of having to sign a government loyalty oath!"

"I'm going to try some of these methods on Sugar! She's been out of control this week."

We pulled into Starbuck's for some coffee to go, and turned toward home. Once home, Marcus took Shug out for a quick walk and I rested and wrote notes on picture post cards of pink art deco hotels till supper time.

"I'll do it, Marcus Parcus," I said, setting the table.

We sat down and broke off pieces of soft Indian bread as he ladled out red lentils with curry, apples and raisins.

"I think abusive relations are about stereotyping," Marcus said, passing coconut and peanuts. "You ought to read about the experiments done by Zimbardo.[17] He wanted to see what behavior stereotyping of people would lead to. So he advertised for twenty-four healthy young males to be part of a study. He told twelve that they were to be prisoners locked up in cells, and the other twelve that they were to be their guards. Would you believe

17   See Zimbardo's website http://www.prison exp.org/ for Phillip G. Zimbardo, "Stanford Prison Experiment: A Simulation Study of the Psychogogy of Imprisonment Conducted at Stanford University."

it was supposed to be a fourteen day study but they had to stop it after two and a half days because the guys in the guard roles got so vicious? It showed that stereotyping of people, in this case as criminals, leads to a distancing that dehumanizes them and causes victimizing."

"Interesting! I will read it." I was feeling lucky to have a son who took my interests seriously.

But what was he up to? While I was too engrossed to notice he had been both listening to me earnestly, and sneaking a mountain of extra lentils on my plate, like one of the three stooges would do. He'd long ago perfected the practice of maintaining two states of mind at once, like a Buddhist. He could simultaneously show serious concern, and be loyal to his birthright as head male of the house to tease his mother and sister.

"Take these lentils back!" I laughed. "I'll be as fat as my granddaughter here! But seriously," I continued, "in the case of the military I think it's intentional—training to dominate by any means necessary. It could be male instinct."

"And you would want to tolerate that kind of treatment because...?"

Marcus shook his head, got up and turned on the vacuum to go after some dropped crumbs, causing Shug to leap startlingly high up and down, outraged, barking and desperate to defend her family against this imminent threat to us and to the whole American way of life as she'd known it. I stripped to my bathing suit and hustled her out for a calming dip in the Atlantic at dusk, my last evening here.

On the flight home I sat back and closed my eyes, relaxing in my sense of well-being from a week immersed in the mother-son relations. I tried once again to think through the fine points of PTSD and our symptoms but ended up stretching and flipping through *Women's Day Magazine.* In no time we were taxiing onto the runway at Logan Airport and I unfolded myself and my belongings and walked out into Boston.

For once I had travelled light enough so that I could manage the subway instead of a $25 taxi ride home. I bumped my new black suitcase down the subway steps several at a time, always an uncertain contest between my balance, the weight of my suitcase, and the pull of gravity. I wheeled it along toward the underground track as the Blue Line inbound whizzed in and sounded its horn. In a couple of stops I changed to the Red Line, heading for Dorchester.

The Red Line route ran west to east from Cambridge past Harvard Square and under the Charles River then on into some of Boston's poor and working class neighborhoods, including mine. I loved the station near the line's beginning at Porter Square where prominent Harvard professors lived. It was like a museum—breathtaking, with a canopy of a hundred shining, moving triangles of glass mobiles overhead, the work of an accomplished sculptor. But now I had ridden far in the other direction and was pulling into Andrew Station, where I could get off and take a bus home. The low-budget design of this station always irritated me. Here in Southie, the white Irish working class enclave of Boston, the subway walls were made of red, white and blue tiles, replicas of the American flag. 'Just throw them a few crumbs of patriotism!' I could hear the planners say. 'They'll love it. Those people are used to getting by on very little anyway.'

VIII

Entitlement

It was June, 1992. As I drove toward the church for our eleventh session, my mind was on Gravy Train Dog Food. In 1971 the General Foods Gravy Train industry in Topeka, Kansas, had opened a new plant based on a "socio-technical design," in which old management hierarchies were flattened and workers did everything from learning formulas to handling customers. They parked in management lots and ate in management cafeterias. They reported much increased satisfaction, and production went up.

Next month, I'll tell the group about experiments like this, I thought. We could change this white elephant factory of ours too if we tried. After eleven sessions we know a lot about how work affects our lives. Our data cries out for organizing, if they've got the fire in the belly to get active.

Only three cars sat waiting in the church parking lot. We were a skeleton crew—Nora, Tom and Hildie and I. Jasmine had returned to first shift, and therefore, to the group, but she, Sean and Suzanne were still on vacation.

"So are you glad to be back?" Nora smiled at me.

I didn't answer.

"That makes four of us still in vacation mode!" said Tom.

Our discussion meandered from one subject to another for most of the two hours, like a long walk in a meadow.

"I have something I have to read to you," I said, hoping this passage would bring them up short. "It sums up what we've been discussing. It's from a speech by the economist Harry Braverman, author of the classic *Labor and Monopoly Capital*.[1] He's describing 20th Century work like ours as it's been over-simplified by Frederick Taylor. Listen:

"...Two worlds of work are created: the work in which a very few managers

1   *Labor and Monopoly Capital: The Degradation of Work in the Twentieth Century* (New York: Monthly Review Press, 1974).

and engineers grasp the process as a whole as their special monopoly...and the work of scheduling clerks, forklift operators and assemblers, each of whom performs simple labor in service to a complex machine, and each of whom is expected to make a working life of from forty to fifty years out of these scraps of duties, none of which can engage the interests or capacities of a mature human or even of a child for more than a few weeks or a few months, after which they become sheer and mindless drudgery.

The individual worker has been incorporated into the collective body of workers, *but this is a body the brain of which has been lobotomized, or worse, removed entirely.*"[2]

I watched for a reaction. I so wanted a reaction—someone to grasp the insult of it, the injustice of it. Tom shifted in his chair and shook his head philosophically.

"Well, I have to remember I only have a short road," he said. "I won't be around more than a couple years more, so I'm not worried. And I personally will not let that happen to me!"

"So do the rest of you feel like Tom does?" I said, trying to keep my expression neutral, "'I'll be okay, I'll be an exception as long as I stick to watching out for myself?'" I felt abandoned by him. How could he suddenly be so nonchalant and detached? I looked at my lap and frowned. Individualism! The curse of the working class! I fumed. It's such a cross to be held up before all kinds of demons!

I looked up, not sure I wanted to hear the answer.

"Absolutely not!" Nora whirled around to face Tom. "Your complete confidence is unbelievable to me! This innate sense in you—that eight hours a day won't affect you! I go out of my way not to let it affect me either, but still I feel so oppressed, so tied up inside that it makes me want to cry when I think about it. Eight hours does so much damage to me I feel that my entire life has been robbed from me."

"Well," Tom grimaced "We said in the beginning we all rationalize things. Maybe I am still doing that."

Nora leaned toward him, her cheeks flushed. "Well *I* don't rationalize it! I feel *completely* oppressed, completely enraged that this is happening to me. I do feel that I'm responsible—I feel I've taken part in my own

2   From a talk given in the spring of 1975, the last before his death, and published as "The Degradation of Work in the Twentieth Century" in *Monthly Review,* May 1982, and again in October 1989, v. 41.

death—I feel we're mentally, spiritually and physically being assaulted and murdered. That's how I feel—I don't rationalize, I don't say it's all right and I don't minimize it. Others feel differently. But I feel that way for *them*."

Thank you Nora! I thought to myself.

It was time to go. Maybe if the group knew that industrial sociologists had in fact designed and run some alternative workplaces that were challenging and beneficial to workers, then they would have some hope. So I proposed that we look at General Foods' Gravy Train in our next session.

Hildie had been unusually quiet during the discussion. Now, as we picked up our belongings to leave, she stopped us at the door.

"Can I ask you all a question? Why would you think it's American's responsibility to keep your mind active? I never really expected anything more."

I felt like something had crumbled around me.

Fire in the belly? I thought as I drove home. It's as if Hildie and Tom said, "What are you talking about, what's your problem?" It's as if all the assumptions we've shared these months are a leaky raft we've been sailing.

There was a faded blue Honda outside my house, which cheered me a little. I remembered that Luke was here. I pulled in under the ash tree and went inside.

Luke was about fifteen years my junior. He was a friend dear to me because of our passage together through the glory days and dark nights of several socialist groups, one of which we ourselves had organized. He was staying with me while he looked for a new apartment. He was tall and gaunt with a well-trimmed sandy gray moustache, high cheekbones, and light blue eyes that seemed fixed on a pregnant reality a little beyond our line of vision. He worked in a shipyard, but if a revolution ever did take place, he would surely be one of its leaders. Women his age couldn't resist his passionate idealism and dedication, his suave sincerity. Fortunately, to me he wasn't irresistible, but he was indispensable.

"Hi, Luke," I yelled, as I went inside. "How are you? What are you doing?" I could hear him at the top of the stairs dragging something, so I went up after him. He was carrying the white louvered folding door I'd bought for my tiny guest room years ago.

"You wanted this up, right? Consider it done!" he said with a debonair bow. "No. On second thought, why don't you let me show you how and we'll do it together," he grinned slyly. *"If you give the people food, they will eat once. If you give them seeds, they will forever feed themselves."*

"You're incurable!" I laughed. "The people need to get their tool box— I'll be right back." I hurried back from the pantry with my tool box, put it down and helped him align the door, then stood around awhile, my mind drifting.

"You're kind of quiet." he said. "Is anything wrong?"

"Well…yes. To be honest, I'm depressed about the group. Despite the damage we've found in ourselves from this work, two out of the three people there today just shrugged it off like they didn't care anymore. Hildie said, 'Why would you think the company had any responsibility for keeping our minds stimulated? I never really expected anything more.' Maybe I should never have agreed to a group that was all study."

He looked at me sympathetically. "But Jean, is that so bad? It's kind of a natural question, isn't it? Hardly anybody in this country thinks that companies have any social responsibility."

"Wait a minute, let's get this door started. Now, the whole thing with a door is to place it level. Got a magazine? See, we put the magazine down and set the door on it to give it just a little clearance from the floor. I mean, this isn't exactly intended as an air tight barrier, is it?"

I frowned at the louvered panels, which I had bought mostly because they looked pretty, wondering just what I had intended them to do.

"It's to give my guests a fig leaf of privacy!" I said promptly. "Particularly from cats." I was back quickly with a quarter inch thick magazine.

Luke was bending over searching for more screws and a Phillips screwdriver in my toolbox. The box had been a Christmas gift from Auntie Phil in 1960. Apparently she had decided I could benefit from some crossgendered skills like hers. She had painted the box red and varnished the surface, to which she had attached magazine cutout letters that spelled out precepts like *Work is the Curse of the Drinking Class. A fair shake for the fair sex!* Wow! Never noticed that before! I squinted at it again. *All that's needed is a willing woman! Only Robinson Crusoe got his work done by Friday.*

"I bought this electric drill—here" I said, and let go of the door. "Oops. See, what really got to me was Hildie saying 'I never really expected anything more.' Why is it that Nora and I do expect something more? We seem to have more sense of entitlement. Does that drive a determination to make a change? I don't know what to do."

"I'm thinking it's not enough to drive it. I'll explain in a minute. For now, could you hold onto this?" he smiled nodding toward the door. I'd gotten distracted and let go of the door again. I closed my mouth and put all my attention toward aligning the hinge flush with the woodwork. Zzzzt—he drilled two holes for the top hinge.

I handed him screw-driver tips for the electric drill, of which I was rather proud, and concentrated on holding the door steady to align the middle hinge with the woodwork while he put in the top screws. I knew that much from work—each screw needed to be tightened in relation to all the other ones.

Luke paused, electric screwdriver in hand, to let me stop and think. "Let me go back to something you said before. When you say *entitlement* what do you mean?"

I smiled, knowing he'd tease me about what I was about to say. "Well, actually, I looked it up in my new writers' dictionary. You know what it means? I love words. It means *the basic sense of having a right to have or do something,* and a second meaning is *to have bestowed upon one a rank of nobility, honor or dignity.*"

He smiled. "So, word lady, your dictionary is saying entitlement can be a matter of rank or class? Is this dictionary red?" He motioned for me to steady the door again while he bent over to put a screw in the middle holes.

I was getting into a little better frame of mind. "Okay," I said, picking up the verbal gauntlet he'd thrown down, "so it could be class privilege, true. But having a sense of entitlement reminds me more of bestowing on your*self* some honor and dignity. In the same way we in the women's movement had to teach ourselves to feel worthy of rights."

He didn't seem to have any trouble affixing screws and talking at the same time, and once more aligned the door for the bottom hinge. "But don't the *guys* in the shop have a sense of entitlement? Do you think the women's movement stuff really fits the working class?"

"Well, yeah, a few guys have *more* than their share of entitlement. But most? I would say no. Hey, over the centuries didn't workers learn to feel subservient and totally dependent on others for their future, just like women did?"

"Good point. And our job is to say no, right?" He grabbed my side of the door to hold it a little straighter, then crouched down and sited the last screws. "Well from your gut as a woman, what do you feel you should do about the group?"

I thought for a minute, leaning against the opposite wall. "Maybe we could back up and ask ourselves where we got our assumptions. I've never really thought about where I got my own sense of entitlement growing up, have you?"

"Don't talk about that to your other Marxist buddies!" he grinned. "All that touchy-feely psychology stuff!" he stood up and struck a pose, hand on hip, "They'd tell you 'workers are tough! Workers don't want feelings! What the workers want is a pay check! Class struggle is economic!'"

"Too bad!" I said. "But do *you* think it sounds too much like therapy?"

"No." He looked at me seriously. "It sounds like *consciencization*. Paolo Freire said that when we begin to question our circumstances, we don't feel so stuck in fate any more, right? He said that then we can see life as a process that can change."

We continued to talk about consciousness development and critical thinking and the kind of dialectical teaching that Paolo Friere had developed while working as a radical teacher with Brazilian peasants. During this, to me, very absorbing discussion, I didn't notice that Luke had finished installing all the screws himself, apparently deciding that giving the people some seeds of knowledge was even better than giving them practical skills.

"Not bad, huh?" he said, surveying the door. "I'm going downstairs and turn on the game, okay?"

I stayed, carrying out a few boxes of papers I'd stored in the guest room. Maybe what's really happened, I thought, is that people are feeling overwhelmed and fatalistic—you can't fight city hall and all that. Maybe I am too. Of course it might be realism not fatalism when you're talking about fighting the whole culture of the military-industrial complex. I gave the boxes a shove into my study.

Or is it a difference in the worlds we've inherited? I thought of Melvin Kohn's poignant observation that among the thousands of men he studied, "men of a higher class position" saw themselves as competent members of an essentially benign society. But those of "a lower class position" saw themselves as "less competent members of an essentially indifferent or threatening society."[3]

Luke was calling from the bottom of the stairs.

"Jean, there's something more." I went down.

"We've always agreed that there is no change without changed consciousness, and you guys have been doing that, right? But you have to look at the other side in the dialectical process. No action without consciousness, Friere said, but also, if there's no action, no advances in consciousness happen. In revolutionary praxis, people develop consciousness out of practical activity—struggles informed by those who see their significance and direction. I think your group needs to ask not just what do we think, but how do we organize."

"I know you're right," I said, "and that's the question that the group has made taboo." I got us some beers and took refuge with him in the last innings of the game.

"There was no such thing as 'rights' growing up in the '50's!" Jasmine said. "That came later."

We were sitting in the back of Averos' Restaurant, a cheap and excellent little Greek place huddled under giant pine trees on the outskirts of town. We'd felt cocky enough to come out of hiding for this group about entitlement and expectations. Tonight was inadvertently a women's night out, since Tom and Sean had to work overtime.

"You know, it's funny about expectations," Jasmine continued. "My great grandmother or somebody had been a slave, and my grandmother expected my mother to do better. So when my mother and father got married they moved to a white neighborhood. White values and expectations became part of us. When I started to work I expected to get a good job, to do well, to always put my best foot forward. But at that time what you could get as a woman was narrow. You could be a nurse or a teacher if you were lucky and went to college, which I didn't. You just followed what was available, and if you failed, it was your fault. Some of the electronics jobs I got in the sixties I'm not sure were through merit—they were through affirmative action. But as I said to Hildie, even if you got them through affirmative action, you were there and you had to know what to do, so if you weren't up to par, you took courses on the outside like I did, so you got qualified fast."

Hildie pulled on the straw in her gin and tonic. "You told me you used to wish you were white!"

"Yeah, till I met lots of working-class white people like you at American and then I realized white people weren't any happier than me!" They laughed.

The waiter brought the *pasticcio* I'd ordered so I could figure out Averos's recipe. I savored the first bite for a minute. Ground beef, not lamb. And maybe a touch of sumac spice along with the Egyptian allspice in the tomato sauce. Nice! I swallowed and got back into the conversation. "You say nurse or teacher. Those were exactly my choices too. But don't you think they were middle-class choices? Compared to men, limited, but compared to other women, those were privileged expectations, don't you think—just handed to us as a right we had? "

"I agree." Hildie said. "It wasn't expressed as rights, but if your father was a doctor, you could expect to become a doctor or a nurse. If you were a working-class person you knew you'd just have to go out and take any job. Just take the path of least resistance."

"I did that too, middle-class or not," I said. "Once my kids were in school, I just took whatever job fell my way. It makes me uncomfortable to think about how I let myself just be dragged along in the stream of life. I came of age right on the cusp of feminism. Maybe part of me is still back on the other side."

"See," Nora pushed her snack-size plate of grape leaves and humus out of the way and rested her chin in her hands, elbows on the table, "I think it *did* make a difference, my being younger and coming after you guys in a more feminist period. I remember from a very early age being angry that I was a woman. I wanted to be a boy, because boys could do everything. And, it's kind of sad, but for a long time I chopped off the marriage and children side of my life because I didn't want that to hold me back."

"I can remember beginning to see things different like that too when I was eleven or twelve," Hildie said. "I can remember wishing I was a boy too."

"It was because of the women's movement that I had the opportunity and felt I had a right to a man's job like I have now," Nora paused to take a bite of pita and humus. "But I was also raised with a sense of rights and expectations by my parents. My father was a scientist and a professor. He used to belittle me a lot and be pretty dominating at home. But in the outside world, I did feel I deserved to be treated in a very civilized manner and to do whatever I found interesting. What I can't stand is to be treated like less than a human at work, especially when I'm trying to do the job right and they don't want me to take the time to do it."

Hildie was looking intrigued. "You thought, 'the world is a pretty nice place—I'm going to go in there and do things the right way and I'll be respected'." She pointed to her place mat as the waiter held up a plate *of shish kebab.* "But I was not brought up to expect the world was going to treat me in any particular way. You were not told you were owed anything. You had to work for it. What you got, you got on your own, nobody gives you anything. We were a working-class family, hard workers. My folks had worked for the WPA at the end of the depression. They knew you couldn't depend on the companies for anything. There were no jobs. The whole system had broken down. Their attitude was take any job you could get, even ditch digging." She slipped her *shish kebabs* off the metal skewers, licked the pink juice from her fingers and continued.

"If your father had a bad day it was probably because one of his experiments went wrong. When my father came home in a bad mood it would be because the boss had yelled at him. Maybe it wasn't easy in middle-class life either, but they *stepped* on you different!" We laughed and nodded.

"As a kid," she continued, "I was always walking around saying, 'Oh I'm not good enough to do that—they're better than me.' My mother would try to encourage me—'You're as good as some and better than most!' But you kind of figured the whole world is a pretty nice place. I'm gonna go in there and do my job the right way and they're gonna think I'm wonderful, and they didn't."

I felt bad for Nora—there was a put-down there. I said to Hildie, "It felt to you like she was expecting too much of life?—that the world owed her a living or whatever?"

"No. She came from a free-thinking arts and college background—it was her parents' expectations. But then in *this* world, the company turns around and says 'we don't pay you to think!' I can see where you'd be ready to tear your hair out. I'm ready to tear *my* hair out and I didn't even grow up with those attitudes."

Suzanne sighed. "I didn't grow up with any expectations—career or any kind. When I was growing up I felt more like a mother than my mother. Finally she left us, like her mother had left her. I was a teenager, and I had a lot on my mind. I ran away all the time. I learned to repress a lot of my feelings. For work I'd take anything I could get. I worked non-union shops and you had to con your way, practically steal your way, fight tooth and nail. I met a fella there who showed me the ropes and he and I fought for our rights all the way. That's where I first learned rights, I guess."

"My mother and grandmother always worked," Ruth said. "They did whatever they could to make a living—wash clothes, pick cotton, clean houses, live off the land when they had no job. Rights on the job? They didn't have any. They couldn't speak up in their jobs if they were treated badly, although they found other ways to get even. Like me, when I was less of a Christian and some old lady in the nursing home where I worked called me a nigger. I put lots of iodine on her bedsores!" We laughed and raised our eyebrows.

"But," she continued, "I learned from my mother and my grandmother how to watch everybody's attitudes—what they'd stand for and what they wouldn't, to be careful what you say. People smile but talk different behind your back."

She hesitated, picking over her salad and spearing a big Greek olive. "I never had anybody to help me do things or think things through. I was programmed negatively—you don't do this, you don't do that. When I was sent to New York to live with my aunt and got beatings, my work was housework and I had no rights. I tried to teach myself to read by reading comic books when I took a break, and she hated me for that. I was her little servant. Now I realize I was abused. My expectations? This is what I tell my kids: 'You're gonna have to learn to take care of *yourself* honey cause nobody's gonna do it for you. Don't let anybody tell you this is free or that's free. *Nothing* is free. And nobody's gonna give you *anything* but a hard time.'"

We were silent.

"Oh well, what can you do?" Ruth said. "So how about you, Jean?"

I didn't want to tell them. I was feeling shame at my background and anguish that inequality sat among us like this. I was wishing we could redistribute our pasts.

"Well, we were lower-middle-class. My dad was very supportive of me. He had a little trouble figuring out how best to encourage a girl. He'd say, 'if you were a boy I'd say you could be president! But maybe you could be president too.' His main message, though, was that being a mother was on a pedestal in his eyes, and better than being president any day. The funny thing was, I don't think he was so much being a chauvinist when he said that as meaning it, since he had lost his own mom when he was seven."

Nora smiled and looked dubious. "But what was your mother like?"

"My mother was very quiet and never expressed any expectations for me. Her own hopes for going to a four year college never came true, because in the depression there was only money in her family for one to go, and even though she was the smartest one in her family, the money went to her brother. Maybe that taught her not to have high hopes if you didn't want to be disappointed. I wonder if I learned that attitude from her?" I looked out across the tables. Diners were coming and going now at the height of the supper hour, dressed mostly in blue denim work clothes. "She never complained but she went to work as a secretary in a bank and put away the money so I could go to college. She showed me you could enjoy having a job, which she did, and still be a good mother.

"I didn't have ambitious career goals either. I planned to become a teacher, but then I became a wife and mother-to-be right after college instead. That taught me you usually had to put yourself second to whatever life handed you."

"On the way over here you said you fell for a myth in college. What was that?" Hildie zeroed in on me.

"What did you mean by that? Give us an example of a myth, Jean," Jasmine said. I was glad that she wasn't embarrassed to ask if she didn't know something, which, I remembered, is a confident habit you pick up in college.

"Okay. How about the cultural myth of the '50's after the war, that women belonged in the home. It was in all the magazines. But just a few years earlier the myth was that women belonged in the factories—Rosie the Riveter—to replace the men who went off to war."

"Yah!" Hildie said. "And if they didn't go back home willingly to make room for the men, returning from the war, they got *thrown* out of their jobs too!"

"Wait a minute—women belonging at home—that's a *white* cultural myth," Jasmine said. "Because black women have always had to work."

"Whoops!" I said. "You're right. Well, other myths would be such things as the belief that anybody in America can be president or a millionaire if they really try hard…."

"Yeah, but what was the myth you swallowed in college?" Hildie pressed me, signaling the waiter for more iced tea.

"Well, it was a very subtle one, and I got taken in by it. In my literature course all the 'great books' chosen by the professor had themes about how 'man cannot fight the gods or the huge social forces against him' (it was always him then). That you better not get into conflict with the powers that be, or *act* on any opinions that you might have, or it would bring down disaster on you."

I paused for a minute and looked around, wondering if it would seem strange to them that a bunch of kids could be influenced to change their behavior by books.

"And?" Hildie prompted me.

"Well, I didn't know at the time that the professor who taught that literature course had just suffered persecution by Senator McCarthy. So maybe, just like working-class parents teach their kids to avoid trouble by being obedient, maybe he was trying to teach us young how to avoid trouble by not criticizing the powers that be, like he had."

Nora dabbed at the corners of her mouth with the red and white napkin and nodded.

"Nobody at Harvard was active—I never knew what a demonstration was till years later," I continued. "It was a class attitude that prevailed throughout Harvard at that time, and I certainly picked up on it, had no clue about being an activist, so I missed out on the good life for fifteen years!"

"But what did they want you to do?" Jasmine was intrigued, listening intently as she cut her *shish kebab*, making her bracelets jangle.

"Well, stay above politics, just shut up, maybe be some kind of analyst of literature or of other things to contribute to the status quo. I learned that my role in life was to be the Observer. In the late 60's I had to consciously recognize that I'd internalized that myth. The writer Denise Levertov helped me there. She was writing poems about her own struggle to overcome the passive observer in herself—to step out of academia into the streets and protest the Vietnam War. Consciousness-raising is so often by chance, isn't it? We owe so much of it to the kindness of strangers."

They all nodded and we ate quietly for a moment, thinking our own thoughts. Then I remembered something more about myself, thanks to our tolerant atmosphere.

"I also owe my consciousness-raising to an inmate at Bridgewater State Prison. He was very brave and leading a class-action suit to be able to wear civilian clothes (which symbolized to them that they had human dignity, and which they won). I say brave because he knew that when he got thrown into isolation as punishment for doing this, the isolation would trigger an attack of the schizophrenia from which he suffered. But he did it anyway. One day I was trying to offer what words of support I could but he objected. He said 'You intellectuals always have your nice ideas and theories, they're all words. But the reason we are *doing* this is to say *no* to this place.' It wasn't long after that I too understood that protest action speaks louder than words. And I still believe that, although of course right now we all are wearing Observer hats!" They ignored that plug for organizing.

Hildie seemed to be following my account with as much interest as she had Nora's. She mopped up lamb juice and stray peas with pita bread, took a bite and said, "Maybe that myth about how you should stay out of the action took with you because you were a woman too. Plus, don't forget that you were going to a school that was brokering power—training Supreme Court Justices and all."

"Right!" How sharp she was. "Sure. They trained the cabinet officials, the federal judges—the ruling class!"

"When you say that about the Supreme Court justices and stuff," Jasmine turned to Hildie, "all of a sudden I thought, well then something's wrong. Because….if they have their own ideas and interests, then the best interests of *us* are not *their* best interests. *We* are not their best interests!"

Nora and I jumped in with the same exclamation: "You hit the nail right on the head!"

"Now we're talking class interests," I said, excited. "And isn't it another myth we're all brought up with that there are no classes in America? We're all the same?"

"Hildie," Jasmine said, "I heard that you said at the end of the last group 'what makes us think that American wants us to have rights?'" Hildie raised an eyebrow about this misinterpretation of 'that it's American's responsibility to keep our minds active' but let it go as Jasmine said with feeling, "Well of *course* the answer is easy. We would *question* too much. They want us to shut up, just like Jean said. They don't *want* us to have rights!"

"Sure!" I said. "They want us to have low expectations about work. They want us to shut up and just work."

Nora pushed back her plate. "Lower expectations about *life*—for intellectual activity or creative activity."

"Because then we don't question our lives, and we don't question what the company does, even when it sends our jobs away!" Jasmine rapped the table, sure of herself now. "They just think about the bottom line!"

"That's why they try to bust the unions!" Suzanne said, sipping from a drink with a pink paper parasol in it.

"The government and the corporations have formed a partnership to bust the unions!" Hildie added.

"So why wouldn't they *owe* us some responsibility for damages?" I asked her, wanting to just leave the thought with her for now, not argue, so I changed the subject. "You know, about the question of rights or entitlement, it sounds like those of us from the middle-class were brought up to feel a little more entitled, but most of you guys had past experience that might have ingrained in you lessons about *necessity* or inevitability, not about rights. But look at us—now we're all a bunch of free thinkers! How did that happen?"

We were almost finished, sitting back and sipping what remained of our drinks. This was apparently an easy one for them.

"It happened to me in American's non-union plant in the South," Suzanne said decisively. "That was where I learned to fight back, like I told you. You had to fight or they'd screw you out of everything."

"I know what changed me too," Jasmine said. "Therapy and school helped me see that everything wasn't my fault—that things on the outside were also preventing me from succeeding."

Ruth nodded her head slowly. "For me it was becoming more religious. There I developed the expectation that people should be what they were created to be, and that they should treat people right!"

"It was the discrimination in police jobs for me," Hildie said. "That was what changed me. I had always thought the government never lied or did anything wrong."

We called for the tab and began to pile our dishes to make it easy for the waitress. Hildie smiled and said, "I guess everybody in their own way gets a rude awakening."

We said goodbye and I got in the car, idling for a moment to enjoy the scent of pine trees in darkness and to sit with the aftermath experience of the group for a while, as I usually needed to do. 'Sooner or later everybody gets a rude awakening.' I like that, I thought. Tonight the rude awakening is mine. When life has made it clear there are no options and nobody's gonna give you anything but a hard time, why would you think you could just take out your sling shot and make the giant give you your due? Do you change all that experience in just a few months? Growth owns itself, and comes in its own sweet time, not mine.

Not long after that, though, I was to come upon growth where I had not dared hope to find it—in changes in the macho and patriotic culture that had always reinforced American's authority.

IX

Changes in Machismo

Machismo and patriotism were the cement that held in place company authority and militarism at American. I use machismo in the current usage, "having a strong or exaggerated sense of power, or the right to dominate".[1] The prevailing machismo at American was like that of Teddy Roosevelt. For those who thought like Teddy and his Rough Riders, male and military prowess went hand in hand. He believed that war releases manly virtues without which the country cannot remain a vigorous organism.[2] It was the swashbuckling machismo of the adventurer, the daring ruffian. It lusted for conquest. It was a serviceable state of mind in 1898 for the expansion of empire,[3] and in 2000 was to enjoy a presidential comeback for the same purpose. But at the plant this warrior machismo was in trouble. The cement was developing widening cracks.

Most women at American, having benefited from at least a decade of popularized feminism, were no longer impressed by warrior machismo. It was the men whom the company expected to carry the standard of militaristic virility. But shop-floor conversations told a different story.

It was 8:30 A.M. and time to stop and chat. Rob was hustling back from the Mold Department, wearing asbestos gloves and carrying a tray of hot units.

1   *Random House Webster's Unabridged Dictionary, Second Edition.* Additional meaning is "having or characterized by qualities considered manly especially when manifested in an assertive, self-conscious or dominating way."

2   Merle Curti, *The Roots of American Loyalty* (New York: Columbia University Press, 1946), 198.

3   For this view, see, for example, the biography of Teddy Roosevelt at http://www.American President.org: "The 'white man's burden' helped to justify Roosevelt's 'New Imperialism' in foreign policy. 'Uncivilized' (colonial or undeveloped) nations would gain eventual independence once they had conformed to the American model of government and democracy. Roosevelt's 'corollary' to the Monroe Doctrine set up the U.S. as 'policeman' in the western hemisphere. Under TR, the U.S. 'empire' extended to include the Philippines, Cuba, Haiti, the Dominican Republic, and Puerto Rico. He also oversaw the building of the Panama Canal, a tremendous feat that enhanced U.S. commerce immeasurably."

"Hey, guess what?" he called "Sandy and Earl had a boy last night!"

We erupted in cheers and whistles. We had watched Sandy and Earl meet in Mold, get married, and now we had all been awaiting this baby.

Rob stood in front of us, hands on the hips of his loose green shorts. He wore a sweatshirt with the sleeves cut off, the kind of old, funky clothes that amiable, self-confident male athletes seem to like. "So!" he challenged us, "What shall we get for a present?"

"How about a nice little white embroidered jacket imported from Portugal?" Joseph turned slightly to speak to us all. Once Joseph had told me a secret: "If I ever get laid off, you know what I'm gonna do? Start child-care in my home for babies. I love little babies!"

Sam leaned back and stretched, expanding his chest, and pulled his navy sweatshirt down to cover his bare midriff. He lowered his voice just enough so it conveyed his quiet authority.

"Well, I don't know. You have to think of the parents' style when you get baby presents. Would they like something formal and European like that for baby clothes, or would they like stuff to make him look like a little casual-type kid?"

"Yeah," Frankie laughed. "We should get the kid a little brown plaid flannel lumber-jack shirt just like Mom and Dad wear all the time."

"Let's get him that. He'll probably grow up to be real tough like The Hammer!" said Hammer, which was Ray's baseball name because of his famous hard drives to the outfield and, he swore, his sexual prowess. Ray was a tall, thin, wiry Norwegian-American with freckles and a receding blonde hairline, which was always hidden under a baseball cap. He enjoyed the prestige of being one of the company's best ball players.

"Okay," Rob said, cutting a slit in a cardboard diode box. "Let's leave buying it up to Sam. Look, he's got good taste, and he lives near them so he can drive it over there after he buys it. Come on, get up the bucks!"

This conversation would never have happened in the early eighties. At that time these men, not long out of high school, were busy establishing their macho prestige at work. There were three rank-and-file male networks that held some authority in most peoples' eyes. There were the athletes, like Rob and Ray, who played on the company-wide baseball teams. They were the popular macho men who got the girls, and hung out with the young managers who played with them on the baseball teams, which gave them extra status because of their access to privileged information. Another network consisted of young partiers like Frankie. They also enjoyed a kind of whispered prestige. They were hip to drugs, alcohol, the coolest music, and they too were privy to special information, since they partied after hours with kindred spirits in management. A third network of influential men were elders, among them Williamson, who "went way back" together. These men consulted each other about how to solve repair problems with old weapons parts, the contracts for which dated back several decades. Only they knew the secrets. The younger men, who had been brought up to respect their elders or get a box on the ears, treated them with affection and respect. There was a junior tier to this group, younger fellows who were especially smart, had some post-high school technical training, and usually worked in the high-paid categories of Test and Research and Development.

Now, I smiled as I listened to yesterday's sportsmen taking charge of choosing baby presents. I wouldn't dream of teasing them for fear of driving these New Males away. I felt I should freeze in my tracks as if at a rare sighting of young antlered bucks grazing in my back yard.

I got up to look for the new job, the 668's, which Williamson had assigned to me. I found the tub with a dozen four-inch coils, and another tub containing more parts—six-inch plastic-coated wire leads, transistors and small PC boards. On the bottom shelf of the move wagon were more tubs containing a dozen metal cases. I pushed the wagon to my bench, still thinking.

What made these fellows change so much in a fairly short time? I wondered. Popular culture showed couples in average households at least attempting gender equality. And the wives of these men were not strangers to modern expectations for women's rights. They tended to be "good catches" themselves, nice young women with good jobs in nursing, teaching, computer programming. "I just tease him when he starts that macho stuff!" Ray's wife giggled behind her hand to me at a company party. "And he's getting plenty of equal opportunity housework too!"

I opened the spec to see how the 688's were to be built. Think about it! I continued talking to myself, everything we've been learning shows that jobs change people. Our fun-loving, freewheeling jocks now have a second job. I used my air hose to blow all bits of wire from my bench, and covered it with white paper towels. A stray bit of metal debris could short out the whole unit. Now they spend eight hours a day alone with a baby or two. Often they're car-key kids. Mom, who works second shift at the plant, will drive the baby to American for 3:30, exchange cars with Dad, and he will drive the baby home for his own second shift. I'll bet the most powerful agents of consciousness change are toddlers. They cry when the dads are too rough, love them unconditionally, and are completely dependent on their nurturing. Think back on our shop culture this year. Our sports heroes have occasionally hired babysitters and played ball after work, but they have been focusing on a different side of themselves—the care-giver—and we've been party to their process of figuring it all out together here at work.

The sports debates that always used to prevail in the shop now alternate with discussions such as how to discipline two-year-olds without being too rough and scaring them. The boys still do their macho bragging, but now it's not so often about athletic and sexual prowess, and more frequently about the excellence of their turkey soup and Portuguese stew, which they bring in for us to sample. They have started nagging us, their bench-mates, to get more sleep. They worry about people who having trouble at home. In a word, they nurture us all, whether we want it or not, for our own good, like we mothers have always done. We tease them about it, and we like it.

Many of the men, amused by this adjustment in gender roles, have made the change graciously. Others have had a rougher time with it and a few are known to be abusive to their wives at home, and can be domineering and angry in the shop. Some, like Ray, sublimate their conflicts.

"Jeannie, I want you to listen to something for the next hour. You have to hear it. Here," Hammer said one morning, and put on me his huge set of yellow earphones which looked like a pilot's headgear. I heard Rush Limbaugh's name. I took off the headphones and tried to think of an excuse to decline this unsavory experience. "Hammer, he's nasty! What do you like about him?"

"Come on, Jeannie, he expresses the way we feel! With our wives working and nagging and all we're expected to do all of a sudden at home? It's too much and we have to strike back somehow. Rush says it all—you all are feminazis!" I was curious so I obliged him and put up with an hour of Rush. The next day Hammer resumed bringing this feminazi his new culinary experiments, and scolding me for not getting some cough medicine.

"Williamson, could you look this over before I send it to Test?" I called. I was proud to have finished wiring the new 688's and anyway it was standard procedure to have the group leader check the work before submitting it to Test.

Williamson was limping a bit today, apparently having a bout of arthritis. I liked him because he was soft-spoken and sweet, good to everybody without favoritism, just like my dad used to be.

"Okay, Jeannie! You did some, huh?' He got close enough to peer carefully over his spectacles at my wiring job.

He stood up and shouted, "Julio, would you mind coming over here a minute? I have to show you something." I saw just the hint of a mischievous grin.

Julio came running, ever the willing witness. "What's wrong, Williamson?"

"I just want you to take a look at this wire here." Williamson pointed with a screwdriver to the wire I had fastened to the wrong terminal.

Julio shook his head, grinning broadly. "I knew it, Williamson!"

"Now, I hate to say it, Julio, I really do, but look at what Jeannie's done now." His eyes twinkled. They nodded gravely at each other and intoned their usual chorus for the benefit of the whole department. "Just like a woman!!"

I rolled my eyes and applied my hot iron to the incorrect joint, sucking up the solder with solder wick, the little spool of soft copper braid used for this purpose. "I know where it should go," I told Williamson, and gently untwisted the wire and re-bent it around the correct terminal.

Are they nostalgic about machismo or mocking it when they play with me like this? I wondered as I soldered. Both, I decided. In the ethereal space of jokes, such ambivalence doesn't have to be resolved.

You had to know Williamson and Julio well, but if you did, you knew that they were not what they pretended to be.

The next year I attended a department retirement party and Williamson and his gentle wife Gladys, themselves now retired, came over to greet me.

"You know, Jean," Gladys said confidentially, "now that we're both retired, I decided that fifty years of cooking and housework were enough. So now he has to do it all."

"Is this true, Williamson?" I inquired grandly. "That would be like a wonderful present for me!"

Williamson peered over his spectacles impishly at me one more time—"Yup."

"Good for her!" I said. "Just like a woman!"

One afternoon as Julio and I were cleaning our completed units, he put down his chloroethane brush.

"Juanita" he said," can I talk to you about something?"

He looked upset. "Of course!" I said.

"I've felt so bad all day. My littlest girl, Liselda, the three-year-old, right? She's tough as nails and she can take care of herself. She's so funny. She tells me off all the time! But Lara, my twelve-year-old, is very sensitive. Last night I read her diary by mistake—it was just there, open. So I read it. She doesn't know. But all day I've felt terrible about intruding on her private space."

Julio's decency and sensitivity were the truth about him. He was a great father for three girls. I couldn't decide whether he played the chauvinist with such delight and extravagance because it amused him to act out Spanish machismo, or because he had grown up as the only boy in a family with five older sisters.

Equal work for equal pay was another area of relations under construction, still being poked and adjusted. For example, late one afternoon I was bone-tired from an assignment to put together a huge transformer. Each of its three coils weighed thirty-five pounds, too heavy for me to carry on one arm. I placed them on the three prongs of one half of a giant E-shaped magnet, then I climbed on a chair and, using a chain lift suspended from the ceiling, I swung the other half of the magnet into place inside the coils too, shoving and wiggling it to be sure I could hear the "clink clink" of the faces coming together. Next I needed to band them tight to just the right torque, using steel banding so heavy I could barely bend it with my fingers.

I walked around to the banding materials shelf, remembering how ten years ago when I worked in the model shop, one of the old guys, who was resentful that women were working there, hid the banding tool and told me bands had to be tightened with bare hands. Now I cut three feet of the three-quarters inch steel band, took it back to my bench and threaded it down between the inside of the first coil and the magnet, out around the bottom of the magnet and up out of the third coil. I fed the band through a buckle, bent it backwards underneath the buckle and squeezed it there with pliers. Then all that remained was to buckle it like a belt and pull hard on the end with the banding tool. The banding tool was a vise with an H-shaped handle. The idea was to bend the band back under the vise, then twist the handles again and again until the band was sufficiently tight. I rotated the handle with my hands, then, when I couldn't turn it anymore, I wedged my arm crosswise between the knobs and forced it some more. I knew my arm would be black and blue tonight.

Julio grinned and shook his head. Sam, who'd apparently been watching too, came over. "Jeannie, let me show you the easy way." He moved my arm, then substituted a hammer, which he wedged crosswise between the two knobs on the handle. He gave it a few quick, easy turns by hand, then took another hammer and tapped the end of the first hammer, effortlessly tightening the resistant banding.

"Oh man, what an improvement! Thank you!" I said. "I have to admit I have weak hands."

"Miss Jean," Dominic said, apparently having been on the observer corps too, "In that physical therapist course I started to take a couple years ago, they had us help patients build strength in their hands by squeezing a tennis ball. Maybe you could do that?"

The next day Hammer brought me a tennis ball.

My lack of mechanical aptitude was particularly stunning, but quite a few of the women were also at somewhat of a disadvantage on the big units. We might shout these fellows down in our battles of the sexes, but in truth we owed more than a little to kindnesses like Sam's.

The ethic in the department was that, if we women got equal pay, we should do the work without help. We women agreed with that. Why, then, did the men offer to help anyway? Outside the plant, on construction jobs in the segregated building trades, white men not only rarely offered help to women or black workers; they sometimes set them up for dangerous accidents, like falling off ladders or down embankments.[4] When women first penetrated all-male jobs at American, the men in those jobs were nasty too. So what accounted for the diminished sexist behavior of men like those in our department? I think that the affirmative action requirement

---

4   See, for example, Susan Eisenberg, *We'll Call You If We Need You: Experience of Women Working Construction* (New York: Cornell University Press, 1998).

in government contracts was partially responsible. Integration on the job, over time, seemed to replace racial and gender prejudice with familiarity.

Male protectiveness, to me one of the more benign forms of chauvinism, was changing. The gender-neutral protectiveness of the buddy relationships remained intact. But male chivalry was yielding to the working-class ethic of abiding by the rules, which were now rules of equal and fair employment without special deference to women. The men seemed to like relating by setting up and negotiating rules, which as studies of boys have shown, is common among males.[5] In the shop, if the rules now were that women had to be treated equally, the men took that up and debated the fairness of their application with the gusto they usually brought to debating umpires' calls. If we women got the same pay, the men should not do extra work such as lifting heavy stuff. (I had some success in introducing the idea of the two-person lift, maintaining, as did O.S.H.A., that none of us, regardless of gender, should lift over twenty-five pounds by ourselves.) On the other hand, if the company broke the rules and denied women equal opportunity for overtime, etc., then the men felt they should stand up for our rights, as long as they perceived us as at least trying to pull our own weight.

One progressive force for fair treatment regardless of gender surprised me: it was working-class family values. This was stated strongly in men's approach to sexual harassment. Joking, flirting and sexual bragging were okay, in fact enjoyed by most people in the shop, as long as it was understood that there were no intentions whatsoever of acting on them. But real and unwanted sexual passes or insults to women's dignity were condemned by most men—"I wouldn't want that to happen to my wife (or daughter or sister)!"

It was fairly likely that wives, sisters, and daughters did in fact work in a nearby department. American was an intricate network of relatives, the opportunity to get a good job for a relative being a fringe benefit as important as our top-of-the-line Blue Cross policy. It was a handsome gift of security for a loved one, and it gave the giver the pleasure of having influence, for a change, about something important. The company benefited from this nepotism, too, because people monitored their kin and made sure they didn't rock the boat that could carry any number of family members to a bright future. "Don't make me look bad, now! Just keep your nose

5   Carol Gilligan, *In A Different Voice: Psychological Theory and Women's Development* (Cambridge: Harvard University Press, 1982), 9-10.

clean, stay away from the radicals, and we'll see that you're taken care of!" Dominic's uncles had told him.

"Mr. Shaunessy, here! Look at these!" Angie summoned Shaunessy and handed him the pictures of Melissa and Marc at my Easter breakfast table. They were balancing their red breakfast plates on their heads and looking cute and goofy. Marcus had Dow Jones draped over his shoulder.

"Miss Jean," she said loudly, "Your daughter's beautiful. She doesn't look anything like you. She looks like a little Italian girl. Must be the ex-husband!"

I shrugged. Shaunessy said "Very nice. The boy is handsome, and he looks tall, like you."

The sharing of family photos was a department ritual, in which all work stopped, bosses joined in the viewing, and everyone expressed admiration. It was an initiation ritual for marginal people like those who were non-white, immigrant, gay, or radical like me. It was a leap of trust, but once you did it, the group was likely to bestow on you a new insider status, like a mafia kiss. You didn't have to have kids or a nuclear family. If you had any kind of relatives and proof you did something with them, you were approved. I'd seen families in saris, families in Portuguese villages, a brother-in-law in front of the Washington Monument who was rumored to be in the C.I.A. There was a nice young woman from another department dressed in a man's suit, her arms around her woman partner and their little girl. It was an iron-clad rule. There was to be no insulting of families here. Families were revered. Period.

Relations in the plant could be nasty and brutalizing, as we've seen. However in periods when the waves of anger subsided, our relations were tinged with the familial, specifically the working-class familial. Working-class familial meant tough nurturing—upholding strict discipline, challenging others to be tough, and giving frequent gruff, blunt advice that was more intrusive and presumptuous than I had been used to. I soon came to experience these words to the wise as an expression of concern, most of the time. I like the bumptious practice and have retained the habit myself, though I have to remember that it doesn't go over well in middle-class circles. Home repairs and family care advice, which were concrete and realistic, began to take the form of men and women teaching each other how to do opposite-gendered tasks at home.

Vets and Machismo

The question of warrior machismo and veterans fascinated me. I had not known any Vietnam veterans before. There were none in the Harvard Square neighborhood where I lived in the sixties, just graduate students and their wives, like me. A few miles away in East Cambridge the vets were coming home, or not coming home, to gray six-family houses that faced onto sidewalks.

In the 1980's, Hollywood produced a series of movies rehabilitating the soldier as an American culture hero, and the return of gender differences and "real" men like the ones who fought in the Vietnam War. *An Officer and A Gentleman, Top Gun* and *Rambo* contributed to a new sentimentalizing and idealizing of the American military man, as Ronald Reagan preferred to conceive him, according to Andrew Bacevich.[6] Cynthia Enloe suggests that *Rambo* conveyed that era's militarized masculinity as an individualistic military adventurer, politically disaffected, betrayed by and flouting his superiors, and keeping an emotional distance from women.[7] These Hollywood macho soldiers were quite different from the Vietnam vets I finally had the opportunity to meet at American. I remember a phone call that typified the support I received from some of the Vietnam vets in 1984 during the John Angelino union reform campaign.

"Alonso!" Shaunessy growled one morning. "You have a call on my phone! From the Lawrence plant. The man says it's an insurance matter. Make it short!"

The Lawrence plant? I thought to myself. I don't know anybody there. There must be some mistake. I wiped the quizzical look off my face and arranged it in a business-like expression, stepping quickly to Shaunessy's desk and grabbing his phone. I edged over to the waist-high wall surrounding his cubicle where he liked to stand, as if on deck, and watch us. I turned my back to him and said tentatively, "Hello?" There was a cackle on the other

---

6   *The New American Militarism: How Americans are Seduced by War* (London: Oxford University Press, 2005), 97-115.

7   *The Morning After: Sexual Politics at the End of the Cold War* (Berkeley: University of California Press, 1993), 74.

end. "Jean. This is Timmy Coughlin. Remember me? We met at John Angelino's party for the campaign at the Knickerbocker Bar."

"Hi! Sure I do!"

"Well me and Tony and a couple other Vietnam vets heard what Mooney did to you, suspending you from your steward's job like that. So get this. We just pulled off a guerrilla tactic." He giggled. "We call Mooney's office and his assistant Business Agent down there too, and your Chief Steward. What's the punk's name, the fat one with the cigar? Scallopini? Anyhow, we call from about four different plants and we say 'We know what you're doing to Alonso, and we're gonna get you when you least expect it. We're everywhere!'"

"Well now that's insurance!" I said, grinning from ear to ear.

"Jean. You hang in there. They came up with the excuse that the union and the company are putting you into receivership as a steward because you spend too much time on the members' grievances? My ass! And don't think it's only because you're an Angelino supporter. What really fries them is that you're a smart woman!"

I love these guys and I don't even know them! They're my kind of people! I thought as I thanked Timmy, pretended to scribble a few insurance prices on a piece of paper and hung up. Shaunessy frowned suspiciously. They were definitely daring, just to be in this campaign. The Business Agent is a vengeful man and, if we lose the first challenge to his machine in thirty-five years, there go our jobs. The company will be only too glad to oblige.

What was it Sean's *Guidebook for Marines* said? "Marines have for years acted as the strong arm of U.S. foreign policy, putting down rebellions and disorderly elements all over the world?" These vets *are* the disorderly elements. They're our platoon leaders in the rebellion. Passionate for democracy! Touched and observing a moment of silence, I sat down at my bench and let my soldering iron lie cold. They're not just Vietnam vets. They are children who came of age in the sixties, too, aren't they. They had their own experiences of betrayal by the U.S. government. Exiled to make history back then, they were deprived of being in our other history, the uprising at home. Hey guys, we have a second chance. This time around, you're old enough to fight.

I was quite sure I was seeing a pattern: the veterans took the strongest stands, among the men, for women's equality. I wondered why. There was Bill Trueblood, for instance, who used to be our foreman. He was quite short and skinny—about one hundred and thirty pounds. He wore his thinning blonde hair down to his shoulders, hippie style. He was no model for command-and-control management.

One day, a cute young woman who had a flirtatious relationship with Bill apparently expected to score points with him by yelling at me: "Jean, you must be a Communist the way you're against the war."

To her surprise Bill turned against her yelling angrily, "I'll have no talk like that in this department! I fought a war so that everyone could be free to speak their beliefs!"

Bill viewed his workers as his equals, which must have come as a culture shock to his superiors. He even gave a lot of hot jobs to us women. "Come over here, girls!" he would say. "I'm gonna show you a trick I had to learn" and he would slant his body against a heavy unit, showing us how to use our whole bodies as fulcrums if we didn't have the upper body strength needed to move a unit.

One day one of the higher echelon commanders-of-a-by-gone-era chewed him out, Patton-style. Bill told the company they could have the job. He quit and drove a cab.

Willy Parks, another Vietnam vet, was a very quiet person who kept to himself. I liked to watch him walk. He had been a semi-pro baseball player and moved with the dancer-like grace of a fine athlete. One day I was having to force myself to campaign for shop steward. I had strong backing from the former steward who had quit in disgust at the union's failure to process his members' grievances, and from his all-male Sheet Metal Department. Usually a big mouth on anybody else's behalf, I was shy and hated to campaign for myself. I had started out for a far-flung corner of the machine shop and realized I just couldn't bring myself to do it. Then I saw Willy sitting in the Mold Department. He had told me he had the black vote going for me. He was sitting alone, eating a sandwich and reading *The Bay State Banner*. The place smelled of hysol glue molds just out of the oven.

"Hi, Willy. Can I talk to you?"

"Sure, Jean" he said with his usual seriousness, pulling up a gray metal stool for me.

"I'm really having trouble making myself be aggressive and go around and ask for votes. I hate it. You need hustle to do this. You've got hustle! You're an athlete. What's it like? How do you get it?"

He smiled and took his time answering, usually a prelude, among certain people I knew, to offering a special piece of old-time wisdom.

"You want to know about hustle, Jean? You've got hustle. You bore and raised two children, didn't you? That's hustle. Just fight for the job like you'd fight for your children!"

Some months later I'd heard Willy was quitting. I ran to catch up with him in the hall.

"Willy, I don't mean to get up in your private business, but I heard you were getting ready to leave. Is it true?"

"Yes." he whispered. "I hate this place, Jean. I'm getting ready to go back to Florida. We were brought up there in segregated schools, you know. Sometimes I think that was better. The teachers cared so much about us and how we learned. These days the kids are headed in a bad direction. I'm going back to my hometown to work with them and see if I can help change that."

"One flew over the cuckoo's nest!" I said. Very few people had the willpower to leave American. The ones who did reminded me of Indian in the Jack Nicholson movie about institutional captivity, the silent man who in the final moments of the movie upends the marble columns of the insane asylum to break out before he is lobotomized.

Another progressive vet was Joe, who was my first ever union steward, in 1978. He had opened the gates of a concentration camp in World War II. He couldn't remember its name but only "the faces on those poor Polish women." Possibly these were women from Ravensbruk, the camp for women and children outside Berlin, who had been transferred to several camps known to be liberated by American G.I.s.

Joe was a wiry, tough and macho-talking Italian, who took in stray animals and kids, was still in love with his wife of forty-five years, cooked favorite recipes and proudly owned his own sewing machine. He led us women of Light Assembly on illegal work stoppages when the company did something wrong. In his youth he and a buddy had tried to organize American into the progressive United Electrical Workers Union, U.E., but had enlisted in the war before the union campaign was finished. After the war he returned to American only to find that it had been organized instead into our present cooperative Brotherhood—without a fight by the company, he had been told, so that it only took about three weeks. Joe was a fine, strong person, and my mentor in how to be "union." He often pushed me to "run for steward some day because we need more women!"

I asked myself, why are these veterans so different? Why do they often choose to express their idealism and rebellion by taking stands for women's equality? Was it that, having proven their manhood in war, they no longer needed to reassure themselves of it with the old privilege of superiority? They did not take part in our department jokes and contests about domination and subordination. Or was it something deeper? Was it a sign of their rejection of militarism itself, with its practice of dehumanizing conquerable objects? What had led them to cross over a line and surrender to feeling someone else's life?

I had been thinking about these questions when I got a phone call from Donny, a former Angelino campaigner. He was a charming, once wild-eyed and unpredictable Vietnam vet, now mellower. He was a well-informed conservative, an intellectual.

"Donny, can I ask you a question?" I said, delighted that he had called just when I had been pondering these questions. "You Vietnam vets seem different from other guys—more sensitive to the plight of others. Am I right? And why?"

"Oh, you noticed that we're different. Yeah. We are. I'm going to explain it to you. I think it's like this. See, things happened to us. Like I remember how one day we came into a village near Da Nang. Everybody was dead. Viet Cong soldiers. Women. Children. Our troops had been there ahead, you know? There was a pregnant woman with a branch shoved up her vagina, through the womb and out her head. We had to look at things like that. I was just a kid from East Cambridge, eighteen years old for Chrissake. But you don't feel nothing. You can't. And then years later when you have a family and kids yourself all of a sudden it hits you. I had a breakdown just a couple years ago when I went and saw my face reflected in the granite around my buddy's name in the Memorial Wall."

Later, at a public reading by the poet, novelist, and Vietnam vet, Doug Anderson,[8] I asked the same question.

---

8   Doug Anderson has been a teacher at the William Joiner Center for the Sudy of War and its Social Consequences at University of Massachusetts, Boston. He is the author of *Blues for*

"Yes. We are different," he said. "We do have a special feeling for women. You see, since the war, we have come to see that the traumas we suffered are an experience that many women share with us."

Women had several approaches to machismo. Our Action Committee tried to counter its more virulent forms plant-wide and as a group. Other women handled it ad hoc and individually. I remember one person, Ella, who was on the case relentlessly on the shop floor.

"Julio, get your brown ass over here!" she commanded one day. I didn't know her well because she had just returned to our department from a lay-off elsewhere. She was stocky with shiny chestnut skin, a broad grin, short Afro and southern accent. She hadn't managed to raise a son alone up north by being shy.

"No! You listen to me, *chica!*" Julio grinned and shook his finger forcefully at her. "You need to learn the rules around here! You don't order me around, because I am the master and you are my slave!"

"Well you come over here," she said, wielding a huge soldering iron, "and I'll brand you right where you'll know whose slave you are!" She grabbed for his crotch. Julio laughed and danced aside, just out of her reach, too gentlemanly to respond in kind.

Most women treated machismo like this—as a joke. It didn't have much currency except as a form of play.

Changes in the attitudes toward machismo, however, were not matched by changes in American's institutional chauvinism. We on the Women's Action Committee conducted various maneuvers against it. Since we were not able to obtain company-wide statistics on gender and job distribution, because the company had them declared company secrets, Action did an informal survey of our own division of about seven hundred and eighty people. The lowest paid Labor Grade (Eleven) was sixty-eight percent women. The middle level Grade Seven (including my Heavy Assembly Department) was seven percent women. Labor Grade Four, which included some advanced testers as well as some tradesmen, was twelve percent women. Labor Grades Three through One, the millwrights and skilled tradesmen, had no women except that Labor Grade Two, thanks to welder Dolly and machinist Nora, had two percent. This was probably typical of

Unemployed Secret Police: Poems (Curbstone Press, 2000) and *The Moon Reflected Fire* (Cambridge: Alice James Books, 1994).

the company as a whole. Sometimes this exclusion of women from good pay grades was because there was special training required that had customarily been obtained by boys but not girls in trade schools. Sometimes it was because bosses or even women were set in their ways and their traditional roles. Lottie was one buddy of mine who broke that barrier.

"Do what your heart tells ya, that's what my mother always said!" Lottie had called me into the ladies' room for break. She was about fifty-nine, Polish, smart and vivacious with a pretty face and curly light brown hair. She was also short, plump and so buxom that her "shelf," as she called her bosom, had often caught cupcake crumbs which had fallen into her units and caused mechanical problems. These were for some time pronounced by the smirking women in Test to be of unknown origin.

"I'm going to do it!" she told me. "I mean, I love Frank—I've worked for him for years, way back when this company was just a little one-building business, but he tries to keep his Light Assembly Department all one little family with him as the Papa. He's always frightening us with stories about how hard the heavy assembly work is and how women can get hurt doing it."

"Right on, Loticia!" I grinned. "You march right in there and take your application to Shaunessy. Why should you be paid eleven dollars an hour when you could be getting fourteen? You're very smart and they know it and that's why they want to keep you in Light Assembly. But if Eleanor and Angie and I can do this work, so can you!"

Lottie was a latter-day pioneer at American. She was a Catholic and generally a conservative person. But wrestling with a personal problem— her husband had run off with a younger woman and left her alone to raise two sons—had brought her out the other side. Like a modern apparition of St. Joan, Lottie became a flaming feminist. She watched everything there was to see about women's issues on Public Television, clipped articles from Woman's Day on women's rights, and gave me jumper cables for Christmas because, she said, women should be able to manage their own cars independently.

"I'm not giving him a divorce, Jean, ever!" she said gleefully of her husband. "I have bought two cemetery plots. One for me and one for Edmond. I'll bury him at my feet, forever!" Several years later she did just that.

Nancy was another pioneer. Structural discrimination remained in the company/union sponsored sports league. Nancy had talked the men into making her the only female coach in the union-company softball league. A divorced mother of two youngsters, she once confided to me that she had a Lesbian sister who had groomed her as a baseball player and fan, and that she had met her second husband tailgating with her kids next to the car where he was tailgating with his kids before a Patriots' football game. She never got to play on a team at American, or on the union all-star team, which got bussed out of state for competitions, wined and dined. There was no such parallel activity for union women.

Over the years Action found that fighting structural discrimination was an uphill battle. We ran a woman for union president, and urged the union to support childcare and flextime. These efforts were not successful. We gathered material for a class-action suit against American for its failure to promote women or give them comparable pay. Our lawyer-advisor was prepared to ask the National Lawyers' Committee for Civil Rights Under Law to sponsor the case. However, in 1989, with the advent of multiple Supreme Court decisions characterized by *The New York Times* as "dealing blow after blow to twenty-five years of progress in Civil Rights laws,"[9] she advised us to put our case on hold rather than chance making reactionary law if we lost to this court.

In 1990, we tried cooperation. We accepted a request not to oppose a slate of officers consisting of the sons of incumbents, in exchange for an official union women's committee and a partnership in policy-making. "Let's go forward into the nineties together!" they said. When they won, they went back on all these promises. Having exclusive power to appoint all committees under the Brotherhood's International Constitution, they appointed a women's committee of their allies, which refused to meet.

It took our lawyer's known presence in the background for Action to win our one big institutional victory in 1989. We persuaded the union to negotiate contract language forbidding sexual harassment at American. The posting of the clause throughout the plants gave women some back-up in warning men to stop offensive sexual behavior that had been open-season previously. Eleven years have made quite a difference, I thought to myself. I was remembering when, in my first months of work, another woman and I had asked the union for help finding work during company shutdown, since we were new and had no vacation pay. The Chief Steward

---

9   June 13, 1989, 1.

had shaken his head and said, "Hey it shouldn't be a problem—you two are a couple a good-looking girls—you're sitting on a gold mine!"

Vestiges of machismo in its extreme form—male supremacy with its obsession with control, power and the use of force—were definitely present at American in the all-male job preserves. And militarized masculinity—having a contemptuous, belligerent, Patton-like personality—was still *de rigueur* among managers. But that was not tolerated in rank-and-file men by women coworkers. We women found commandist machismo either laughable or alarming. Many of us knew from experience that male contempt, over-control and belligerence were hallmarks not of the hero but of the batterer.[10]

We were aware of cases of domestic violence in American's families, but not of its extent. This would have been interesting to know in light of 1993 statistics on elevated levels of domestic violence in military homes. According to a *New York Times* article, May 23, 1994, one child or spouse of a person in uniform died from it per week. Cynthia Enloe has questioned whether this might be caused by the process of militarizing a man's sense of his own masculinity. She comments that it may be that the nurturing parent role is incompatible with the profession designed to wield violence in the name of the state.[11] We have no way of knowing whether those who still espoused American's militarized masculinity also experienced violent impulses at home.

On the whole, the men in gender-integrated departments at American gave me heart. Among rank and file men, to be domineering, to insist on hierarchical values and absolute power, and to suppress empathy were no longer adaptive at home or at work. Most men seemed to be finding the character of the militaristic male outmoded.

---

10   See, for example, *When Men Batter Women: New Insights Into Ending Abusive Relationships* by Neil Jacobson and John Gottman (New York: Simon and Schuster, 1998). "Contempt and belligerence are particular forms of anger that are emotional or verbal abuse, vs. regular anger." 22. "Belligerence refers to taunting, challenging remarks designed to provoke another person. Contempt refers to insulting, demeaning behavior directed toward the partner." 65.

11   *Maneuvers: The International Politics of Militarizing Women's Lives* (Berkeley: University of California Press, 2000), 190.

X

Changes in Patriotism

War correspondent Chris Hedges has written that myths always accompany wars to engage citizen support, but "wars that lose their mythic status with the public, as with Korea and Vietnam, are doomed to failure because war is then exposed for what it is—organized murder."[1]

Our permanent business of war at American was accompanied by permanent patriotic myths. They were the cultural cement reinforcing both the legitimacy of war and the authority of the company. Was it still holding in the nineties?

The production of weapons gave a higher meaning to the lives of many workers. Since 1914, modern weapons have gradually replaced individual warriors as the real winners of war.[2] Weapons can be, in effect, patriotic heroes, and their builders can be heroes too. I heard a story illustrating this in 1991, during the Gulf War.

"What did you start to tell me yesterday about your weekend at the Cape?" I asked Dominic, who was hammering heavy leads flat so that they wouldn't touch their metal case and short out the unit.

He beamed, put his arm around me and his head on my shoulder, grinning for public consumption. "Remind me, Miss Jean?"

"I was asking you something else—if you minded building weapons—then we got interrupted."

"Oh, right. No, I don't mind! I feel honored! I'm proud of doing stuff for my government. I love it. Especially last weekend. I walked into a bar on the Cape and I forgot I was still wearing my American security badge. Somebody spotted it and yelled out that I worked at American and he started to clap and all the people there stood up and cheered for me! Someone

---

1   *War is a Force that Gives Us Meaning* (New York: Public Affairs, 2002), 21.
2   *Ibid.*, 85-6.

came up to me and said, 'You saved my brother's life!' It was wonderful. I was so proud!"

It was no secret that I wasn't proud, but I needed to better understand this point of view and try to empathize with how people were feeling as long as I was presuming to ask. Back at my bench I turned around to Joseph, who was sanding paint from wire leads. I knew he had been in the Portuguese army as a youth.

"Do you wish you were a soldier again and over there fighting for America in Desert Storm?" I asked him.

He bent for a sip of his coffee and whispered "No. Promise not to tell anyone if I tell you something, Jean?"

"I promise."

"Every Wednesday around five o'clock I stand outside my church with a candle in a vigil for peace. My church believes that war is wrong."

Several weeks later, in February, 1991, the Gulf War ended, pronounced a success by the media. Far fewer American lives were lost than opponents had predicted. American basked in the limelight of its missile, but there was something of a letdown too. As I picked up a new job, a bunch of connectors, which were two-inch silver cups, and bundles of leads needing to be attached inside the cups. Once assembled inside the case, they would turn into prongs outside—a power supply with a plug, probably for a missile, I thought irritably. I stopped my rickety metal move cart next to Howie's bench.

"Hi, Howie, how are you? Are you sorry the war's over?" Howie was a nice man who was rather withdrawn, assigned the same job he'd done for years—the outsized units, which carried a certain prestige. He had to use a chain lift to move the huge magnetic cores. He'd come here as a young sailor, fresh out of the Korean War. Now, after almost forty years, his wavy short hair was gray. He shook his head and beckoned for me to bend down.

"I'm glad the war's over." he whispered. "All along I was feeling awful for all those women and the little children that got killed." I nodded, surprised.

Back at the bench, I lined up bunches of labeled wire leads and rows of silver connectors. I had to stick each lead tip in a cone inside the connector, apply a miniscule amount of solder, and solder it in carefully. If the solder overflowed and ran out or made sharp points, it would arc with electricity, shorting the unit. If you removed your soldering iron before the solder was hot enough, it could result in what was called a "cold solder joint" that would not conduct electricity. I started to assemble the leads, still thinking.

Patriots Who Made Sacrifices For Their Country

If Joseph and Howie had negative feelings about the war, what about other veterans? I thought of asking them a question about whether they would want their children to go to war. I suppose the ultimate measure of patriotism would be the willingness to give your life for your country. If you were a warrior, chauvinist kind of patriot, then risking your life would prove your masculine courage. Or if your patriotism was of the patriarchal variety, coming from feelings of piety and indebtedness to God, father and country, then giving your life, or offering your child as a sacrifice, like Abraham, would seem the ultimate proof of your loyalty, the ultimate tribute you could pay. I looked up in time to see Sam on his way out for a cigarette.

"Can I ask you something real quick?" He smiled and nodded.

"Sam, if there's another war when your boy is eighteen—what's he now, thirteen?—would you encourage him to sign up for the service like you did? Would you expect him to be ready to die for the country?" His face grew dark and serious.

"No. And if he got drafted I'd drive him to Canada. No kid of mine is going to fight in another U.S. war." He got out a cigarette and went for the hall without further comment.

Billy, who had seen action in Vietnam, was coming toward me, pushing a wagonload of experimental units from the model shop and holding his jaw square and combat-ready as usual. Maybe he noticed me looking at him. Our conversations usually amounted to him scolding me for my bad attitude.

"Hi, Billy. How are things in the model shop today?"

"Oh, not bad. Donovan's at a managers' meeting. How are you? Are you working hard or hardly working?"

"Hardly working," I smiled. "I'm good. I'm in one of my curious moods. Would you mind if I asked you a question I've been asking other people?"

"No, go ahead. What's up?"

"When your son grows up, would you encourage him to be patriotic and go fight a war just like you did?"

I expected a quick affirmative but he seemed to be having trouble with the question. He looked at his feet for a while and then looked up.

"You mean honestly, huh? Honestly, I don't want my kid ever to get involved in a war."

I was taken aback. "Would you mind if I asked why?"

He said nothing, smoothing down wires in the units he was transporting, and then arranging them in a neat row. He was quiet for what seemed like a long time. He appeared to be struggling with something inside himself, maybe whether or not to trust me. When he looked up his eyes had filled with tears and I could barely hear what he said.

"Jean, they made me pour napalm into a trench filled with women and children, okay?"

I just shook my head in silence. "Oh, Billy, I'm so sorry."

He shrugged and walked away.

I stayed behind for break, wanting to be alone. My heart went out to Billy. How much you're carrying, man, I thought. How much more you know about life at its breaking point than most of us do. And you never mention it. How many more are there like you?

American hired a great many veterans, whom they undoubtedly expected to set a standard of patriotic militarism. All the weekend-warrior managers, the officers in the Reserves, did so very vocally. But the veterans of combat were silent. In fact, it struck me that I had not heard a single war story in my fourteen years at the plant. Perhaps that was the real war story. Perhaps this munitions plant, with its large population of combat veterans, contained a powerful, though silent, witness against war.

I looked toward the empty Mold Department wishing the thoughtful Willy Parks still worked there so that I could ask him the same question, and also the other Vietnam vets now gone—Bill Trueblood and Tim Coughlin. They never bought the company and the union's cold-war patriotism. Nor did they subscribe to the common pious kind of patriotism, in which people felt indebted to country and authority. I'm sure they felt their debt of loyalty to be more than paid. They spoke with their own authority, and rendered their loyalty to democratic principles in whatever unorthodox way they chose to. They were among the few here who had a sense of entitlement. What kind of combat would it take for others to feel empowered too?

I poured myself some coffee, cautioning myself not to spill on the units, and thought of my welder friend, Dolly. She too had let go of feelings of indebtedness to American in favor of a sense of earned entitlement. I had told her about some of our group's discoveries about the developmental hazards of our jobs. One day she said to me: "You know, Jean, when you used to talk about flextime in the Action Committee, I thought you were nuts! We were so lucky to have this good pay, what right did we have to ask for more? But when we got some promise of flextime in the contract, I realized we could have it, and that maybe we had influenced the union to negotiate it by speaking up for it. I also realized that we had a right to ask, because we had already sacrificed so much."

Working Without The Patriotic Myth: "Did I Have a Part In That?"

People were coming back from break. Eleanor leaned over to slip me a large frosted brownie and some gossip.

"Listen here. I've got something to tell you. I've just had a chat with Betty Boop!" She chuckled at her own apt characterization of the little-girl voice of American's long-time Pentagon customer service representative. "It's definite. They're going to be closing one of the biggest plants, but she wouldn't say which one."

"Eleanor, could you please take back part of this beautiful looking thing with the calories? What do you think that means for us? Are they selling off parts of the company? Do we get to build air traffic control parts instead of this stuff? Or do we just quietly hit the street?"

"Well, you and I won't hit the street—not with fourteen years' seniority. But there's bound to be bumping."

We settled into the silence of the last segment of the afternoon. People were putting on their Walkman headphones, and I put on mine too, taking up a small pair of needle-nosed pliers with rounded tips, which could bend lead wires without nicking them. The veterans who have no more patriotic illusions about war, I mused, do they also see the instruments of death that lie beneath our hands every day without illusions? It was really a taboo subject for the shop floor. I had avoided thinking about it much myself until the group got into it recently. I felt like hearing that again, and I could, since I had with me a cassette of the discussion. I was in the habit of carrying around the most recent tapes so that I could listen while I worked, and then summarize them for our next session. I snapped it into my Walkman, fast-forwarding a little. Nora was speaking.

"I feel like we're more oppressed than normal people who are not in the defense industry," she was saying, "because we're bought off. Even though in a certain way we're aware that the defense industry is running this country, you have to be saying 'this is all right' just by the fact that you're working here. But it's not all right."

Jasmine replied, "I've felt that way myself. I felt.....you know, I'm for peace, not making war, trying to negotiate, then I find myself working for a company that makes weapons or potential weapons, me who feels bad about even killing a flea. I wanted to quit but I had a small kid to support and I said, 'what am I going to do?' So I had to rationalize it and pretend that the stuff I was making was going to a hospital. You know, like some of the stuff American makes that is for medical technology. Then during Desert Storm I really felt good when it looked like we were saving lives. Until I found out that they fell on all those people who were killed, and I felt terrible, and I said, 'Oh Lord, did I have a part in that'?"

"So what's your take on being for peace but building weapons, Jean?" Tom was asking me.

"How come you're asking the hard questions today? Is Hildie asleep?"

"I'm listening. Make it good!"

"Well, I had a rationale when I came here. I still agree with it. I didn't believe individual moral gestures like abstaining from defense jobs did any good, unless you were confronting an opponent with a conscience that you could appeal to. But we were dealing with an amoral industry and an amoral administration in Washington. They only care about profits and world power. The only way to influence them might be to hurt them in the pocket book. I think it would take a national upsurge against war, and demanding defense money for citizens' needs. I think we would have to be militant enough to shut down industries if the demands were not met."

"Oh, sure!" Hildie said.

I paused the tape and applied flux to one of the neat curved wire joints I'd made. The flux heated the metal, drawing impurities and oxidation away from it so that the solder flowed smoothly and evenly around the wrapped terminal. I remembered what else I had thought, but hadn't said to the group. I'd thought that for me to be overly sensitive about getting my hands dirty with weapons work would be to retreat into my middle-class, protected life. Working people have always had to do the dirty work—stoke the dangerous furnaces, work the flaming steel smelting rooms, slaughter the stock and clean up after the sick and the dead. And fight the wars. I searched the buttons for "play" to listen to more of the voice that sounded odd outside my head.

"I used to feel resentful that the peace people didn't seem to understand the world of working people and our limited options when they looked down on us for making weapon parts. Once I met a doctor on a plane, who was traveling to the same peace demonstration I was, and he said to me, 'Well sometimes I have bad days but at least I don't make weapons for a living,' and he turned around and didn't speak to me for the rest of the flight.

"On the other hand, the peace people know so much that most of us don't. Remember the local people who used to stand in the vigil outside the plant? There were Catholic war resisters, and a lawyer and a nurse, and researchers in the SANE-FREEZE movement. I still have a flier they gave out that said the U.S. has 9000 nuclear warheads on our missiles and the Soviet Union has only 7000. It said that's like comparing two boys standing in a garage with gasoline all over the floor, and one boy has six matches and the other has seven. Who's ahead? If just one match is lit and dropped it won't matter."

"The truth is, though," Tom said, "life is a series of compromises, isn't it? We have to support our kids, and so we are a part of this arms industry. We make weapons. But, hey, if I work for Smith and Wesson making thirty-eight caliber rifles and some guy buys one and shoots someone in downtown Springfield, I didn't know he was going to do that. I don't really feel responsible for what's done with them. I don't approve of it. Now if they were going to put these missiles we make into storage in case there's a real need to defend ourselves, that's one thing. But instead they go around the world with these missiles using them on little countries that can't defend themselves, busting them up like they're Rodney King!" (The shocking March 3, 1991 video that caught Los Angeles cops beating the unarmed King was still fresh in our minds.)

Eleanor elbowed me, indicating with her eyes that I needed to listen to something behind us. I took off the headphones.

"Alonso!! I've been calling you. Do you have to take notes while you work? What are you doing, trying to learn the words to some rock and roll? Concentrate on the job!"

I nodded obediently, took off my headphones but kept writing and exchanged a mischievous grin with Eleanor, who knew my habits.

I didn't answer the real question, though, I thought to myself. I talked to them about my thinking when I first took the job. But how do I feel right now about these weapons parts in front of me? What is the first thing that comes to mind?

That they're not there. That's my most honest answer.

But they are there, so what just happened? I sat back for a minute, contemplating the apparatus I was wiring. 'It isn't weapons' the other half of me said again. 'It's just pieces of metal and tempered steel.' Apparently, over time, my familiarity with these pieces of metal had won out over my rational knowledge of their final use. I was quite sure it happened to most people.

I concluded later that night that what took place in me was dissociation, described by Robert Jay Lifton as a psychological aberration common among people involved with weapons production or genocidal activity, like Nazi doctors. I was not happy to find myself in that league. Lifton's book, *The Genocidal Mentality*, had been gathering dust on my bookshelf but now I needed to consult it. I really wanted to confront my reaction, this "psychic numbing."[3]

Lifton quoted Carol Cohn, a feminist scholar who experienced psychic numbing as she spent time with nuclear weapons intellectuals, whose culture she was studying. She reported that these men, whom she found smart and likeable, used euphemistic language as defensive dissociation. Typically they used technical, obscure and sexual language when talking about the weapons they worked on.[4] They even made a habit of patting

3   Robert Jay Lifton and Eric Markusen, *The Genocidal Mentality: Nazi Holocaust and Nuclear Threat* (New York: Basic Books, 1990), 13.
4   *Ibid.*, 215.

the missile like a cute pet. Cohn said that, in spite of herself, she stopped experiencing the human consequences of these weapons until "over and over I found that I couldn't stay connected, couldn't keep human lives as my reference points."[5]

I put the book back and thought about how neutralized language was a means of dissociation for us too, with our "units" and "products" that had no names, only numbers.

Buscando America

In addition to avoiding my feelings about building weapons parts, I had avoided thoughts about my own patriotism, until one day when I received an invitation to speak at a labor workshop about being an American and an activist. What could I say about being an American? I certainly did not espouse the narrow-minded, conformist patriotism around me. I was capable of feeling loyalty and dedication, but not usually to authority figures, which left me out of the pious, filial kind of patriotism so common at the plant. I had such bitter feelings about the way late-stage American imperialism conducted itself that I, in effect, hadn't been on speaking terms with my country in years. I decided any patriotism I once had was extinguished.

"I just can't do this speaking thing, Julio. I don't feel like I have anything special to say," I confessed to him one afternoon when my distress overcame my common sense about opening myself up to his teasing. "I don't even know how I feel about being American. Mainly I'm ashamed of what my country has done around the world. It's a villain, and it's my home."

"You shouldn't give up Juanita," he said. "You should try to do things that are hard for you."

The next morning he arrived just as the buzzer rang. He slid into his chair, slipped out of his New York Yankees jacket and sat back pretending he'd been there for a while.

"Hey *hombre*," I whispered, "what happened to eighty miles an hour?"

He just smiled, turned on his soldering iron and passed me something.

"Here Juanita," he said with uncharacteristic seriousness, "I made this for you last night because I think it might help you."

5   *Ibid.,* 192.

It was a tape. I thanked him and put it in my Walkman. I heard a soft sound of waves lapping a shore and seagulls calling, then a dramatic big-band introduction. I only understood the title line: *"T'estoy buscando America* [I am looking for you, America]."[6] The music was gently tender and intense like a love song.

"This song is *numero uno* in Puerto Rico this week, so you have to like it Juanita!" Julio said. "Did you ever hear of Ruben Blades?"

The melody was beautiful. At home that night, I translated the lyrics, stopping the tape phrase by phrase to look up words. It was in the intimate *"tu"* form, used in Spanish for family and loved ones.

Estoy buscando a América	I am searching for America
Y temo no encontrarla	And I fear not finding her
Sus huellas se han perdidas	Her footprints have gotten lost
Entre la oscuridad	In darkness and obscurity
Estoy llamando a América	I am calling to America
Pero no me responde	But she does not answer
La han desaparacido	They have disappeared her
Los que temen la verdad	Those who fear the truth
Viviendo en dictaduros	Living in dictatorships
Busco pero no t'encuentras	I search but do not find you
Tu torturado cuerpo	Your tortured body,
No saben donde esta	They don't know where it is
América, te han sequestrado	America, they have kidnapped you,
Y amordazado tu boca	And bound your mouth
Y a nosotros nos toca	And it falls to us
Ponerte en libertad	To set you free.

The sophisticated and sensitive understanding of politics and of me that this gift represented touched me. It was one of those fleeting revelations that once or twice escaped from under the cavalier Julioismo. This anthem was a good enough expression of my patriotism, this ballad of longing for an America nowhere to be found, with its grief about atrocities perpetrated on a captive country, and its commitment to liberation.

Tarnished Patriots

My tires made a crunching sound on the driveway pebbles as I rolled to a stop in the church parking lot. I was hesitant to get out, hesitant to go forward with the day. I sat for a minute without turning off the motor. I should have been relieved. I was relieved. No more work to prepare these sessions. This was the last one. I turned to the back seat and pulled up a white plastic bag with a Bob Slate Stationers logo on it, smiled at its secret contents and tucked it in my beach bag. A picnic would be nice on this lovely warm September day. Our topic, patriotism, was a popular issue for us. Walden Pond, which had been Suzanne's idea, held as much emotion for me as this rupture of our communications did, this slow and necessary death of a good thing. We had gone past our agreed-on ten sessions, to fifteen, after all. But it felt like breaking a bond, breaking faith. How life moved on, with its disconnections. Twenty-nine years ago Thoreau was the center of my universe, along with baby Melissa and her brother. I had read all twelve volumes of his Journals, studied his Buddhist texts, absorbed *Walden* for five years while writing a master's thesis about it, and I had hardly thought of him since.

"Hi Jean!" the chorus of sisters with picnic baskets fast-forwarded me. Suzanne, Hildie, Nora and Jasmine were slamming car doors and arranging their baskets in a row in the driveway. We knew Ruth couldn't be with us because of her new classes in drafting, and Sean would be late because he had to work over-time.

"Here he is!" Nora clapped as Tom pulled up in his wife's green Dodge van, still sparkling with water droplets, apparently fresh from the car wash.

"I'm not going!" Hildie said. "It's so clean somebody will think we stole it!"

"For our last trip together, I thought we should go in style!" Tom said, helping us up and in, and stacking the picnic gear in the back. We pulled out of the driveway and headed for Main Street. "Jeez, that sounds like last rites, doesn't it!"

"So did you bring us a bunch of Thoreau's sayings, Jean?" Nora cocked her head at me and smiled knowingly.

"You know, I can't remember any!" I said, and then turned to the others. "She knows I studied Thoreau and he meant a lot to me. But that was 'back in the day.'"

"Done and gone, huh?" Suzanne smiled.

"Right. But anyway, I did bring you a different quote," I said. "Kind of an epitaph, to go with your last rites Tom—a famous statement about what work does to people, written in 1776."

"Well that sounds patriotic!" Tom shouted above the traffic. "Hey, let's get underway with the discussion while we drive! Read it loud, Jean, okay, so I can hear it over the traffic?"

"Okay. But it's from England of 1776 and you'd have to be very rich to feel patriotic about it. It's one of your favorite economists, Tom—Adam Smith! Listen." I couldn't stop myself from making one last attempt at provoking a rage to organize. I pulled out my notes and read the famous passage:

> The understanding of the greater part of men is necessarily formed by their ordinary employments. The man's whole life is spent in performing a few simple operations and he naturally loses, therefore, the habit [of solving problems] and generally becomes as stupid and ignorant as it is possible for a human creature to become... But in every improved and civilized society this is the state into which the laboring poor, that is, the great body of the people, must necessarily fall.[7]

"The working people were seen as no better than bulls in the field!" Tom shouted. "Coming from Adam Smith, it doesn't surprise me at all. And the same cynical, feudal attitude toward us holds today!" He leaned on the horn.

"Move, damn you!" The kid in the car ahead of us was reaching to turn up his radio. He was rocking in the driver's seat and jutting his jaw out and back in time to the music, oblivious of the green light.

"Oh, oh, road rage!" Hildie yelled and gripped the seat-back in front of her.

At the sound of the horn the kid's car lurched forward and we continued on the tree-lined route to Concord.

"Look!" Tom tilted his head so his voice carried back toward us. "We're discussing patriotism, right? On what grounds do they expect us to be

7   "Of the Expence of the Institutions for the Education of Youth," Book V, Chapter 1, Part III, Article 2, *The Wealth of Nations,* Intro., Alan B. Krueger (New York: Bantam Classics, 2003), 987.

patriotic? You might not remember it, but in the fifties when most people were patriotic, they always promised us that our jobs wouldn't be replaced. Now they're taking them away. The cynicism is bigger than just American."

"When I say stuff like what I'm going to say," Jasmine, who was keeping Tom company up front, turned around back toward us, "people say I'm a communist. It's not that. I'm not. It's that it's a capitalistic system that the U.S. deals under. If we had a different system in place…. a democratic system like this is supposed to be… But it's a democracy set up to have lower levels—people like the blacks and the lower class and the working class for those people to make their profits from, and to work at low wages and buy their stuff."

There was an analysis I liked! I kept quiet though, looking sideways out the window at the working-class neighborhoods and small Cape Cod and ranch houses like the one in which I grew up. They had neat round shrubs, one on each side of the front door, and, in many yards, American flags with their poles surrounded by red, white and purple petunias.

"I agree it's a government thing," Nora tucked her feet up under her. "But I think that it's also carried out in the educational system, which is set up for two different tracks—one for the families of more affluent people who have been programmed to go on to college, and be part of the system. The other for the working-class people who have their minds and creativity closed down. I think the system does that to everybody, but especially to the working class. And I don't know how you all feel, but I see it as being cross-racial. It's infuriating! I don't know how it's going to change unless the whole system changes, and I've felt a part of it since I was a little kid. So I rejected the system and went to work in a factory."

"You wanted to reject the system by working in the factory, but it's still here!" Suzanne grinned. "I've been a factory worker most of my life and that hasn't made it go away yet!" We laughed, some harder than others.

"I'm hot!" Tom said. "Mind if we stop for a minute for me to have a quick coke?" He pulled over under the shade of a maple tree, wiping his forehead with a handkerchief.

Suzanne grinned and tossed cokes to each of us. Mine fell through my hands to the floor and spouted like a fountain when I opened it.

"Nora, polarization is the word," Tom took a long pull on his coke, "and I don't think it happened by chance. I am really pissed off all right; I am pissed at some things I've been reading. Do you know that in the last twelve years, from 1978 to 1992, the number of Americans at the poverty level in this country—in 1990, $12,00 for a family of four by the way—has grown exponentially? The top 1% has made a killing under Reagan and Bush!" He fortified himself with the rest of his coke. "Now to do that" he continued, "it had to come from somewhere. Wealth isn't like rain, you know, that you just have every once in a while. It's squeezed from someone else. If I acquire a great deal of wealth I have to take it from working people. They have sucked us dry. They have siphoned off our ability to make ends meet!".

He nodded toward the road. "Shall we head out?"

"I feel depressed" Suzanne said. "What is there to look forward to? Your job's on the line. You give all your life, coming up, pay your social security, and then when it comes your turn to be on the receiving end, there's nothing there. Now they just want to get rid of the elderly. We're the only country that does that to our elderly. It's a disgrace."

"Listen to this!" Tom said as he pulled out onto Route Two toward Concord. "I heard the best description of modern capitalism. It said that in the U.S.A., the power structure of this country controls the military and the police for one reason—to protect the ultra-wealthy from the lower working classes in the event of revolutionary radicalism and upheaval."

"Sure!" Jasmine turned around again. "And they control you by throwing you in jail, putting you on welfare, or pitting the races and classes against each other. But what can you do, overthrow the system?"

"Sure!" I said, shaking my raised fist. I had no idea she thought like this.

"You can't do that," she shook her head at me. "I used to be so angry at this, but now I'm resigned. It's too big for me. So the only thing you can do is vote people in who have your same frame of mind, and try to take back to the community what you've learned."

Now the lawns I could see from the road were broad and the houses, several hundred years old, were neatly if unimaginatively landscaped, with Yankee thrift. We were in historic territory.

"I don't belong in this discussion." Hildie spoke up now. "All right, you don't like the capitalist democratic society, but what do you propose as an alternative to it?"

"I'll tell you what I'd propose," Tom shot back over his shoulder, "I want to see a system that, instead of waving a flag of democracy and freedom and free enterprise, says to a lot of these countries—our dictatorships that we call friends—'Any country on this planet that is not making an honest effort at raising the standard of living in their country is no friend of ours!'"

There on the side of the road was a green state sign that pointed to Walden Pond. "Here we are!" I said, "which will temporarily spare you hearing what I'd propose."

As we turned down the country road another sign said that we were entering Walden Pond State Reservation, and we were suddenly quiet.

I hadn't been here for twenty-eight years. Not since I brought the children to sit their small bottoms by the water's edge, to pat the pond as it lapped their pudgy feet, and to dig little shovels full of some of the yellow-iron colored sands of Walden, still "singularly agreeable" as when Thoreau described them. Now there were seven parking lots carved out of the woods, and a tasteful gift shop. Still, the hundred-and-fifty-year-old trees seemed to humble those of us who came and went beneath their towering venerability.

We picked up baskets and coolers in silence and started for the road that led to the pond.

"Look!" Nora led us away from the main path and pointed through the trees where a tiny ten by fifteen foot shingled cabin sat. We went up to it. It had only a cot, cast iron stove, writing table and three chairs, and was—without a door—open to the elements. A few feet from the cabin was a beautiful, craggy man contemplating his cupped hands. He was all jagged bronze surfaces, as if made of mud and sand foliage. "Henry." I said.

We crossed the road and walked the dirt path that wound downhill to the pond. For a weekday afternoon there was quite a crowd on the small beach. A neatly built stone wall and seven steps surrounded the sand, and the pond was roped off with buoys to mark approved swimming areas. We looked at each other without a word and turned away, following Tom along a dirt path till we came to a small deserted sandy area with a sign that warned: "unguarded."

"Hey let's take a quick dip first, what do you say?" Tom suggested.

We anchored down my pink tablecloth, stripped to our bathing suits, and raced into the water. Nora could wear a bikini just fine while the rest of us looked well under water. It wasn't important any more. Hildie skimmed the heel of her hand across the water toward Jasmine, who ducked Tom. They swam a few laps to cool off and get refreshed, and headed for the beach.

The water was warm and so pure that the grains of sand at my feet were there for viewing. Birches and cardinal red maples seemed to float on the surface. I touched them gently and the pond rippled, creating shimmering hexagons of sun-gold light, like frames awaiting stained glass, or awaiting nothing, hexagons that dissolved and reformed as the surface trembled. I couldn't leave.

A pebble broke the surface, which I knew was to remind me that I was daydreaming on the job again. I walked slowly toward the shade behind Suzanne and Jasmine, who were stretched out to let their tropical print bathing suits dry in the sun.

"Okay, let's get down to our discussion again," Tom said, and everyone sat up. "Patriotism. But first, I'm curious Jeannie. What did you start to say for a proposal after I gave Hildie a piece of my mind in the car?"

"A piece might be all you've got to give!" Hildie said brightly.

"Well," I said. "What would I replace this system with? I'd have an out-and-out socialist system. Surprise, right? After a short revolution accomplished with the use of some of the world's finest missiles in the hands of the people, I'd institute immediate reforms. I'd mandate national health care and free college for all, like most of the industrialized world has. I'd take from the Scandinavians their little fjord-front cottages free for all the elderly, and their workplace psychosocial health laws that require companies to organize work in a non-oppressive way. From the former East Germany, free high quality day care. From Cuba, advanced medicine, and music and art lessons for every child. And from China, its former system of democratic street and neighborhood committees. Then, after giving the people these simple little things that they deserved all along, I'd ask them to decide and design what else they'd like."

"That's nice," said Hildie. "And how would you pay for all this?"

"Easy!" I flicked my hand. "The national health care would save one third to one half the money our health care costs now by taking out all the middlemen, the clerical and billing duplications, the unfair drug profits. That's a well-known fact. The other middleman I'd save billions by removing is…American! I'd immediately, my first day in office, nationalize the defense industry!"

"All right!" they laughed and cheered. Hildie raised an eyebrow and smiled.

"Hey, this is a picnic!" Tom said. "Should we take a break and get it out?"

"Come on," Hildie said. "Let's get this product moving! Here!" She slapped cold cuts on a plate for Tom, handed Jasmine a bag of rolls, gave Nora the pickles and onions and tomatoes and lettuce to arrange at the end of the line. "And here!" she grinned at Suzanne, handing her serving spoons and shoving the cooler of salads in her direction.

We each had one plate, loaded, in hand within four minutes.

Suzanne took a forkful of potato salad and said, "This is delicious, Jas. You used some pickle juice, right? About patriotism. Did you mean toward your country or your job? I think of it as devotion to the job. I certainly don't feel devotion to 'my country right or wrong!' When I was a little stupid kid I wrote poems about America. But now they just seem to be digging a hole and getting us deeper into it. With all this patriotism I don't hear anyone talk about all the racism that's rampant in this country!" We all nodded vigorously.

"Oh," I was very pleased. I'd remembered something from Thoreau. "You know what Thoreau said about the governor of Massachusetts not speaking up when soldiers from Virginia seized the fugitive slave Anthony Burns, who was a citizen of Massachusetts? He said, "I listened to hear the voice of the Governor. I heard only the creaking of crickets…He was no governor of mine! He did not govern me!"[8] They laughed and Tom hit the crook of his elbow and raised his fist.

"To me patriotism is devotion to your country," Hildie said. "I am patriotic. I was very idealistic when I was growing up. But I didn't see my country could forsake things, or lie to us. It happened gradually, in Korea and in the Vietnam War, and in the corruption of the politicians. I'm a tarnished patriot."

She passed the barbecued chips we'd forgotten, and continued.

"All the secret stuff our country is involved in—the Cold War, the CIA, Interpol—all the undercover stuff that goes on in the belly down there. We live in two different worlds. There's the one out here for all of our people to see, and then there's the ugly world down there where everybody is fighting tooth and nail.

Tom and I exchanged glances.

8   "Slavery in Massachusetts: An Address Delivered at the Anti-Slavery Celebration at Framingham, July 4th, 1854," *Civil Disobedience and Other Essays* (New York: Dover Thrift Editions, 1993), 20.

"And the Gulf War? I was embarrassed when the President went on TV and gave his speech about us. The war was a weapons test. Before we put any more money into them, we had to find out if they worked." She paused to take another bite of her sandwich. "So we give Saddam Hussein an opportunity to buy some weapons. The French sell some. We have a little conflict and see whose weapons work. It was contrived. You don't think all those countries wanted anything to do with that war, but they had to do what we tell them because the big bully on the block told them to, and we're the big bully now. We really depleted ourselves in doing that."

"Yeah," I said, "like we used to say when police beat up protesters, 'The whole world is watching!'"

"That's right," Hildie sighed. "And now it's a world economy too. I don't feel that there's much we can do but change little pieces of it. I like the bumper sticker that says, 'Think globally—Act in your neighborhood.' Our U.S. war economy falls in on itself by not making a product that's going to circulate. We need to change over to a peacetime economy."

"Hildie, you're too smart. Did you ever consider a career in the C.I.A.?" Tom cracked, "or can you neither confirm nor deny that?" We laughed.

"I hate to break it to you," I said, "but you're out for that job. I'd say you've come over into radical territory now, what do you think Tom?"

"Oh definitely!" he grinned.

Nora passed some cokes and took her turn. "I had to look up patriotism. The dictionary says it's love of one's country and a dominating, zealous loyalty that, no matter what your country does, you're loyal. I have recently realized I'm very patriotic in that I really do love our country. But I don't qualify as patriotic because I'm not zealously loyal. I feel free to disagree with what the government does. I feel true patriotism is manifested in being thoughtful and trying to be aware of what's going on in your country, and letting your opinions be known. I feel betrayed by our government for the unjust things it does, not just to me but to other people, especially people of less means."

We all nodded. It felt good to be having the same reactions again.

"It was the working class to go off to war," Nora continued. "it's always the working class that die, the working class that's deprived of good education, of opportunities—it's a crime that that's how our government operates. I want the government to tell the truth, not perpetuate myths for business as it did in the Gulf War. We are in a dangerous situation. I'm afraid of us becoming a non-democratic country. I feel that to be patriotic we need to take back our country, to be informed and speak out. To me, talking is resisting."

"Yes," I said. "I agree that talking is resisting—not allowing ourselves to be deceived, and maybe spreading the word for others to resist too. But don't we have to be careful that then it doesn't become 'just talk?' Without turning it into an organized movement for change, couldn't it be in danger of just drying up and blowing away?"

"But, Jean, talking in this group did produce change. It has allowed us to resist what was happening to us at work," Hildie said. "It's been therapy."

"Yes, exactly!" Tom and Jasmine agreed.

"Remember that passage we read?" Nora asked, "It was about the need to bridge the gap between workers' lives inside the factory and their lives outside the gates? Coming into the group was the first time I sort of bridged that gap and started to feel like...well, you know, I've had individual friends. But I've never felt like I had a group of people that were not just my friends, but that we'd talk about work and have the same sort of understanding about what we were going through. And by talking to everybody I've felt like I'm not crazy and I'm not all alone and I feel stronger to deal with things inside the plant. I feel more optimistic about everything."

The others smiled and nodded. We neatened up, put used napkins and paper plates in a bag before getting out the cookies that were favorites on the shop floor, Suzanne's Chocolate Window Panes.

"Okay," said Hildie, turning to me. "Isn't it about time you got to work on our book, now that we won't be meeting any more? Keep in mind that I have a tiny waist and am svelte!"

"I think the book has already begun to take shape," I said. "And that's why I have these. They're for you. I want to call the book 'The Patriots' because, to tell you the truth, that's how I think of you guys." I rattled my Bob Slate Stationers' bag toward them.

"Gold pens!" Nora said. "Cool!"

"Gold plate, like American would give you at retirement if you were in management!" I smiled. "I wanted a way to recognize you as the writers!"

"Oh no you don't!" Hildie said. "No way! We were just coming along for the discussions!"

"Too late," I said. "You've already spent fifteen months putting the unspeakable into words. What do you call that?"

"All right you commies, clear out before we haul you in and give you a night in the slammer for being in an unauthorized area!" a voice came through the trees behind us. It was accompanied by the scraping sound of a cooler.

"Sean!" I said. He sat down hard on the sand, took off his shoes and shirt, rolled up his pants and dashed to wade knee-deep and christen his face and head with Walden Pond. Then he raced back and slid home into our tablecloth, shaking water on us like an Irish setter. Suzanne and Jasmine shrieked and put their hands up to shield their faces from the drops. Hildie and Nora made him a plate of food.

"I have to tell you I brought some Guinesses for us to celebrate. I didn't see any signs forbidding Guinness, did you?"

"Of course not!"

"Listen to this!" he waited till we quieted down. We were listening expectantly because, being a millwright who moved heavy equipment, Sean got around to all the plants and usually had inside information.

"They're definitely closing the Lawrence plant!"

"No!" we exclaimed. This was a big plant and big news.

"The old-timers still can't accept it, even though the doors close next week. American is definitely downsizing to try to deal with the peace economy now that Russia isn't a threat."

Jasmine smiled. "Peace economy. You better be careful what you wish for!"

Sean added extra onions to his sandwich and continued. "All this year in this group we've been looking at how we've been imprisoned in the company's environment. Now I'm watching the company being dismantled. Even upper management is being brutally dismantled. The god-son of the C.E.O., the sons of the original brain-trust of the company—they're all panicked about their jobs."

People snorted and Sean went on.

"They're getting their just punishment. The circle has come around. All these years, they've set the values of what was right for us, and we had no input even though it harmed us. We had no value. Now we know that their values weren't real values at all—they were just industrial theories set up by some individual on a whim fifty years ago, and now they're disappearing too. Everything is crumbling. We're crumbling from within in this country, like the Roman Empire. The leadership in Rome failed to look at the needs of society. Here and in Russia also, we cannot sustain a society that will tolerate wars any longer."

"Think about that!" Nora said. "That's wonderful!"

Jasmine sat back, reflecting. "This is completely different from any other time in our lives!" she said. "We're so much in touch with people now, that we don't see other people as being our enemies. We're not going to be so warlike because we're not going to have an economy based on wars anymore."

We nodded and sat for a while watching ripples in the pond. None of Thoreau's loons or Canadian geese were here, but a small and cheeky baby chipmunk came to our picnic and made off with a tiny pawful of ham.

"Very inquisitive," Hildie laughed.

"Let's send him to do a little investigation of the nut supply at Corporate!" Sean grinned.

We collected our trash and sat looking out over the water in silence.

"Seriously," Sean began again, "I think we're coming to our knees in this country. We always thought we were perfect. But we can be duplicated throughout the world now. The human mind has the beautiful capacity to develop anywhere, with enough education, regardless of race, color or creed. Any part of the spectrum of greatness can be produced anywhere."

"To the beautiful capacity of the human minds here!" I said, raising my glass. "And to you, Sean. A patriot in the radical tradition!"

"Is that what I am? Well then give me a pen! Let me sign something! And what do you mean by the radical tradition?"

"Internationalism that opens its arms to human greatness anywhere. High expectations that your nation will practice equality not domination, and peace not war. And fearless criticism of it when it fails its ideals. Martin Luther King, Thomas Jefferson, Eleanor Roosevelt are in this tradition.

"And Tom Paine. Or me!" said Tom, raising his can. "But you, Jeannie?" he looked at me quizzically.

"Well," I said, "in these particular times, I think my patriotism is more like a vigil, a candle set in the window for the missing."

"You know something?" Tom said after a pause. "We're avoiding the end, aren't we? We don't want this to end."

We nodded.

"To me, it's okay" Nora said. "To me we are somewhat like Thoreau because we set out on this experiment to think very deliberately about certain things and we did it. As the plaque said, "I went to the woods because I wished to live deliberately."

"...To front only the essential facts of life," Tom finished the quote.[9]

"Well," said Sean, raising his Guinness, "We did confront some essential facts of life. And quite a few that weren't essential too!"

"Like American," Hildie grinned, and raised her glass toward the full moon.

9   "Where I Lived and What I Lived For," *Walden* (New York: Modern Library Classics, 2000), 86.

XI

After American

"At my last job, the boss told me I wasn't getting paid to think!" Hildie told her new boss, the teacher in charge of the Plant and Animal Growth Greenhouse, who said, "Well here, we want you to do all your thinking on the job!"

When most of the patriots were scattered in a huge lay off, which began in February 1993, Hildie retrained for a year in a college biotechnology course. *The Brockton Herald* ran a story about her, headlined "Grandma gets all A's!" Now, after workdays at the local high school green house, she is the treasurer of the city's Garden Club.

"There are flower arrangers and there are diggers in our club," she told me. "I'm a digger. We plant flowers in public places." She is also treasurer of the D.W. Field Park Association, which has preserved her favorite park and has fought to have it listed on the state historical register.

From 1993 to 1999 Suzanne continued to work at American, and won union elections first for union Executive Board member, and later for Recording Secretary. She was a union delegate to the Massachusetts A.F.L.-C.I.O.'s state convention, served on the union contract negotiating committee, was a delegate to the state Gompers-Murray-Meany Institute and received certificates from the Massachusetts Labor Guild School of Industrial Relations. She retired in 1999. Now she spends her time rebuilding a family vacation house and caring for two little grandsons. She is a member of our community labor committee.

Nora left American when the division in which she worked closed. She moved to a small town, which welcomed artists by making available to them low-priced lofts in a building next to the town's new art museum. She has begun to create sculptures again.

"I'm so happy!" Nora told me. "This is a real community for me, with artists all over the place to talk to. The friendliness radiates out of the lofts and into the surrounding community. The museum does projects with community people. Recently they offered kids big spools from the historic textile mills in town and asked them to use them for wheels to build race-cars. They held a race—the mayor and everyone was there—but the prizes were for creativity, not speed. They raced on an aluminum track, fourteen feet wide and sixty feet long, that I built for them along with two other artists. It was such fun!"

Sean continued to work at American on the day shift. In the evening he pursued his passions, democratic politics and education for all. He won election to the city's School Committee twice. According to the Chairman of the School Committee, Sean was appreciated for his strong opinions and for his surprise check-ups on contractors remodeling the schools. "Pity the contractor that tried to cheat the kids or the taxpayers!" he said. Sadly, that conversation was at a wake. Sean died of a heart attack on Father's Day, June, 2003.

Tom has finally walked that bridge to a perpetual weekend—retirement. He said he loves living in Florida, and pursuing his interest in history by working part-time as a tour guide.

To tell you about Dominic's present work would compromise his anonymity. I have been unable to locate Ruth and Jasmine at their old addresses, or on "Facebook." Where have they gone? Has Ruth finally gone back to the south and established her plantation? Where's our invitation?

On the morning of my last day at American I turned on my fluorescent bench lamp to find a loaf of bread and red roses from Nora. It was March, 1993, and I had accepted a retirement package offered by the company to facilitate downsizing. For me, it would facilitate writing. I spent most of that day sniffling. Frankie and Rob organized my retirement lunch party. Everybody was there, the patriots incognito. Back at the bench as 3:30 drew near, Rudy said, for the benefit of the department, "Ah, all these years together and look at them now, they are like a pile of snow that melts in an hour. Already her face is fading."

In the process of writing this book, a question came to preoccupy me. What, exactly, was the nature of the similarity I was sensing in U.S. foreign policy backed by the military, and our experience of what that military might was like at work?

We found that the military model of domination and expediency on the shop floor bred withdrawal from the community, clinical symptoms including chronic stress, and constriction of our abilities and perspectives. Psychologist Michael Baseeches has said of conventional organization of work like ours, "perhaps smooth organizational functioning is being maintained at the expense of most workers' development."[1] Nevertheless there is little evidence that the U.S. government or defense industrialists are in the least concerned about the consequences of their methods of production, except perhaps in certain new high-performance job sectors that require more developed "human capital." Workers are expendable.

The U.S. design for supremacy in the world is no longer just an alarming idea, as it was for me when it appeared in the *New York Times* in 1992. We now know that the statement leaked to the *Times* at that time came from the secret "Defense Planning Guidance" paper prepared for Richard Cheney by I. Lewis Libby and Paul Wolfowitz.[2] It was revised to emphasize U.S. control of the world's strategic resources, and was made public on September 17, 2002, as the National Security Strategy of the U.S.A. (NSSUSA).[3] Thousands of American and Iraqi lives have been lost because of U.S. contention for domination of Iraq's resources.[4] Citizens and soldiers are expendable.

It is the ethic of expendability that haunts me: if the underdevelopment of some populations or the death of others is required for accumulation, according to its proponents, so be it. Here is an illustration. The United Nations estimated that during the U.S. embargo, from 1992-98, half a million children died mainly of infections that were preventable by restoration of the infrastructure for water, sanitation and electricity after the war.[5]

---

1   He begins by asking, "Are work organizations maintaining their equilibrium by keeping workers in jobs for which they have the requisite abilities, but not giving them opportunities to develop more powerful structures of reasoning? If, as I would hypothesize, in most cases [this is so]...it means smooth organizational functioning is being maintained at the expense of most workers' development." *Dialectical Thinking and Adult Development,* Publications for the advancement of theory and history in psychology, Vol. 3, (Stamford, CT: Ablex Publishing Corp., 1984), 358-9.

2   Research Unit for Political Economy of Bombay, India, *Behind the Invasion of Iraq* (New York: Monthly Review Press, 2003), 70. To be referred to hereafter as *B.I.I.*

3   *Ibid.,* 67.

4   *Peacework*, a publication of the American Friends Service Committee, July-August 2004, Vol. 31, Issue 347, 5.

5   *B.I.I.,* 46.

The Defense Department of Intelligence predicted this outcome twice
in 1991 and, I believe for strategic reasons, did nothing.[6] Three successive
UN Humanitarian and Food Coordinators for Iraq resigned in protest,
charging genocide.[7] On May 12, 1996, Leslie Stahl asked Secretary of State
Madeleine Albright, on CBS television, whether the price of the war—the
deaths of half a million children, "more than died at Hiroshima"—was
worth it. The Secretary answered, "I think this is a very hard choice, but
the price, we think the price is worth it."[8]

It appears that cynical policies of malign neglect similar to those of the
Defense Department of Intelligence in 1991 continue. In August, 2004,
Christian Parenti reported from Iraq that vital reconstruction of Iraqi sanitation, water and power systems had once more been delayed, this time for
one year by U.S. contractor Bechtel Corporation. People were again getting
sick from the pollution. Not a cent of the $2.8 billion of U.S. taxpayers'
money earmarked for re-building Iraqi infrastructure had been spent on
health care, water treatment or sanitation projects. No explanation for this
failure was available.[9]

In our evening at Walden Pond in 1993 we, like millions around the
world, were hopeful for peace. In 2007 the administration has continued,
without reckoning the costs, to pursue its strategy for domination of re-
source-rich regions, as it was laid out in 1990 and 2002:

"Our first objective is to prevent the re-emergence of a new rival...which

---

6   See the following important information, from *B.I.I.*, 42: "That the United States was
quite clear about the consequences of such a bombing campaign is evident from intelligence
documents now being declassified. "Iraq Water Treatment Vulnerabilities," dated 22 January,
1991 (a week after the war began), provides the rationale for the attack on Iraq's water supply
treatment capabilities: "Iraq depends on importing specialized equipment and some chemicals to
purify its water supply...Failing to secure supplies will result in a shortage of pure drinking water
for much of the population. This could lead to increased incidence, if not epidemics, of disease."
Even more explicitly, the U.S. Defense Intelligence Agency wrote a month later: "Conditions
are favorable for communicable disease outbreaks, particularly in major urban areas affected by
coalition bombing...Current public health problems are attributable to the reduction of normal
preventive medicine, waste disposal, water purification/distribution, electricity, and decreased
ability to control disease outbreaks. Any urban area in Iraq that has received infrastructure
damage will have similar problems."
7   *Ibid.*, 46-7.
8   *Ibid.*, 47.
9   What little has gone to restoration of the health and sanitation infrastructure has come
from Iraqi oil money managed by the U.S. controlled Development Fund for Iraq, a successor
to the U.N.-run Oil for Food program. The August, 2004 report on growing pollution and the
failure to repair infrastructure, by Christian Parenti, "Fables of the Reconstruction," appears in
The Nation 8/30-9/6/04, 18.

requires preventing any hostile power from dominating a region whose resources would under consolidated control, be sufficient to generate global
power. These regions are western Europe, East Asia, the territory of the former Soviet Union, and South west Asia [i.e., the oil producing region] Finally,
we must maintain the mechanisms for deterring potential competitors from
ever aspiring to a larger regional or global role."[10]

We are once again at war. As of 2007 the Opinion Research Business
survey has reported 1,033,000 Iraqi deaths due to the conflict. The U.S.
Department of Defense reported 3,658 U.S. troops dead. 500 U.S. troops
have undergone amputations and 62% of critically injured soldiers returning to Walter Reed Hospital suffered brain injuries.[11] The September
Eleventh bombing of the World Trade Center was a double tragedy, killing
2,752 innocent civilians and releasing the Bush administration from public
constraints on wars of conquest in the Middle East. Osama Bin Laden has
been perhaps too convenient a pretext for the conquest of the Middle East
to expedite his capture. Under the radar, American workers and their social
institutions are feeling the strain of twenty years of U.S. funds needed for
cities and towns being drained for the war, and trickle-down, neo-liberal
draconian tactics for surplus productivity. The fifty-four hour week of the
1920's mills has returned for some.

I think back to what we called, in the seventies, "revolutionary hope."
I still have that. I believe it lies in honorable people joining hearts and
minds worldwide to work, as Albert Einstein said to another generation
in 1949, "to overcome and advance beyond the predatory phase of human
development."[12]

10   Information is from *"Iraq War Facts, Results and Statistics at August 23, 2010,"* compiled
by Deborah White for About.com. Facts given herein were reported in 2007.
11   "Casualties of the Iraq War/Wounded In Action"; Wikipedia.org. This is source for
both amputations and brain injury numbers.
12   "Why Socialism," Albert Einstein, reprinted in *Monthly Review,* May 2004. Originally
published in the founding issue of *Monthly Review,* May 1949.

Afterward

Four years have passed since I finished writing *The Patriots*. Its final progress was delayed by an illness, cancer. I find that surviving cancer sweetens life and also focuses one's perspective.

It remains clear to me that the harms caused by working-class manufacturing or office jobs that are rote and have command-and-control relations are wrongful. They subject people to the risk of life-long clinical symptoms and underdevelopment that can, in all likelihood, be detected in physical changes in the brain.

Now, as a nation, we are in a time of poverty and unemployment. It would appear to be necessary for many people to take just any job and not worry about its quality. Survival has forced people into devastating work in other eras, as in the years of slavery and child labor. But unless the time has come for the complete collapse of capitalism, the economy will slowly improve and new kinds of work will be created. Workers and their allies—all of us—should call for the redesign of work. The groundwork has been laid for this in years of study and experimentation.[1] And in 1977 the government of Norway established a landmark Occupational Health and Safety Act which regulates psychosocially hazardous work.[2]

To change long entrenched ways of work in favor of brighter prospects for working people will require public education, conviction and a passionate movement. There is some reason to be optimistic about that. We have known a time when lynchings were common in the south, when domestic violence and sexual harassment weren't even concepts, and equal opportunities for minorities and women had no legal standing.

---

1   See, for example, Robert Karasek and Tores Theorell, *Healthy Work: Stress, Productivity and the Reconstruction of Working Life* (New York, Basic Books, 1990), Melvin Kohn, "Unresolved Issues in the Relationship Between Personality and Work" in *The Nature of Work, American Sociological Association Presidential Series* (New Haven, Yale University Press, 1990), or Daniel Zwerdling's *Workplace Democracy* (New York: Harper Torchbooks, 1978).

2   Reference is made particularly to Paragraph 12 of the Act in Karasek and Theorell, *Ibid.*, 221.

The militarism that malformed our work relations also disfigures U.S. media culture, in which television programs, video games and movies glorify violence, conquering and the debasement of those who don't conquer. The defense industry and the Pentagon sustain and lobby for the empire building that has caused the deaths of 5,644 American soldiers in Iraq, seriously wounded 32,965 more, and killed 1,359 American soldiers in Afghanistan.[3] It has killed, as well, 1,421,933 Iraqis[4] and 1,271 Afghan civilians.[5] It has cost $1 trillion as of May, 2010.[6] Part of that money goes to projecting American power and supremacy with 1,077 bases[7] world-wide. War's advocates have, as usual, ignored the collateral damage of rising numbers of the hungry, impoverished and sick without care in our own country.

Can we do anything to end war and the militarism of our culture? I have misgivings about this and they are reinforced by those of two men who were formerly part of the military establishment. The late Chalmers Johnson, an academic China specialist and consultant to Richard Helms and the CIA, states at the end of his book, *The Sorrows of Empire: Militarism, Secrecy and the End of the Republic*: "This book was not easy to write. I do not like what it has to say about my country. It is because I do not like stating that the U.S. is probably lost to militarism that this book is so heavily documented."[8] Historian and former U.S. Army Colonel Andrew Bacevich concludes that the "Washington rules" or policy of permanent war that he has documented "are likely to remain securely in place for the foreseeable future" because of the enormous number of institutions and individuals to whom these rules "deliver profit, power and privilege." The one possible out he sees is that "the strain laid on a military perpetually at war and on an economy propped up by perpetual borrowing causes one or both to collapse."[9]

One of the things that I learned in my years at "American" was that it was the veterans of actual combat who were the most deeply anti-war. Perhaps the overthrow of war will have to come, not from those who rule,

3   See "www.defense.gov/news/casualty.pdf."
4   See "www.justforeignpolicy.org/iraq."
5   See "www.justforeignpolicy.org/node/669."
6   See "afsc.org/action/1-trillion-war-spending-milestone."
7   See "original.antiwar.com/engelhardt/2011/01/09/all-bases-covered."
8   (New York: Henry Holt and Company, 2004), 367.
9   *Washington Rules: America's Path to Permanent War* (New York: Henry Holt and Company, 2010), 229.

but from the people enlisted to produce it. Even now the Iraq Veterans Against the War, increasing numbers of Afghanistan War soldiers and the Veterans for Peace are taking stands. The Veterans for Peace issued this statement on November 11, 2009:

> Armistice Day was a reminder of the insane, horrific cost of war paid by soldiers at the front, those who ministered to the dead and wounded, and their families back home. It was a day to reflect on that memory and vow to learn to live in a world without war.[10]

Jean Alonso
Boston, 2011

---

10   See "www.veteransforpeace.org/Armistice_day_statement_2009.vp.html."

The Patriots

Acknowledgments

At the beginning I was a person long on experience and short on creative writing skills. Each of these acknowledgments recalls with gratitude the people whose kindness and confidence in my project kept me pursuing it.

The William Joiner Center for the Study of War and Its Social Consequences at University of Massachusetts, Boston, holds two week conferences every June to affirm and hone the skills of people with shared concerns about war and other social harms. Joiner's staff and residents created a protective community to which I was fortunate to return for several years. Demetria Martinez, poet, author of *Mother Tongue*, and one of my teachers there, had many good precepts to guide us.

To Joiner's Lady Borton I owe my safe passage into the realm of writing. In her writing and in ours, she could hear the spirit behind events and personages, and she urged on to try to make that palpable. School bus driver, farmer, AFSC Representative in Ha Noi, person who led the first reporters to the site of the My Lai massacre, author of two memoirs about her close relationship with the Vietnamese people (*After Sorrow* and *Sensing the Enemy*) and writing teacher with exquisite perception and respectful communications--she is a visionary and wonderful person.

Lady Borton referred my work to Al Silverman, former senior editor at Viking Press and long-time C.E.O. of the Book of the Month Club, who gave advice about publishing at Joiner summer workshops. I was unbelievably fortunate to have his encouragement and editorial advice for months on the first four chapters of the book. A sports writer (most recent of ten books is *Yankee Colors*), he well understood what it took to do writing in a popular vein. He is a generous and progressive man who has made a practice of lending his talents to a number of earnest but green writers like me. I remember him with great warmth and gratitude.

Cynthia Enloe, a professor and author of numerous books on women and militarism, most recently of *Nimo's War, Emma's War: Making Feminist Sense of the Iraq War*, asked to read my manuscript as primary material from inside a defense plant. Her appreciation of it kept me writing for quite a while. She has been most generous in sharing contacts in the book world and in endorsing *The Patriots*. She is well known for her kindness and generosity, and for her democratic emphasis on the importance of ordinary women in the military-community complex that bolsters the global advance of U.S. militarism.

The Divers, the writers' group that grew out of Lady Borton's workshop, sustained me for a number of years. All committed to social justice as well as writing, we practiced solidarity instead of competition, and did meticulous, respectful readings of each others' work. Others belonged briefly to this group, but the mainstays, who helped shape the book and encouraged the author, are my friends Susan Freireich, Linda Stern, Nancy Teel, Deborah Schwartz, Molly Watt, Bette Steinmuller, Joan Ecklein and Gretchen Klotz.

Friends Vivien Shalom, a writer and illustrator of children's books, Judith Baker, an astute teacher and activist, Paul Mc Lennan, a writer and community organizer, and Steve Meacham, a pioneer organizer against foreclosure evictions, each gave very careful readings of the manuscript and made recommendations that changed the book. Each one brought the understanding of long-time political activism of their own. Suzanne Hodes, who is a painter, extended her friendship and expert advice about the cover.

My children have loved me and urged me on over the years, even when they were young and learned I was changing my life work. Melissa Alonso was my never-failing support for womanist strength, self-assertion and perseverance. Marc Alonso, who has done desk-top publishing professionally, dedicated his spare time for six years to the format and lay-out of various drafts of the book, to designing the cover, and most importantly to applying his refined literary intelligence to criticism and editing of the manuscript.

Writing a book out of nothing makes you fear, at first, that you are on a fool's errand.

The story, emerging from the mists, begins to talk back and argue for its own existence. But it is the generous faith of friends, family and advisors that something important may be developing that keeps a book afloat. I hold you all in my heart and hope for your own creative successes.

JEAN ALONSO worked in a defense plant from 1978 to 1993 building parts for missiles. She holds a B.A. in English from Harvard, an M.A. in English from Tufts and an M.A. in Psychotherapy and Social Change from Goddard College. She has published articles in *The Women's Review of Books* and *The Monthly Review*. As a public mental health worker she founded an alternative school, a temporary shelter program for homeless teens, was a storefront crisis counselor and a psychotherapist in a prison treatment center. She came to feel that inequality and poverty were at the root of much of the damage she saw in this work. So she joined the '70's movement for social change that was seeking the support of working-class people by meeting and working side by side with them in America's industries.

Jean Alonso lives in Boston, Massachusetts, where she is a community activist. She has two grown children.

Made in the USA
Charleston, SC
04 September 2011